Learn C++ on the PC

Learn C++
on the
PC

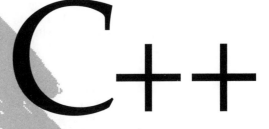

INCLUDES
SPECIAL VERSION
OF A BESTSELLING
C++ COMPILER

Dave Mark

Addison-Wesley Publishing Company
Reading, Massachusetts • Menlo Park, California • New York
Don Mills, Ontario • Wokingham, England • Amsterdam
Bonn • Sydney • Singapore • Tokyo • Madrid • San Juan
Paris • Seoul • Milan • Mexico City • Taipei

Many of the designations used by manufacturers and sellers to distinguish their products are claimed as trademarks. Where those designations appear in this book, and Addison-Wesley was aware of a trademark claim, the designations have been printed in initial capital letters or all capital letters.

The authors and publishers have taken care in preparation of this book, but make no expressed or implied warranty of any kind and assume no responsibility for errors or omissions. No liability is assumed for incidental or consequential damages in connection with or arising out of the use of the information or programs contained herein.

Library of Congress Cataloging-in-Publication Data

Mark, Dave.
    Learn C++ on the PC / Dave Mark.
      p. cm.
    Includes index.
    ISBN 0-201-62622-5
    1. C++ (Computer program language)   2. Microcomputers-
-Programming.   I. Title.
    QA76.73.C153M32   1993
    005.26'2--dc20
                                       93-33538
                                         CIP

Sponsoring Editor: Keith Wollman
Project Editor: Elizabeth G. Rogalin
Production Coordinator: Gail McDonald Jordan
Cover design: Ted Mader Associates
Icons in book designed by Crystal Sarno, Graphic Perspectives, Inc.
Set in 11 point Palatino by Rob Mauhar and Lenity Himburg, CIP

1 2 3 4 5 6 7 8 9 -MA- 9796959493
First printing, December 1993

Addison-Wesley books are available for bulk purchases by corporations, institutions, and other organizations. For more information please contact the Corporate, Government and Special Sales Department at (617) 944-3700 x2915.

*This book is dedicated to
Deneen J. Melander,
yin to my yang . . .*

Contents

Chapter 10   Moving On   291

Appendices

Preface

Some time ago, maybe 1988 or 1989, I remember reading an article written by a well-known C++ programmer. The article was addressed to all programmers of a certain personal computer, and talked about the future of software development. Back then, the vast majority of programs were written in either C or Pascal. Sure, there might have been a little Basic here, and a little C++ there, but these languages were viewed as the fringe—a definite minority.

Anyway, this article went on to describe the wonders of object-oriented programming and of C++ in particular. Normally, I would have turned the page, since I was perfectly happy programming in C and Pascal, my personal languages of choice. But this article quickly captured my attention. As I read, I began to realize something basic was happening. This article wasn't just an interesting discussion of an alternative development methodology. It was a warning shot across my bow. Major developers like Microsoft, Borland, and Symantec were making a real commitment to object programming and to C++. At development conferences, the message was clear. More and more, Windows developers are expected not just to understand, but to embrace object programming.

Pay attention to this message: Object programming is the future, and C++ is the language for object programming. Why C++? Go to your favorite bookstore and check out the programming titles. Chances are, the vast majority are dedicated to C and C++. The premier Windows development environments all feature C++ as their language of choice. When Symantec announced their cross-platform development library, Bedrock, they made it clear that Bedrock would be written entirely in C++.

Once you've made the commitment to learn about Object Programming and C++, you're ready to take the next step. Bring this book home with you (pay for it first) and start reading. *Learn C++ on the PC* will do the rest.

Oh, and by the way, if you feel like getting in touch, I'd love to hear from you. Get on CompuServe, type **GO MACDEV** and leave a message in the *Learn Programming* section (section 11). In the meantime, turn the page, and let's get started...

D.M.
Arlington, Virginia

Acknowledgments

I'd like to take a few moments to thank all the people who made this book possible. First and foremost, I'd like to thank my good friend Steve Baker for his invaluable assistance. Steve put in a lot of long hours to put this book together. Whether he was fine tuning the table of contents or tinkering with one of my C++ sample programs, Steve's heart and soul run through this book. By the way, thanks also to Steve's family, Kelly, Michael, and Matthew, for patience and understanding above and beyond the call of duty.

Thanks to Keith Wollman, my editor, for his incredible patience and understanding. Keith, you are truly an author's editor!

Thanks to Elizabeth Rogalin, my friend, confidante, and project editor, for seeing this book through. Thanks, Elizabeth!

Thanks to Gail McDonald Jordan for doing a superb job handling the production of this book.

Thanks to Brian Weed at Symantec for putting together THIN C++ and for answering all my questions.

Thanks to Crystal Sarno for her excellent artwork. Crystal designed the icons sprinkled throughout the book.

Thanks to Jean Peck for an incredible job copyediting the book.

Thanks to Carlos Derr for guidance and friendship.

Thanks to Daniel for all of his help editing the manuscript. Book?

Finally, thanks to Deneen Joanne Melander, for companionship, love, and understanding. LFUEMISHOK?

Chapter 1

Welcome Aboard

Interested in learning how to program in C++? Well, you've come to the right place. Grab your PC, hop into your most comfortable chair, and read on...

This Chapter
at a Glance

WELCOME! BY PURCHASING THIS BOOK/DISK PACKAGE, you've taken the first step toward learning the C++ programming language. As you make your way through the book, you'll learn one of the most popular and powerful programming languages in the world today—you've definitely made a wise investment.

Before we start programming, we first need to address a few questions.

What's in the Package?

Learn C++ on the PC is a book/disk package. The book is filled with interesting facts, figures, and programming examples, all of which are designed to teach you how to program in C++.

In the back of the book is a floppy disk that contains all the software you'll need to run each of the book's programming examples on your own computer. Included on this disk is THIN C++, a customized version of one of the leading Windows development environments, created especially for this book. The disk also includes each of the programs presented in the book so that you don't have to type the examples yourself. Such a deal!

Why Learn C++?

There are a lot of reasons for learning C++. Perhaps the biggest reason is the popularity of C++ as a programming language. Go to your local technical bookstore and count the books dedicated to each programming language. Ten years ago, you would have found that the most popular language out there was Pascal. Five years ago, the pendulum shifted and C became the most popular language. Now, the move is toward C++.

You'll find support for C++ everywhere. There are C++ compilers for Unix, the Macintosh, DOS, and, of course, Windows. Symantec recently announced Bedrock, a cross-platform development vehicle written completely in C++. The number of C++ programming texts is growing by leaps and bounds. Opportunities for a good C++ programmer are endless.

The bottom line is this: C++ is *the* language of the nineties. Major computer companies like Microsoft, Apple, and Sun are basing their future operating system designs around C++. Knowledge of C or Pascal just isn't enough anymore. In my opinion, C++ is a must!

What Should I Know to Get Started?

There are two prerequisites to using this book. First, you must have a basic knowledge of DOS. Do you know how to start up an application? Do you know how to use a word processor like Microsoft Word? If you can use a PC to run programs and edit documents, you're halfway there.

Second, you should have a working knowledge of C. If you're just getting started with programming or if your language of choice is a language other than C, you might want to pick up a copy of *The C Programming Language* by Brian Kernighan and Dennis Ritchie. Be sure to get the second edition. If you just need a quick C refresher course, check out Chapter 3 of this book. Once you have these two skills in hand, you're ready to tackle C++.

What Equipment Do I Need?

While it is possible to learn C++ just by reading a book, you'll get the most out of this book if you run each example program as you read and discover how it works. To do this, you'll need a PC. If you don't have one, borrow one from a friend. You'll need a PC with at least a 386-based processor and 2MB of memory. The compiler included with this book, THIN C++, will run with most versions of DOS. (You'll hear more about THIN C++ in Chapter 2.)

If you can, upgrade your PC to the latest version of DOS. At the same time, see whether you can get hold of a couple of extra megabytes to bring your PC up to 4 megs or more. The extra breathing room will help.

The Lay of the Land

This book was designed with several different readers in mind. If you're new to programming, you'll want to read each and every chapter. Try not to skip over material that seems fuzzy. If you get stuck, find a C++ programmer who can answer your questions. Most C++ programmers are friendly and are usually more than glad to help someone just getting started. Make a commitment to finish this book. You can do it!

If you're a C master, you might want to skip the C review in Chapter 3. Do *not* skip Chapter 2, however. Chapter 2 walks you through the THIN C++ installation process and ensures that you copy all the sample code to the right spot on your hard drive.

The Chapters and Appendices

This book is made up of ten chapters and eight appendices. This chapter provides an overview of the book and gets you started down the right path.

Chapter 2 introduces the disk part of this book/disk package. You'll learn about THIN C++, the C++ programming environment designed especially for use with this book. You'll install THIN C++ on your hard drive and test out the software to make sure it's installed properly. In Chapter 2, you'll run your first C++ program. No matter what previous programming experience you have, don't skip Chapter 2!

Chapter 3 contains a refresher course in C. Even if you're a seasoned C programmer, you might want to take a quick look through this chapter just to make sure everything in it looks familiar.

Chapter 4 introduces the basic syntax of C++. It covers topics ranging from C++ operators and keywords to reference types and function name overloading.

Chapter 5 introduces you to the basics of object programming, the heart and soul of C++. You'll learn all about classes and objects and the C++ mechanisms that allow you to create classes and objects of your very own.

Chapter 6 takes the concept of classes one step further. It shows you how to use one class as the basis for a new, derived class. Derived classes play a critical role in extending an existing set of C++ classes.

Chapter 7 introduces the concept of operator overloading. C++ allows you to overload its built-in operators, customizing them to work with objects you define. For example, you might overload the + operator, enabling you to add two arrays together.

Chapter 8 introduces `iostream`, C++'s equivalent of C's `stdio` library. Just as routines such as `printf()` and `scanf()` allow you to build a portable user interface in C, the `iostream` functions allow you to build a portable C++ interface.

Chapter 9 takes you down the homestretch by exploring a potpourri of miscellaneous C++ topics. When you finish this chapter, you'll have completed the first phase of your C++ education.

Chapter 10 wraps things up. It prepares you for the next step on your programming path. You'll learn about class libraries like the Microsoft Foundation Class Library and the Object Windows Library. You'll also read about some of the books and reference materials that you'll want by your side as you start your own C++ development efforts.

Appendix A is a glossary of the technical terms that are used in this book.

Appendix B contains a complete listing of each of the examples used in this book. This section will come in handy as a reference, as you write your own C++ programs. Need an example of an overloaded operator? Turn to the examples in Appendix B.

Appendices C, D, E, and F contain listings of the files `<iostream.h>`, `<fstream.h>`, `<strstrea.h>`, and `<iomanip.h>`, respectively. These files are all critical parts of the `iostream` library. If you'll be using `iostream` in your own applications, you'll find these appendices helpful.

Appendix G describes Symantec C++ for Windows, the full version of the development environment used in this book.

Appendix H is a bibliography of useful programming titles.

The Conventions Used in This Book

As you read this book, you'll encounter a few standard conventions that make the book easier to read. For example, technical terms appearing for the first time are displayed in **boldface**. (You'll find most of these terms in the glossary in Appendix A.)

All of the source code examples in this book are presented using a special font, known as the `code font`. This includes source code fragments that appear in the middle of running text.

Occasionally, you'll come across a block of text set off in a box, like this. These blocks are called *tech blocks* and are intended to add technical detail to the subject currently being discussed. Each tech block will fit into one of five categories: "By the Way," "Style," "Detail," "Definition," and "Warning." Each category has its own special icon, which will appear to the left of the tech block. As the names imply, "By the Way" tech blocks are intended to be informative but not crucial. "Style" tech blocks contain information relating to your C++ programming style. "Detail" tech blocks offer more detailed information about the current topic. "Definition" tech blocks contain the definition of an important C++ term. "Warning" tech blocks are usually trying to warn you about some potential programming problem, so pay attention!

Strap Yourself In...   That's about it. Let's get started!

Chapter 2

Installing
THIN C++

Before we charge into C++
programming, you need to
install the C++ development
environment included with
this book. This chapter
takes you step-by-step
through the THIN C++
installation process.

This Chapter at a Glance

Installing THIN C++
Testing THIN C++
What's Next?

TUCKED INTO THE BACK OF *LEARN C++ ON THE PC* IS A floppy disk containing THIN C++, a collection of tools that provide you with everything you'll need to work with the programming examples presented in this book.

THIN C++ was created especially for this book by Symantec. In PC programming circles, Symantec is known best as the maker of Symantec C++ for Windows.

THIN C++ includes a C++ compiler and linker that you'll use to build each of the book's sample programs. Of course, all of the source code found in the book is also included as part of THIN C++. Finally, just in case you don't have access to a full screen text editor, THIN C++ includes a shareware text editor called *VDE* (remember, if you use VDE, honor the license agreement).

**Installing
THIN C++**

Before you do anything else, make a backup copy of the THIN C++ disk and place the original disk in a safe place. From now on, only work with the backup copy of THIN C++. That way, when your dog uses your backup disk as a teething ring, you'll still have the original tucked away to make a new backup from.

Next, insert the THIN C++ backup disk (you did make a backup, didn't you?) into your floppy drive. There are three files on the disk: `install.bat`, `thincpp.exe`, and `vde.exe`. To install THIN C++, you'll execute the batch file `install.bat`. If you are running Windows, either exit Windows or spawn a DOS shell. At the DOS prompt, type

```
A:
```

to change from your main drive to your floppy drive. You *must* run the install script from the A drive!

Next, type

```
install c:
```

to run the install script in `install.bat`, copying the files to your C drive. If you'd prefer to install THIN C++ on a different drive, substitute that drive's letter for the `c:` in the install command line.

If you get an error message telling you that you are "out of environment space," you should make a slight modification to your `config.sys` file (increasing the number of bytes allocated for environment variables) and then run the install script again. Here's the line I added *at the end* of my `config.sys` file:

```
shell=\c:command.com /p /e:1024
```

You'll have to reboot before the change takes effect.

install.bat creates a new directory, called thincpp, at the top level of your hard drive. Inside thincpp, you'll find four directories: bin, projects, lib, and include. lib and include contain various files that go along with the compiler and linker. bin contains the compiler, the linker, the VDE shareware editor (as well as some support files for VDE), and, finally, a very important batch file called setthin.bat.

setthin.bat makes sure your DOS search path includes the appropriate THIN C++ directories and sets up some variables needed by THIN C++. You *must* run setthin.bat each time you restart your machine. You'll probably want to add the line

```
\thincpp\bin\setthin.bat
```

to your autoexec.bat file. If you have a preferred place to add the line, go ahead. Just be sure it is run each time you reboot your machine.

If you plan on using the shareware editor VDE, you should start out by reading the file vde.doc located in the bin directory. Also, be sure to run the program vinst to customize VDE to your machine. Use cd to change to the bin directory before you run vinst.

Testing THIN C++

Now that you've installed THIN C++, you're ready to take it for a test drive. In DOS, type the command

```
c:
```

to get back to your C drive. Then, type

```
cd \thincpp\projects
```

to move into the projects directory, where all the source code for the book is kept. Next, type

```
dir
```

to get an idea of how the projects are organized. As you can see, the programs are organized by chapter, and there's a directory for every program in the book. Now, type

```
cd chap2_1
```

to move into the directory for our test program, `hello`.
 Next, type

```
dir
```

again. A listing of the files in this particular directory will appear. The file `hello.cpp` contains the source code for our test program.

> The other files that accompany the source code file in each directory are provided just in case you have a full version of Symantec C++ for Windows. They'll enable you to run the programs inside the Symantec C++ environment.

To take a look at the `hello` source code, type the command

```
type hello.cpp
```

Here's what the source code looks like:

```cpp
#include <iostream.h>

int main()
{
    cout << "Hello, world!";

    return 0;
}
```

Don't worry about how this program works. We'll get started with C++ in Chapter 4. For now, let's make sure this puppy compiles. Type the command

```
sc hello.cpp
```

This command compiles and links the source code in `hello.cpp`, producing two files as output: `hello.obj` and `hello.exe`. As you'd guess, `hello.obj` contains the object code and `hello.exe` the executable. Typing the command

```
hello
```

runs `hello.exe` and produces this line of output:

```
Hello, world!
```

If you ran into any problems with this process, try deleting the `thincpp` directory (use the `deltree` command if you've got DOS 6.0 or later), make sure you have enough environment space, and rerun the install script. Be sure `hello` runs properly before you move on.

What's Next? That's about it for our THIN C++ intro. Are you ready to get started? Get comfortable, and turn the page. Here we go!

Chapter 3

Remembering C

One of the basic assumptions made in this book is that you are already acquainted with the C programming language. This chapter contains a quick refresher course in C. Even if you're a seasoned C programmer, you might want to take a few moments to look over this material.

This Chapter at a Glance

BEFORE WE GET STARTED WITH C++, IT'S IMPORTANT that you have a good grasp of the C programming language. This chapter offers a review of the primary features of C. Since C is a subset of C++, you'll want to make sure you feel comfortable with all the material covered here. As you read through the chapter, build yourself a checklist of the C features you need to bone up on. Then grab your favorite C reference and plug away.

Literal Constants

This section covers the various forms you can use to represent a constant in C.

Integral Constants

Integral constants (constants that represent mathematical integers) can be represented in decimal, octal, or hexadecimal format. Decimal constants appear as plain numbers. Octal (base 8) constants always start with a leading zero. Hexadecimal (base 16) constants always start with the two characters 0x.

The size in bytes of an octal or a hex constant is determined by the number of characters that appear in the constant. For example, since there are two characters to every hex byte, this constant is 4 bytes long:

```
0x00FF00FF
```

Decimal constants default to the size of an int.

To represent a decimal constant as a long, tack an L (in either upper or lower case) at the end:

```
205L
```

To represent a decimal constant as an unsigned int, tack a U (in either upper or lower case) at the end:

```
205U
```

The characters UL (in either upper or lower case) are used to denote a decimal constant of type unsigned long:

205UL

The characters U and L can also be used at the end of octal and hexadecimal constants.

Floating-Point Constants

Floating-point constants represent signed, real numbers. A complete floating-point constant consists of an integer portion (to the left of the decimal point), a fractional portion (to the right of the decimal point), and an exponent. For example, the constant

103.75e2

represents 103.75 times 10 to the second power, or 10,375.

To qualify as a floating-point constant, either the decimal point or the exponent (or both) must be present. All of the following are legal constants:

100.e2
.5e2
100.5
.5
100e5

Normally, floating-point constants are represented as a double. To represent a floating-point constant as a float, tack an F at the end:

125.7F

To represent a floating-point constant as a long double, tack an L at the end:

125.7L

float, double, and long double are the three floating-point types offered by C. For more information on these types, read the section on variables a few pages down the road.

Character Constants

Single-byte character constants are represented by enclosing a character in single quotes, like this:

'a'

The \ character (backslash) is used to create special single-byte character constants. If the first character following the \ is a zero, the remainder of the constant is interpreted as an octal ASCII character code. If the first character following the \ is an x, the remainder of the constant is interpreted as a hexadecimal ASCII character code. For example, both of the following constants represent the ASCII bell character:

'\007'
'\x7'

In addition, there are 11 backslash combinations that represent single-byte characters (Figure 3.1). For example, the constant '\a' represents the ASCII bell character.

The most frequently used backslash sequence is the newline character, represented by the sequence '\n'. When placed at the end of a string sent to the console, the newline character forces the cursor to the beginning of the next line of output.

Finally, the constant '\0' represents a single byte with a value of 0. This constant is used as a terminator for C character strings.

FIGURE 3.1

Single-byte backslash characters.

Constant	Meaning
\a	Bell
\b	Backspace
\f	Formfeed
\n	Newline
\r	Return
\t	Horizontal tab
\v	Vertical tab
\\	Backslash
\?	Question mark
\'	Single quote
\"	Double quote

String Constants

String constants are formed when a set of zero or more characters is surrounded by double quotes, like this:

```
char  *nickname = "Apple dumpling";
```

Each character in the string consumes 1 byte of memory. A null terminator (' \0 ') is automatically placed at the end of the string. The \ combinations presented in the previous section are particularly useful when placed inside a string constant.

Enumerations

Enumerations are types declared using the enum keyword and a list of enumeration constants. These constants provide an alternative to the #define mechanism (described later in the chapter) by allowing you to declare a series of constants with a single statement. Here's an example:

```
enum  weekDays { monday = 2, tuesday, wednesday,
   thursday, friday }
```

By default, the first constant starts with a value of 0, and following constants increase in value by 1. Any or all of these constants can be initialized automatically. In the example just given, monday is initialized to 2, tuesday to 3, wednesday to 4, and so on.

Variables

Variables can be defined within any block of code. The basic variable types are char, int, and float. All three of these can be defined as signed or unsigned. A signed variable can represent either a positive or a negative number, while an unsigned variable is limited to nonnegative numbers. For example, a signed char can hold values ranging from −128 to 127 and an unsigned char can hold values from 0 to 255.

In addition to signed and unsigned, an int can be defined using the qualifier short or long, as in these examples:

```
long int    myLong;
short int   myShort;
```

Most programmers prefer the shorthand notation, using long for long int and short for short int:

```
long    myLong;
short   myShort;
```

It should be pointed out that the ANSI standard does not specify the size of the int data type, leaving that decision up to the development environment.

Just as char, short, and long represent a steadily increasing sequence of integral types, float, double, and long double are a steadily increasing sequence of floating-point types.

According to the ANSI standard, a double is at least as large as a float, and a long double is at least as large as a double. Typically, a float is 4 bytes long, and a double, appropriately enough, is 8 bytes long. On most machines, a long double is the same size as a double.

Arrays

Any variable data type can form the basis of an array definition. Array definitions consist of a *type*, an *identifier*, and a *dimension*, as in the following:

```
short myShortArray[ 10 ];
```

Arrays can be multidimensional. For example, the code

```
unsigned char bytes[ 10 ][ 20 ];
```

defines an array named `bytes` that totals 200 bytes in size. `bytes` is actually an array of 10 arrays, each of which is 20 bytes in length.

In real life, multidimensional arrays are seldom necessary. In most cases, an array of pointers serves the same purpose and allows the size of each "row" to be specified independently, as opposed to the fixed row size of a multidimensional array.

Initialization

Here are a few examples of variable and array initialization:

```
char    firstLetter = 'a';
char    *name = "Dave Mark";
short   value = 0xFFAA;
float   numbers[ 5 ] = { 10.0, 20.0, 35.0, 6.7, .2 };
```

Structures

Structures allow you to group a set of variables under a single name and are declared using the `struct` keyword. The individual variables in a `struct` are known as *fields*. To access a `struct` field, use the `.` operator, as shown in the following example:

```
struct
{
  short   myFirstField;
  float   mySecondField;
} myStruct, *myStructPtr;

myStruct.myFirstField = 20;
```

To access a `struct` using a pointer, use the `->` operator as follows:

```
myStructPtr = &myStruct;

myStructPtr->myFirstField = 20;
```

Unions

Unions allow you to interpret the same block of memory in more than one way. Unions are declared using the same format as a structure declaration, but the `union` keyword is substituted for the `struct` keyword. In a union, however, enough memory is allocated to hold the largest of the declared fields. The contents of the union are interpreted based on the field you reference. Here's an example:

```
union short_or_long
{
  short   myShort;
  long    myLong;
}

union short_or_long myUnion;
```

The union declaration just given merges a `short` and a `long` into a single entity. If you refer to

```
myUnion.myShort
```

the first 2 bytes of the union will be interpreted as a short. If you refer to

```
myUnion.myLong
```

all 4 bytes of the union will be used as a long. The size of the union is determined by the largest of the union's fields.

Typedefs

Typedefs are used to create new variable types from existing types. For example, the typedef statement

```
typedef short    MyType;
```

creates a new type called MyType, which can be used in future variable definitions, such as the following:

```
MyType   myVariable;
```

Typedefs are frequently used in combination with structure and union declarations. Here's a struct example:

```
typedef struct
{
   short shortField;
   long  longField;
} MyStructType;

MyStructType  myStruct;

myStruct.shortField = 20;
```

The typedef statement in this example creates a new symbol with the name MyStructType, which can then be used to define a struct named myStruct.

Automatic Type Conversion

When an operator joins two operands of differing data types, the operands are converted to a common type before the operation is performed. Here's an example:

```
short    myShort = 20;
long     myLong = 10;
long     result;

result = myLong + myShort;
```

In this code, the + operator joins a `short` (2 bytes) and a `long` (4 bytes). Since the `long` is larger than the `short`, the `short` is converted to a `long` before the addition is performed, producing a `long` as a result.

This example typifies C's approach toward automatic type conversion. In general, a small type will be converted to a larger type, rather than the other way around. In this way, no information is lost by truncating a value.

If an operator's operands are built-in C data types (one of `char`, `short`, `int`, `long`, `unsigned`, `unsigned long`, `float`, `double`, or `long double`), the following rules are used to guide the automatic type conversion:

- First, if either of the operands is a `char` or a `short`, that operand is converted to an `int`.
- Next, if the operands are of different types, the shorter of the two operands is converted to the longer of the two types.
- Finally, the result of the operation is converted to the type of the l–value.

For example, if the operands were an `int` and a `double`, the `int` would be promoted to a `double` before the operation was performed. A comparison between a `float` and a `char` would first see the promotion of the `char` to an `int`, then the promotion of the `int` to a `float`.

The rules change when the operands are pointer types instead of built-in types. With one exception, pointer types need to match exactly. If they don't, you'll need to cast one of the pointers to the type of the other pointer.

The exception to this rule involves the void pointer (void *). The void pointer was designed to serve as a generic pointer type, pointing to a block of data whose type may not be known at compile time. In an expression where one of the two operands is a void pointer, no typecasting is necessary. This means that the following code will compile (even if it doesn't do very much):

```
void     *voidPtr;
short    *shortPtr;

voidPtr = shortPtr;
shortPtr = voidPtr;
```

When we get to the topic of automatic type conversion in C++ (see Chapter 4), you'll find that these rules change slightly.

Typecasting

Typecasting offers a more direct method for translating one variable data type to another. A typecast is a combination of types and * operators embedded in parentheses that determine the order of casting. The following code casts a short to a long:

```
(long)myShort
```

The next code casts a short pointer to a long pointer:

```
(long *)myShortPtr
```

The const Qualifier

When a variable is defined using the const qualifier, an initial value must be provided in the definition, and that value cannot be changed for the duration of the program. Here are two examples:

```
const float serialNumber = 523.5876;
const char  myName[] = "Dave Mark";
```

Storage-Class Specifiers

The storage-class specifiers `auto`, `extern`, `static`, `register`, and `volatile` define the mechanism used to create the associated variable. A variable marked as `auto` has the same properties as a local, nonstatic variable. This means that space for the variable is allocated when the defining block is entered and the same space is deallocated when the block is exited.

The `extern` specifier tells you that space for a variable is allocated outside the current scope. `static` variables retain their value even after the block they're defined in is exited. `register` variables are allocated using a register, if the current implementation allows for it.

Finally, `volatile` is a little used qualifier that marks a variable as modifiable from outside the program. `volatile` is implementation dependent. For more information on it, check the manual that comes with your development environment.

Pointers

A variable defined as a pointer is designed to hold the address of a variable or function of a specific type. The * operator combines with a normal variable definition to create a pointer variable, as in the following example:

```
long     myLong;
long     *myLongPtr;
```

These definitions create a `long` and a pointer to a variable of type `long`. To make the pointer point to a `long`, use the & operator. The unary & operator returns the address of its operand:

```
myLongPtr = &myLong;
```

To retrieve a value from a pointer, use the * operator. The * operator takes an address and returns the value at that address:

```
myLong = *myLongPtr;
```

As mentioned earlier, the -> operator can be used with a pointer to a struct to access one of the struct's fields. The * and . operators can be used in the same way. The code

```
myStructPtr->myField
```

has the same effect as the following code:

```
(*myStructPtr).myField
```

Pointers are frequently used to step through an array. To do this, you'll make use of the +, ++, -, and -- operators (described in the section on operators). The + and ++ operators increase the value of a pointer based on the size of the pointer's base type. The - and -- operators do the reverse. For example, + will increment a char pointer by 1 byte, a short pointer by 2 bytes, and a long pointer by 4 bytes. This is precisely the amount of memory you want to increment a pointer to move it from one element of an array to the next element.

Pointer arithmetic comes in especially handy when you're working with character strings, which are implemented as an array of chars. For example, the following code copies one character string to another:

```
void  CopyString( char *source, char *dest )
{
  while ( *source != '\0' )
  {
    *dest = *source;
    dest++;
    source++;
  }
  *dest = '\0';
}
```

This example copies each byte of source to the corresponding byte in dest until source's terminating null byte is encountered. The ++ operator is used to bump the pointers along the character strings.

STYLE

Here's a version of the preceding string-copying example that's preferred by many C programmers:

```
void CopyString( char *source, char *dest )
{
    while ( *dest++ = *source++ )
        ;
}
```

The key to this code is the combination of the =, *, and ++ operators inside the `while` clause. Take a few minutes to analyze this code. This method of copying a null-terminated string is so common (and elegant, in my opinion) that you may want to add it to your personal toolbox.

Operators

At the heart of C is an extensive set of operators that allow you to build complex expressions. Some of the operators work with a single operand. Others require two or more operands. Some operators are mathematical in nature. Some are comparative. This section lists the complete set of ANSI C operators.

Arithmetic Operators

The arithmetic operators are +, −, *, /, and %. Each of these operators is binary (takes two operands). +, −, and * perform addition, subtraction, and multiplication, respectively. / performs integer division, truncating its result to an integral value. % divides its first operand by its second and returns the remainder.

Assignment Operators

All of the assignment operators are binary. The = operator copies the value of its right side to the variable on its left side. All of the other assignment operators combine = with some other operator, as in this example:

```
leftSide += rightSide;
```

This expression is equivalent to the following statement:

```
leftSide = leftSide + rightSide;
```

The augmented assignment operators are +=, -=, *=, /=, %=, >>=, <<=, &=, |=, and ^=. Each of these operators follows the pattern just described. The operator portions of the augmented assignment operators are described individually throughout this section.

Bitwise Logical Operators

The bitwise logical operators are &, |, ^, <<, >>, and ~. ~ is a unary operator (takes a single operand). The remainder of the bitwise logical operators are binary. ~ produces a one's complement of its operand. & performs a bitwise AND, | a bitwise OR, and ^ a bitwise EXCLUSIVE OR on their two operands.

<< and >> perform a left and a right bit shift, respectively, on the left-hand argument. The right-hand argument determines the number of bit positions to shift.

The bitwise OR operator (|) is typically used to change the value of a specified bit to 1. For example, suppose you had a byte with a value, in binary, of 00001111, and you wanted to set its high bit to 1. Use the bitwise OR operator, along with the binary value 10000000:

```
unsigned char   highBitIsOne = 0x80;
    /* 10000000 */
unsigned char   myByte = 0x0F;
    /* 00001111 */

myByte |= highBitIsOne; /* Now myByte
    is 10001111 */
```

The bitwise AND operator (&) is typically used to test whether a bit is set to 1 or to change a bit (or bits) to 0. Consider these two variables:

```
unsigned char   highBitIsOne = 0x80;
   /* 10000000 */
unsigned char   myByte = 0x0F;
   /* 00001111 */
```

To test whether the high bit of myByte is set, use the bitwise AND operator:

```
if ( (myByte & highBitIsOne) ==
   highBitIsOne )
```

This expression will evaluate to true only if the high bit of myByte is set to 1.

This line of code will set the high bit of myByte to 0:

```
myByte &= 0x7F;   /* 0x7F == 01111111 */
```

The Conditional Operator

The conditional operator (? :) is C's only ternary operator (requiring three operands). The operator takes the following form:

```
expression1 ? expression2 : expression3
```

The first expression is evaluated. If it evaluates to true, the second expression is evaluated and that result is the result of the entire ? : operation. If, however, the first expression evaluates to false, the third expression is evaluated and that result is the result of the entire expression.

Increment and Decrement Operators

The increment and decrement operators offer a quick way to increment or decrement a variable. Both of these operators are unary. The increment operator (++) increments its operand by 1.

The decrement operator (--) decrements its operand by 1. Applying either of these operators to an array pointer changes the value of the pointer to point to the next element (either up or down) in the array.

These two operators may be placed before the operand (prefix notation) or immediately after the operand (postfix notation). In prefix notation, the increment or decrement operation is performed before the enclosing expression is evaluated. In postfix notation, the increment or decrement operation is performed after the enclosing expression is evaluated.

Logical Operators

The three logical operators are &&, ||, and !. They manipulate their operands using Boolean logic according to the table in Figure 3.2. && and || are binary operators and perform logical AND and logical OR operations, respectively. ! is a unary operator and performs a logical NOT operation.

FIGURE 3.2

Logic table for the &&, ||, and ! operators.

A	B	!A	A&&B	A‖B
True	True	False	True	True
True	False	False	False	True
False	True	True	False	True
False	False	True	False	False

Relational Operators

The six relational operators are >, >=, <, <=, ==, and !=. All are binary operators and compare the first operand with the second. > returns true if the first operand is greater than the second. >= returns true if the first operand is greater than or equal to the second. < returns true if the first operand is less than the second. <= returns true if the first operand is less than or equal to the second. == returns true if the two operands are equal. != returns true if the two operands are not equal.

The Comma Operator

The comma operator (,) is used to fuse two expressions into a single expression. For example, the line of code

```
i++, j++;
```

increments the variables i and j. The expressions that surround the comma operator are evaluated from left to right. The result of the operation is the value of the rightmost expression.

The sizeof() Operator

Although it appears to be a function call, sizeof() is actually a C operator that takes a single parameter. sizeof() returns the size in bytes of the argument. If the argument is a variable, sizeof() returns the number of bytes allocated for that variable. If the parameter is a type, sizeof() returns the number of bytes necessary to allocate a variable of that type.

Operator Precedence

All of C's operators are ranked according to precedence. In this expression

```
6 + 3 * 5
```

the order in which the two operators are evaluated has a definite effect on the expression's value. If + has a higher precedence than *, the expression will evaluate to 45. If * has a higher precedence, the result will be 21 (the correct answer is 21, by the way).

Two factors determine the order in which an expression's operators are evaluated. If one operator has a higher precedence than another, that operator is evaluated first. If the operators have equal precedence, the operators are evaluated from either left to right or right to left, depending on the operators. The chart in Figure 3.3 ranks each of C's operators and, for each grouping of equal operators, tells whether that group is evaluated from left to right or right to left.

FIGURE 3.3
C operators listed in high to low precedence.

Operators (High to Low Precedence)	Order
->, .	Left to right
Typecast, *, &, unary + and -, !, ~, ++, --, sizeof	Right to left
Arithmetic *, /, %	Left to right
Arithmetic + and -	Left to right
<<, >>	Left to right
>, >=, <, <=,	Left to right
==, !=	Left to right
& (bitwise AND)	Left to right
^	Left to right
|	Left to right
&&	Left to right
||	Left to right
?:	Right to left
=, +=, -=, *=, /=, %=, >>=, <<=, &=, |=, ^=	Right to left
,	Left to right

Statements

C statements are terminated by a semicolon (;). They can be grouped into blocks by using a matching pair of curly braces (left { and right }). Figure 3.4 lists the keywords that can be used in the construction of ANSI C statements. You should be familiar with each of these keywords.

FIGURE 3.4
C statement keywords.

ANSI C Keywords				
auto	do	goto	short	typedef
break	double	if	signed	union
case	else	int	sizeof	unsigned
char	enum	long	static	void
const	extern	register	struct	volatile
continue	float	return	switch	while
default	for			

Functions C statements can be grouped into individual functions. Every program contains at least one function, `main()`. `main()` is automatically called to start the program. When the program starts, `main()` takes two parameters, `argc` and `argv`. `argc` and `argv` are known as *command-line* arguments. `argc` specifies the number of parameters embedded in the second argument, `argv`. `argv` is an array of parameters.

Functions can take parameters, and those parameters may be passed by value or by reference. Each function can also return a value of a specified type. If you don't specify a return type, `int` is assumed by the compiler. The predefined type `void` indicates an absence of a return type or an absence of parameters. A function with no parameters and no return values might look like this:

```
void  GoodForNothing( void )
{
}
```

Typically, functions are declared at the top of the program file (or in a header file) by using function prototypes. Function prototypes allow you to specify a function's return type as well as the type of each of its parameters, adding an extra layer of type-checking to your program.

The Ellipsis

Used at the end of a function's argument list, the ellipsis (`...`) indicates that a variable number of arguments may be passed to the function. For example, consider the following function declaration:

```
void  MyFunc( short atLeastOne, ... );
```

`MyFunc()` requires at least one parameter but may take more than one. The type of the first parameter is `short`. The type of any additional parameters is unspecified.

The classic example of ellipsis use is in the declaration of `printf()`:

```
int printf( char *format, ... );
```

The first parameter is a text string containing the format specification. The remaining arguments (if there are any) are determined by the format string.

Preprocessor Directives

Traditional C compilers compile your program in two passes. The first of these two passes is known as the *preprocessor pass*. There are a number of commands that you can place in your code to instruct the compiler to take a special action during this pass. These commands are known as *preprocessor directives* and always start with the pound sign (#).

Two widely used preprocessor directives are `#define` and `#include`. `#define` takes two parameters and asks the preprocessor to substitute the second parameter for the first throughout the remainder of the code. Since this substitution happens during the first compiler pass, the substitutions are in place for the second pass.

`#include` includes the specified file in the source code, also in time for interpretation by the second pass of the compiler. Typically, the name of the included file ends in `.h` (instead of C's traditional `.c`). These files are known as *header files* and contain `typedefs`, `#defines`, function prototypes, and other useful nonexecutable statements.

Other preprocessor directives include `#elif`, `#else`, `#endif`, `#error`, `#if`, `#ifdef`, `#ifndef`, `#line`, `#pragma`, and `#undef`.

Comments

The character combinations `/*` and `*/` have a special meaning in C. `/*` marks the beginning and `*/` marks the end of a source code comment. When the compiler encounters these characters in your code, it will ignore all characters in the comment, including `/*` and `*/`.

C comments cannot be nested. This means that you can't put a comment block inside another comment block. Also, /* and */ lose their meaning when placed inside a string or character literal.

Summary   It is downright impossible to describe the entire C language in one chapter. However, if you understand the concepts presented here, you are definitely ready for C++. If you ran into trouble anywhere along the line, pick up a copy of the second edition of *The C Programming Language* by Kernighan and Ritchie. Better yet, hook up with your local neighborhood C guru or ask your teacher for help. You'll get much more out of this book once you understand C.

When you're ready, turn the page. C++, here we come!

Chapter 4

Introducing C++

Welcome to the world of C++. This chapter covers all the basics, from operators and keywords to reference types and function name overloading.

This Chapter at a Glance

NOW THAT YOU'VE GOT A REVIEW OF C UNDER YOUR BELT, you're ready to tackle C++. C++ supports all the features of C, with a few twists and a lot more features thrown in.

This chapter starts with a comparison of C and C++, focusing on changes you'll need to make to compile your ANSI C code with an ANSI C++ compiler. It then moves on to some features unique to C++.

Getting C Code to Run under C++

Think of C++ as a superset of C. For the most part, every single feature you've come to know and love in C is available in C++ (albeit with a few changes). As in C, C++ programs start with a `main()` function. All of C's keywords and functions work just fine in C++. If you've ever written a C program that takes advantage of the command-line arguments `argc` and `argv`, you'll be glad to know that they're still around in C++.

In fact, with only a few tweaks here and there, your C programs should run quite well in the C++ world. Try not to get too wrapped up in this section. While it is important that you be aware of each of the issues discussed, some of this stuff is pretty subtle and you may never run into it in your own code. You may want to skim the rest of this section, then come back to it for a quick review once you start coding. Be sure you're back on full alert, however, when we get into new features of C++.

Function Prototypes Are Required

In C, function prototypes are optional. As long as there's no type conflict between a function call and the same function's declaration, your program will compile.

In C++, a function prototype is *required* for each of your program's functions. Your C++ program will not compile unless each and every function prototype is in place. As in C, you can declare a function without a return type. If no return type is present, the function is assumed to have a return type of `int`.

Automatic Type Conversion

If you haven't already, turn back to Chapter 3 and review the section that describes C's automatic type conversion. C++ uses the same rules as C for automatic type conversion, but with a slight twist.

Although a void pointer can be assigned the value of another pointer type without explicit typecasting, the reverse is not true. For example, although the following code compiles properly in C, it will *not* compile in C++:

```
void    *voidPtr;
short   *shortPtr;

voidPtr = shortPtr; /*  <-- This line is just
                            fine... */
shortPtr = voidPtr; /*  <-- This line is fine in C,
                            but WILL NOT compile in C++ */
shortPtr = (short *)voidPtr;  /*  <-- This works in
                                      C++ */
```

Scope Issues

There are several subtle differences between C and C++ involving **scope**. A variable's scope defines the availability of the variable throughout the rest of a program. For example, a global variable is available throughout a program, while a local variable is limited to the block in which it is declared. Though C++ follows the same scope rules as C, there are a few subtleties you should be aware of.

For example, take a look at the following code. Try to guess the value of size at the bottom of main():

```
char   dummy[ 32 ];

int main()
{
  long   size;
```

```
struct dummy
{
  char  myArray[ 64 ];
};

size = sizeof( dummy );

return 0;
}
```

In C, `size` ends up with a value of 32; the reference to `dummy` in the `sizeof()` statement matches the global variable declared at the top of the program. In C++, however, `size` ends up with a value of 64; the reference to `dummy` matches the `struct` tag inside `main()`.

In C++, a structure name declared in an inner scope can hide a name in an outer scope. This same rule holds true for an enumeration:

```
enum color { red, green, blue };
```

In C++, this enum creates a type named `color` that can be used to declare other enums and would obscure a global with the same name.

Here's another example:

```
int main()
{
  struct s
  {
    enum { good, bad, ugly } clint;
  };

  short good;

  return 0;
}
```

An ANSI C compiler will not compile this code, complaining that the identifier `good` was declared twice. The problem here is with the scope of the enumeration constant `good`. In C, an enumeration constant is granted the same scope as a local variable, even if it is embedded in a `struct` definition. When the compiler hits the `short` declaration, it complains that it already has a `good` identifier declared at that level.

In C++, this code compiles cleanly. Why? C++ enumeration constants embedded in a `struct` definition have the same scope as that `struct`'s fields. Thus, the enumeration constant `good` is hidden from the `short` declaration at the bottom of `main()`.

A third example involves multiple declarations of the same variable within the same scope. Consider the following code:

```
short    gMyGlobal;
short    gMyGlobal;   /* Cool in C, error in C++ */
```

The C compiler will resolve these two variable declarations to a single declaration. The C++ compiler, on the other hand, will report an error if it hits two variable declarations with the same name.

def'ə nish' ən

It's useful to be aware of the difference between a **declaration** and a **definition**. A declaration specifies the types of all elements of an identifier. For example, a function prototype is a declaration. Here are some more declarations:

```
char name[ 20 ];
typedef int myType;
const short kMaxNameLength = 20;
extern char aLetter;
short MyFunc( short myParam );
```

As you can see, a declaration can do more than tie a type to an identifier. A declaration can also be a definition. A definition instantiates an identifier, allocating the appropriate amount of memory. In this declaration

```
const short kMaxNameLength = 20;
```

the constant `kMaxNameLength` is also defined and initialized.

New Features of C++

OK, here comes the good stuff! The remainder of this chapter will take you beyond C into the heart of C++. While we won't explore object programming in this chapter, we will cover just about every other C++ concept.

The // Comment Marker

C's comment block markers, /* and */, perform the same function in C++. In addition, C++ supports a single-line comment marker. When a C++ compiler encounters the characters //, it ignores the remainder of that line of code. Here's an example:

```
int main()
{
    short numGuppies; // May increase suddenly!!
}
```

As you'd expect, the characters // are ignored inside a comment block. In the following example, // is included as part of the comment block:

```
int main()
{
    /*    Just a comment...
    //    */
}
```

Conversely, the comment characters /* and */ have no special meaning inside a single-line comment. The start of the comment block in the following example is swallowed up by the single-line comment:

```
int main()
{
    // Don't start a /* comment block
       inside a single-line comment...
       This code WILL NOT compile!!! */
}
```

The compiler will definitely complain about this example!

Handling Input and Output

In a standard C program, input and output are usually handled by Standard Library routines such as `scanf()` and `printf()`. While you can call `scanf()` and `printf()` from within your C++ program, there is an elegant alternative. The `iostream` facility allows you to send a sequence of variables and constants to an output stream, just as `printf()` does. Also, `iostream` makes it easy to convert the data from an input stream into a sequence of variables, just as `scanf()` does.

Though the `iostream` features presented in this section may seem simplistic, don't be fooled. `iostream` is actually quite sophisticated. In fact, `iostream` is far more powerful than C's standard I/O facility. The material given here will allow you to perform the input and output you'll need to get through the next few chapters. Later in the book, we'll explore `iostream` in more depth.

`iostream` predefines three streams for input and output. `cin` is used for input, `cout` for normal output, and `cerr` for error output. The << ("put to") operator is used to send data to a stream. The >> ("get from") operator is used to retrieve data from a stream.

def'ə nish' ən

The << operator is known as the **insertion operator** because it allows you to insert data into a stream, and the >> operator is known as the **extraction operator** because it allows you to extract data from a stream.

Here's an example of the << operator:

```
#include <iostream.h>

int main()
```

```
{
  cout << "Hello, world!";

  return 0;
}
```

This program sends the text string `"Hello, world!"` to the console, just as if you'd used `printf()`. The include file `<iostream.h>` contains all of the definitions needed to use iostream. Since `<<` is a binary operator, it requires two operands. In this case, the operands are `cout` and the string `"Hello, world!"`. The destination stream always appears on the left side of the `<<` operator.

Just like the & and * operators, >> and << have more than one meaning (>> and << are also used as the right and left shift operators). Don't worry about confusion, however. The C++ compiler uses the operator's context to determine which meaning is appropriate.

As with any other operator, you can use more than one `<<` on a single line. Here's another example:

```
#include <iostream.h>

int main()
{
  short   i = 20;

  cout << "The value of i is " << i;

  return 0;
}
```

This program produces the following output:

```
The value of i is 20
```

`iostream` knows all about C++'s built-in data types. This means that text strings are printed as text strings, `shorts` as `shorts`, and `floats` as `floats`, complete with decimal point. No special formatting is necessary.

An iostream Output Example

Here's an interesting example of `iostream` and output. Start up your PC and, if you are running Windows, spawn a DOS shell. Use `cd` to move into the `projects` directory and then into the directory named `chap4_1`. The source code for this example is in the file named `cout.cpp`. To check out the source code, you can enter the DOS command

```
type cout.cpp
```

If you are feeling adventurous, you might want to try your hand at customizing these examples once you've seen them run a few times. If you've upgraded to the full version of Symantec C++ for Windows, you've probably already discovered the nifty built-in source code editor that comes with the compiler. If you have MS-DOS 5.0 or higher, you also have access to Microsoft's built-in text editor, Edit (enter the DOS command `Edit cout.cpp`).

If you don't have access to Edit or the built-in Symantec C++ editor, you can use VDE, the shareware editor included on the floppy in the back of the book.

Whichever method you used to examine the source code in `cout.cpp`, here's what the code should look like:

```
#include <iostream.h>

int main()
{
    char    *name = "Dr. Crusher";
```

```
      cout << "char:     " << name[ 0 ] << '\n'
           << "short:    " << (short)(name[ 0 ]) << '\n'
           << "string:   " << name << '\n'
           << "address:  " << (unsigned long)name;

   return 0;
}
```

Compiling cout.cpp

Compile and link the source code by typing this line at the DOS prompt:

```
sc cout.cpp
```

The compiler will compile your source code, and the linker will link it into an executable file named `cout.exe`. Run your newly created executable by typing

```
cout
```

at the DOS prompt. You should see something like this:

```
char:    D
short:   68
string:  Dr. Crusher
address: 422445152
```

The executable produced by the compiler is designed to be run under DOS. If you are trying to run these programs from inside Windows, you might be surprised by what you see. Windows will spawn a DOS shell and then run the program inside the shell. The trouble is, once the program exits, the shell disappears before you can see your output. If this happens to you, add these two lines at the end of each of the example programs:

```
cout.ignore();
cout.getchar();
```

Basically, these two lines will flush the input buffer and then wait for you to hit a carriage return. Remember, you need to add these lines only if you are running under Windows and your output is disappearing before you get a chance to see it.

The cout Source Code

The program starts by initializing the char pointer name, pointing it to the text string "Dr. Crusher". Next comes one giant statement featuring eleven different occurrences of the << operator. This statement produces four lines of output.

The following line of code

```
cout << "char:     " << name[ 0 ] << '\n'
```

produces this line of output:

```
char:     D
```

As you'd expect, printing name[0] produces the first character in name, an uppercase D.

The next line of code is

```
<< "short:    " << (short)(name[ 0 ]) << '\n'
```

The output associated with this line of code is as follows:

```
short:    68
```

This result was achieved by casting the character 'D' to a short. In general, iostream displays integral types (such as short and int) as an integer. As you'd expect, a float is displayed in floating-point format.

The next line of code

```
<< "string:   " << name << '\n'
```

produces this line of output:

```
string:  Dr. Crusher
```

When the << operator encounters a char pointer, it assumes you want to print a null-terminated string.

The final line of code in our example shows another way to display the contents of a pointer:

```
<< "address: " << (unsigned long)name;
```

Again, name is printed, but this time is cast as an unsigned long. Here's the result:

```
address: 422445152
```

Anytime you encounter an address, take it with a grain of salt. Since your computer and mine are probably quite different, your addresses will probably be different from those shown in the book.

As you can see, cout does what it thinks makes sense for each type it prints. Later in the book, you'll learn how to customize cout by using it to print data in a specified format or teaching it how to print your own data types.

According to the ARM (*The Annotated C++ Reference Manual*), main( )'s type is implementation dependent. Traditionally, main() is declared to return an int. If main() doesn't return a value, the compiler assumes its type to be void. Consider this code:

```
main()
{
}
```

Different compilers deal with this code in different ways. Some print a warning message, telling you that a return value from `main()` was expected, while at least one compiler (Symantec's) refuses to compile this code, generating a compile error.

All of the programs in this book declare `main()` to return an `int`. To avoid compile warnings/errors, each `main()` ends with the line

```
return 0;
```

To avoid repetition, I ignore this line in the code walk-throughs. Just thought you'd like to know why it's in there.

An iostream Input Example

Our next example explores the flip side of `iostream` by reading data in as well as printing it out. Use `cd` to move back up to the `projects` directory and then into the directory named `chap4_2`. The source code for this example is in the file named `cin.cpp`. Compile and link the source code by typing this line at the DOS prompt:

```
sc cin.cpp
```

The compiler will compile your source code, and the linker will link it into an executable file named `cin.exe`. Run your newly created executable by typing

```
cin
```

at the DOS prompt.

First, you'll be prompted to type in your first name. Type in a single name (don't type in any spaces, tabs, or other white space characters) and hit return. Next, you'll be prompted for three numbers: a `short`, a `long`, and a `float`. Type all three numbers on the same line, separating each by a space, and then press enter. `cin` will list your name, as well as each of the three numbers you typed in:

```
Type in your first name: Dave
Short, long, float: 747 123456789 3.14159

Your name is: Dave
myShort: 747
myLong: 123456789
myFloat: 3.14159
```

If things didn't go exactly as planned, try running the program again. This time, when prompted for your first name, be careful to type only a single word containing no white space characters. Next, be sure that the three numbers are in the proper order, a `short`, followed by a `long`, followed by a `float`. As you'll see, `cin` is pretty picky about the format of its input data.

The cin Source Code

As is always the case when you use `iostream`, the program starts by including the file `<iostream.h>`. Next, the constant `kMaxNameLength` is defined, providing a length for the `char` array name:

```
#include <iostream.h>

const short kMaxNameLength = 40;

int main()
```

When a variable is defined using the `const` qualifier, an initial value must be provided in the definition, and that value cannot be changed for the duration of the program. Although some C programmers tend to use `#define` instead of `const`, C++ programmers prefer `const` to `#define`.

cin uses cout and << to prompt for a text string, a short, a long, and a float. cin and >> are used to read the values into the four variables name, myShort, myLong, and myFloat:

```
{
  char   name[ kMaxNameLength ];
  short myShort;
  long   myLong;
  float myFloat;
```

The next line uses << to send a text string to the console:

```
cout << "Type in your first name: ";
```

Next, >> is used to read in a text string:

```
cin >> name;
```

Type your first name and hit a carriage return. Be sure to type your first name only. When the >> operator reads a text string, it reads a character at a time until a white space character (like a space or a tab) is encountered.

Now, three more pieces of data are read using a single statement. First, display the prompt

```
cout << "Short, long, float: ";
```

Then, read in the data, separating the three receiving variables by consecutive >> operators:

```
cin >> myShort >> myLong >> myFloat;
```

Be sure to separate each of the three numbers by a space (or some white space character). Also, make sure the numbers match the type of the corresponding variable. For example, it's probably not a good idea to enter 3.52 or 125000 as a short, although an integer like 47 works fine as a float.

Finally, display each of the variables we worked so hard to fill:

```
cout << "\nYour name is: " << name;
cout << "\nmyShort: " << myShort;
cout << "\nmyLong: " << myLong;
cout << "\nmyFloat: " << myFloat;

return 0;
}
```

More on iostream Later

So far, `iostream` might seem primitive compared to the routines in C's Standard Library. After all, routines like `scanf()` and `printf()` give you precise control over your input and output. Routines like `getchar()` and `putchar()` allow you to process one character at a time, letting *you* decide how to handle white space.

Be patient. I promise you that `iostream` is awesome. The trouble is, to unleash `iostream`'s true power, you must first come up to speed on object programming. The `iostream` concepts presented here are the bare minimum you'll need to get through the sample programs in the next few chapters. Later in the book, we'll examine `iostream` with an electron microscope. For now, basic input and output are all we need.

Default Argument Initializers

C++ allows you to assign default values (known as **default argument initializers**) to a function's arguments. For example, here's a routine designed to generate a tone at a specified frequency:

```
void  GenerateATone( short  frequency = 440 )
{
    // A frequency of 440 is equal to an A note
}
```

If you call this function with a parameter, the value you pass in is used. For example, the call

```
GenerateATone( 330 );
```

will generate a tone with a frequency of 330 beats per second, which, in musical notation, is equivalent to an E note. If you call the function without specifying a value, the default value is used. The call

```
GenerateATone();
```

will generate a tone with a frequency of 440, which represents an A note.

This technique works with multiple parameters as well, although the rules get a bit more complicated. You can specify a default value for a parameter only if you also specify a default for all the parameters that follow it. For example, this declaration is cool:

```
void  GotSomeDefaults( short manny, short moe=2,
  char jack='x' );
```

Since the second parameter has a default, the third parameter *must* have a default. The next declaration *won't* compile, however, because the first parameter specifies a default and the parameter that follows does not:

```
void  WillNotCompile( long time=100L, short stack );
```

Default parameter values are specified in the function prototype rather than in the function's implementation. For example, here's a function prototype, followed by the function itself:

```
void  MyFunc( short param1 = 27 );

void  MyFunc( short param1 )
{
  // Body of the function...
}
```

Many C++ programmers create a separate #include file for their function prototypes. Gathering all the function declarations, including parameters and default values, into a single list makes a handy reference tool. I keep my prototypes in alphabetical order and follow each one with a comment telling me where the actual code for that routine is. Here's an example:

```
void MyFunc( short param1 = 27 );
   // MyFile.cpp
```

A Default Argument Initializer Example

Let's take default argument initializers out for a quick spin. Use cd to move back up to the projects directory and then into the directory named chap4_3. The source code for this example is in the file named prototst.cpp. Compile and link the source code by typing this line at the DOS prompt:

```
sc prototst.cpp
```

The compiler will compile your source code, and the linker will link it into an executable file named prototst.exe. Run your newly created executable by typing

```
prototst
```

at the DOS prompt. Here's what you'll see:

```
MyFunc( 1, 0, 0 )
MyFunc( 1, 2, 0 )
MyFunc( 1, 2, 3 )
```

Let's take a look at the source code.

The prototst Source Code

The key to prototst.cpp lies in the function MyFunc() and its default-laden parameter list. After the obligatory #include of the file <iostream.h>, you'll find the prototype for MyFunc():

```
#include <iostream.h>

void  MyFunc( short param1,
         short param2 = 0,
         short param3 = 0 );
```

Notice that defaults are provided for the second and third parameters only. Both of these parameters have a default value of 0.

main() calls MyFunc() using three different calling sequences. Since no default is provided for MyFunc()'s first parameter, all calls to MyFunc() *must* include at least one value. Calls like

```
MyFunc();
```

or

```
MyFunc( , 1 );
```

will cause the compiler to complain bitterly.

The first call of MyFunc() passes a single value, forcing MyFunc() to rely on its default values for the second and third parameters. The call

```
MyFunc( 1 );
```

produces this line of output:

```
MyFunc( 1, 0, 0 )
```

Notice that the default value of 0 is used for the second and third parameters.

Next, the code

```
MyFunc( 1, 2 );
```

produces this line of output:

```
MyFunc( 1, 2, 0 )
```

In this case, values are passed in for the first and second parameters, while the default value of 0 is used for the third parameter.

Finally, the code

```
MyFunc( 1, 2, 3 );
```

produces this line of output:

```
MyFunc( 1, 2, 3 )
```

In this last case, the three values passed in override all of the parameter defaults.

The function `MyFunc()` uses `iostream` to print the current values of `MyFunc()`'s three parameters:

```
void  MyFunc( short param1,
         short param2,
         short param3 )
{
  cout << "MyFunc( " << param1
    << ", " << param2
    << ", " << param3
    << " )\n";
}
```

Notice that the defaults are specified in the function prototype and not in the function title.

Reference Variables

In C, all parameters are passed by value as opposed to being passed by reference. When you pass a parameter to a C function, the value of the parameter is passed on to the function. Any changes you make to this value are *not* carried back to the calling function.

Here's an example:

```
void  DoubleMyValue( short valueParam )
{
  valueParam *= 2;
}

int main()
{
  short number = 10;
```

```
   DoubleMyValue( number );

   return 0;
}
```

`main()` sets number to 10, then passes it to the function `DoubleMyValue()`. Since number is passed by value, the call to `DoubleMyValue()` has no effect on number. When `DoubleMyValue()` returns, number still has a value of 10.

Here's an updated version of the program:

```
void  DoubleMyValue( short *numberPtr )
{
   *numberPtr *= 2;
}

int main()
{
   short number = 10;

   DoubleMyValue( &number );

   return 0;
}
```

In this version, number's address is passed to `DoubleMyValue()`. By dereferencing this pointer, `DoubleMyValue()` can reach out and change the value of number. When `DoubleMyValue()` returns, number will have a value of 20.

The Reference Variable

Reference variables allow you to pass a parameter by reference, without using pointers.

Here's another version of the program, this time implemented with a reference variable:

```
void  DoubleMyValue( short &referenceParam )
{
   referenceParam *= 2;
}
```

```
int main()
{
    short number = 10;

    DoubleMyValue( number );

    return 0;
}
```

Notice that this code looks just like the first version, with one small exception. DoubleMyValue()'s parameter is defined using the & operator:

```
short &referenceParam
```

The & marks referenceParam as a reference variable and tells the compiler that referenceParam and its corresponding input parameter, number, are one and the same. Since both names refer to the same location in memory, changing the value of referenceParam is *exactly* the same as changing number.

Some people declare their reference variables and parameters like this:

```
short  &referenceParam
```

placing the & next to the variable. Some others do it this way,

```
short & referenceParam
```

leaving white space in between the two, and others like this:

```
short& referenceParam
```

placing the & directly after the type. All of these will work. Use whichever one you prefer; just be consistent.

A Reference Variable Example

Here's an example that should make things a little clearer. Use `cd` to move back up to the `projects` directory and then into the directory named `chap4_4`. The source code for this example is in the file named `refrence.cpp`. Compile and link the source code by typing this line at the DOS prompt:

```
sc refrence.cpp
```

The compiler will compile your source code, generating a pair of identical warning messages along the way. For the moment, ignore these warnings. We'll get to them in a bit. Despite these warnings, the linker will still link your code into an executable file named `refrence.exe`. Run your newly created executable by typing

```
refrence
```

at the DOS prompt. Here's what you'll see:

```
&number:       120726708
&longNumber:   120726710

&valueParam:   120726702
After ByValue: 12

&refParam:     120726708
After ByRef( short ): 24

&refParam:     120726714
After ByRef( long ): 12
```

The nine-digit numbers shown here are addresses. Unless you snuck in here and have been using my PC, your addresses will probably be different.

Let's take a look at the source code.

The refrence Source Code

`refrence.cpp` starts with a pair of function prototypes. Just like the routine `DoubleMyValue()` presented earlier, both of these routines take a single parameter and double its value:

```
#include <iostream.h>

void  CallByValue( short valueParam );
void  CallByReference( short &refParam );
```

Notice that `CallByValue()` takes a `short` as a parameter using the standard by-value parameter passing mechanism, while `CallByReference()` takes a reference variable as a parameter passed by reference.

main() starts by defining two variables, a `short` and a `long`, initializing each to a value of 12:

```
int main()
{
  short number = 12;
  long  longNumber = 12L;
```

Next, the address of both variables is printed in the console. When a parameter is successfully passed by reference, the calling and receiving parameters will have the same address:

```
cout << "&number:      " <<
  (unsigned long)&number << "\n";

cout << "&longNumber: " <<
  (unsigned long)&longNumber << "\n\n";
```

Perhaps you noticed that `refrence` prints its addresses in decimal, rather than hexadecimal, format. Later in the book, you'll learn how to customize `cout` to print data in any format you like. For the moment, we'll print out addresses by casting them to `unsigned longs`.

Next, number is passed by value to `CallByValue()`:

```
CallByValue( number );
```

`CallByValue()` prints the address of, and then doubles the value of, its parameter. number's address, which we printed earlier, was `120726708`. The address of the value parameter is `120726702`. Clearly, this parameter was not passed by reference, which explains why number's value is not changed by the call to `CallByValue()`. As proof, the value of number is printed again. As you can see by the output, the value stays at 12:

```
cout << "After ByValue: " << number << "\n\n";
```

Then, number is passed to `CallByReference()`:

```
CallByReference( number );
```

`CallByReference()` also prints the address of its parameter. When we compare this address with the address printed earlier, they match exactly. number's address (printed earlier) was `120726708`. The address of `CallByReference()`'s parameter is also `120726708`. This call by reference was successful! As proof, when the value of number is printed for a third time, its value doubles to 24:

```
cout << "After ByRef( short ): " << number
  << "\n\n";
```

Finally, a `long` is passed to `CallByReference()`:

```
CallByReference( longNumber );
```

Since `CallByReference()` declares its parameter as a reference to a `short`, the compiler is faced with an interesting problem. Reference variables work only if the type of the variable being referenced agrees with the type of the reference variable. When this isn't the case, the compiler creates a temporary variable that is referenced by the reference parameter in the called routine. When a change is made to this parameter, the change is made to the temporary variable and not to the matching parameter in the calling function.

In this case, the value of the `long` is passed on to `CallByReference()`. As proof, compare the address of `longNumber`, which is 120726710, with the parameter address printed out by `CallByReference()`, which is 120726714. As you can see, the addresses don't match.

> When you compiled `refrence.cpp`, the compiler generated warnings that referred to this line of code:
>
> ```
> CallByReference( longNumber );
> ```
>
> The problem here is that `longNumber` is a `long`, but `CallByReference()` expects a `short` reference variable. Since the types don't agree, the compiler prints a warning and then creates a temporary variable.

To add more proof to the pudding, when the value of `longNumber` is printed upon `CallByReference()`'s return, it remains at 12, unchanged from its original value:

```
cout << "After ByRef( long ): " << longNumber << "\n";

    return 0;
}
```

> Reference variables are frequently used as call-by-reference parameters. However, they can also be used to establish a link between two variables in the same scope. Here's an example:
>
> ```
> short    romulus;
> short    &remus = romulus;
> ```
>
> The first line of code defines a `short` with the name `romulus`. The second line of code declares a reference

variable with the name `remus`, linking it to the variable `romulus`. Just as before, the `&` marks `remus` as a reference variable.

Now that `remus` and `romulus` are linked, they share the same location in memory. Changing the value of one is *exactly* the same as changing the value of the other.

It's important to note that a reference variable must be initialized with a variable as soon as it is declared. The following code will not compile:

```
short     romulus;
short     &remus;  // Will not compile!!!

remus = romulus;
```

The reference variable must also be of the same type as the variable it references. The following code won't work:

```
short     romulus;
long      &remus = romulus; // Type mismatch!!!
```

In addition, once established, the link between a reference and a regular variable cannot be changed as long as the reference remains in scope. In other words, once `remus` is linked to `romulus`, it cannot be set to reference a different variable.

Function Name Overloading

The next feature up for discussion, **function name overloading**, allows you to write several functions that share the same name.

Suppose you needed a function that would print the value of one of your variables, be it `long`, `short`, or a text string. You could write one function that takes four parameters:

```
Display( short   whichType,
         long    longParam,
         short   shortParam,
         char    *textParam );
```

The first parameter might act like a switch, determining which of the three types you were passing in for printing. The main code of the function might look like this:

```
if ( whichType == kIsLong )
  cout << "The long is:  " << longParam << "\n";
else if ( whichType == kIsShort )
  cout << "The short is: " << shortParam << "\n";
else if ( whichType == kIsText )
  cout << "The text is:  " << text << "\n";
```

Another solution is to write three separate functions, one for printing `longs`, one for `shorts`, and one for text strings:

```
void  DisplayLong( long longParam );
void  DisplayShort( short shortParam );
void  DisplayText( char *text );
```

Each of these solutions has an advantage. The first solution groups all printing under a single umbrella, making the code somewhat easier to maintain. On the other hand, the second solution is more modular than the first. If you want to change the method you use to display `longs`, you modify only the routine that works with `longs`; you don't have to deal with the logic that displays other types.

As you might expect, there is a third solution that combines the benefits of the first two. Here's how it works.

As mentioned earlier, C++ allows several functions to share the same name by way of function name overloading. When an overloaded function is called, the compiler compares the parameters in the call with the parameter lists in each of the candidate functions. The candidate with the most closely matching parameter list is the one that gets called.

def'ə nish' ən

A function's parameter list is also known as its **signature**. A function's name and signature combine to distinguish it from all other functions. Note that a function's return type is not part of its signature.

A Function Name Overloading Example

Earlier, we looked at two solutions to our multitype printing problem. As promised, here's a third solution that takes advantage of function name overloading. Use cd to move back up to the projects directory and then into the directory named chap4_5. The source code for this example is in the file named overload.cpp. Compile and link the source code by typing this line at the DOS prompt:

```
sc overload.cpp
```

The compiler will compile your source code, and the linker will link it into an executable file named overload.exe. Run your newly created executable by typing

```
overload
```

at the DOS prompt. Here's what you'll see:

```
The short is: 3
The long is:  12345678
The text is:  Make it so...
```

Let's take a look at the source code.

The overload Source Code

overload.cpp starts with three function prototypes, each of which shares the name Display():

```
#include <iostream.h>

void  Display( short shortParam );
void  Display( long longParam );
void  Display( char *text );
```

Notice that each version of Display() has a unique signature. This is important. You are *not* allowed to define two functions with the same name and the same signature.

main() starts by defining three variables: a short, a long, and a text string:

```
int main()
{
  short myShort = 3;
  long  myLong = 12345678L;
  char  *text = "Make it so...";
```

Next, Display() is called three times. First, a short is passed as a parameter. Since this call exactly matches one of the Display() routines, the compiler doesn't have a problem deciding which function to call:

```
Display( myShort );
```

Similarly, the calls passing a long and a text string to Display() match perfectly with the Display() functions having long and text string signatures:

```
Display( myLong );

Display( text );

return 0;
}
```

The signatures of these three versions of Display() feature a short, a long, and a text string, respectively:

```
void  Display( short shortParam )
{
  cout << "The short is: " << shortParam << "\n";
}

void  Display( long longParam )
{
  cout << "The long is:  " << longParam << "\n";
}

void  Display( char *text )
{
```

```
    cout << "The text is:   " << text << "\n";
}
```

Matching Rules for Overloaded Functions

The preceding example was fairly straightforward. The compiler had no difficulty deciding which version of `Display()` to call because each of the calls matched perfectly with one of the `Display()` functions. What do you think would happen if you passed a `float` to `Display()`?

```
Display( 1.0 );
```

When the compiler can't find an exact match for an overloaded function call, it turns to a set of rules that determine the best match for this call. After applying each of the rules, unless one and only one match is found, the compiler reports an error.

As you've already seen, the compiler starts the matching process by looking for an exact match between the name and signature of the function call and a declared function. If a match is not found, the compiler starts promoting the type of any integral parameters in the function call, following the rules for automatic type conversion described in Chapter 3. For example, a `char` or a `short` would be promoted to an `int` and a `float` would be promoted to a `double`.

If a match is still not found, the compiler starts promoting nonintegral types. Finally, the ellipsis operator in a called function is taken into account, matching against zero or more parameters.

In answer to our earlier question, passing a `float` to `Display()` would result in an error, listing the function call as ambiguous. If we had written a version of `Display()` with a `float` or a `double` in its signature, the compiler would find the match.

The new and delete Operators

In C, memory allocation typically involves a call to `malloc()` paired with a call to `free()` when the memory is no longer needed. In C++, the same functionality is provided by the operators `new` and `delete`.

Call new when you want to allocate a block of memory. For example, the following code allocates a block of 1024 chars:

```
char   *buffer;

buffer = new char[ 1024 ];
```

new takes a type as an operand, allocates a block of memory the same size as the type, and returns a pointer to the block. To return the memory to the heap, use the delete operator. The next code frees up the memory just allocated:

```
delete [] buffer;
```

The brackets in the preceding line of code indicate that the item to be deleted is a pointer to an array. If you are deleting something other than a pointer to an array, leave the brackets out:

```
int  myIntPtr;

myIntPtr = new int;

delete myIntPtr;
```

new can be used with any legal C++ type, including those you create yourself. Here are a few examples:

```
struct Wobble
{
  short    papaWobble;
  short    mamaWobble;
  long     littleBabyWobble;
} ;

short           *shortPtr;
long double     *longDoublePtr;
Wobble          *wobblePtr;
```

```
shortPtr = new short;
longDoublePtr = new long double;
wobblePtr = new Wobble;
```

Here's an example of a *bad* use of new:

```
short *shortPtr;

shortPtr = new 1024;   // Will not compile!!!
```

Though you can pass a constant to malloc(), a constant is not a type and has no place in new.

What to Do When new Fails

Every program that allocates memory runs the risk that its request for memory will fall on deaf ears, most likely because there's no more memory left to allocate. If your program uses new to allocate memory, it had better detect, and handle, any failure on new's part.

Since new returns a value of 0 when it fails, the simplest approach just checks this return value, taking the appropriate action when new fails:

```
char   *bufPtr;

bufPtr = new char[ 1024 ];

if ( bufPtr == 0 )
  cout << "Not enough memory!!!";
else
  DoSomething( bufPtr );
```

This code uses new to allocate a 1024-byte buffer. If new fails, an error message is printed; otherwise, the program goes on its merry way.

This approach requires that you check the return value every time you call new. If your program performs a lot of memory allocation, this memory-checking code can really add up. As your programs get larger and more sophisticated, you might want to consider a second strategy.

C++ allows you to specify a single routine, known as a new handler, that gets called if and when new fails. Design your new handler for the general case so that it can respond to *any* failed attempt to allocate memory.

Whether or not you designate a new handler, new will still return 0 if it fails. This means you can design a two-tiered memory management strategy combining a new handler and code that runs if new returns 0.

To specify a new handler, pass the handler's name to the function set_new_handler(). To use set_new_handler(), be sure to include the file <new.h>:

```
#include <new.h>

void   NewFailed();

int main()
{
  set_new_handler( NewFailed );
     .
     .
     .
}
```

One possible memory allocation strategy is to allocate a block of memory at the beginning of your program, storing a pointer to the block in a global variable. Then, when new fails, your program can free up the spare memory block, ensuring that it will have enough memory to perform any housekeeping chores that it requires in a memory emergency.

A new Example

Our next sample program repeatedly calls new until the program runs out of memory, keeps track of the number of memory requests, and then reports on the amount of memory allocated before failure. This program uses the spare memory scheme just described. Use cd to move back up to the projects directory and then into the directory named chap4_6. The source code for this example is in the file named newtestr.cpp. Compile and link the source code by typing this line at the DOS prompt:

```
sc newtestr.cpp
```

The compiler will compile your source code, and the linker will link it into an executable file named newtestr.exe. Run your newly created executable by typing

```
newtestr
```

at the DOS prompt. Here's what you'll see:

```
Installing NewHandler...
Number of blocks allocated: 33
```

The number of blocks you can allocate before you run out of memory depends on the amount of memory available to your program. Don't be too surprised if your number differs from the number of blocks shown in this example.

Let's take a look at the source code.

The newtestr Source Code

newtestr.cpp starts by including both <iostream.h> for access to the iostream library and <new.h> for access to the set_new_handler() function:

```
#include <iostream.h>
#include <new.h>
```

Next come a pair of declarations, creating values for the constants false and true:

```
const int    false=0;
const int    true=1;
```

NewFailed() is the function we want called if new fails in its attempt to allocate memory:

```
void  NewFailed();
```

newtestr makes use of two global variables. gDone acts as a flag, initially set to false, but set to true when we're ready to exit our memory allocation loop; gSpareBlockPtr is a pointer to the spare block of memory we allocate at the beginning of the program:

```
char   gDone = false;
char   *gSpareBlockPtr = 0;
```

main() uses two local variables. myPtr acts as a pointer to the blocks of memory we allocate; numBlocks tracks the number of blocks we allocate before new finally fails:

```
int main()
{
  char   *myPtr;
  long   numBlocks = 0;
```

Next, we'll send an appropriate message to the console:

```
cout << "Installing NewHandler...\n";
```

set_new_handler() is called to set NewFailed() as the routine to be called if and when new fails:

```
set_new_handler( NewFailed );
```

Then, the spare block of memory (20 kilobytes) is allocated, and a pointer to the spare block is stored in gSpareBlockPtr:

```
gSpareBlockPtr = new char[20480];
```

> Your C++ environment most likely has a fixed limit on the size of a single block of memory. Many environments limit a single block to 32 kilobytes. If you need more memory than your environment allows, design a workaround using multiple blocks.

Next, we enter an endless loop, allocating a 1-kilobyte block and incrementing numBlocks:

```
while ( gDone == false )
{
  myPtr = new char[1024];
  numBlocks++;
}
```

> Notice that we don't squirrel away the pointers to these allocated blocks. Once we allocate a new block, we lose the pointer to the previously allocated block. That block can never be deleted and is lost forever. Not a particularly good memory management scheme, eh? Make sure you balance every use of new with a corresponding delete.

Once we've allocated all the available memory, new will fail and NewFailed() will be called. NewFailed() sets gDone to true, and the memory allocation loop exits. Once the loop exits, we print out the number of blocks we were able to allocate:

```
cout << "Number of blocks allocated: " <<
  numBlocks;

return 0;
}
```

NewFailed() starts by checking to see whether gSpareBlockPtr actually points to a block of memory. After all, new might fail when we first try to allocate the spare block. If we were able to allocate the spare block, NewFailed() uses delete to return the block to the heap and gSpareBlockPtr is reset to 0:

```
if ( gSpareBlockPtr != 0 )
{
  delete gSpareBlockPtr;
  gSpareBlockPtr = 0;
}
```

Finally, gDone is set to true:

```
gDone = true;
}
```

The Scope Resolution Operator

The next feature we'll examine is C++'s **scope resolution operator** (::). The scope resolution operator precedes a variable, telling the compiler to look outside the current block for a variable of the same name.

Suppose you declare a global variable and a local variable with the same name:

```
short    number;

int main()
```

```
{
  short    number;

  number = 5;      // local reference
  ::number = 10;   // global reference

  return 0;
}
```

Inside main( ), the first assignment statement refers to the local definition of number. The second assignment statement uses the scope resolution operator to refer to the global definition of number. This code leaves the local number with a value of 5 and the global number with a value of 10.

A Scope Resolution Operator Example

Our next sample program offers a quick demonstration of the scope resolution operator. Use cd to move back up to the projects directory and then into the directory named chap4_7. The source code for this example is in the file named scopetst.cpp. Compile and link the source code by typing this line at the DOS prompt:

```
sc scopetst.cpp
```

The compiler will compile your source code, and the linker will link it into an executable file named scopetst.exe. Run your newly created executable by typing

```
scopetst
```

at the DOS prompt. Here's what you'll see:

```
yourValue: 5
yourValue: 10
yourValue: 5
```

Let's take a look at the source code.

The scopetst Source Code

scopetst.cpp defines a global variable with the name myValue, initializing it to a value of 5:

```
#include <iostream.h>

short myValue = 5;
```

main() defines a local variable named yourValue and assigns it the value in myValue:

```
int main()
{
   short yourValue = myValue;
```

Then, yourValue is printed out, showing it with a value of 5, the same as the global myValue:

```
   cout << "yourValue: " << yourValue << "\n";
```

Next, a local with the name myValue is defined and initialized with a value of 10. When myValue is copied to yourValue, which variable is copied, the local or the global?

```
   short myValue = 10;
   yourValue = myValue;
```

As you can see from the output, the reference to myValue matches with the local declaration, showing yourValue with a value of 10:

```
   cout << "yourValue: " << yourValue << "\n";
```

Then, the scope resolution operator is used to copy myValue to yourValue. When yourValue is printed again, it has a value of 5, showing that ::myValue refers to the global declaration of myValue:

```
   yourValue = ::myValue;
   cout << "yourValue: " << yourValue << "\n";

   return 0;
}
```

WARNING

> The scope resolution operator can be applied only when a match is available. Applying the scope resolution operator to a local variable without a corresponding global will generate a compile error. To see this for yourself, add the following code to the end of `main()` and try to compile it:
>
> ```
> ::yourValue = 20;
> ```
>
> Since there is no global named `yourValue`, the code will not compile.

Inline Functions

OK. One final topic, then we'll move on to object programming. Traditionally, when a function is called, the CPU executes a set of instructions that move control from the calling function to the called function. Tiny as these instructions may be, they still take time. C++, however, provides **inline functions**, which allow you to bypass these instructions and save a bit of execution time. Here's how this feature works.

When you declare a function using the `inline` keyword, the compiler copies the body of the function into the calling function, making the copied instructions a part of the calling function as if it were written that way originally. The benefit to you is a slight improvement in performance. The cost is in memory usage. Why? If you call an inline function twenty times from within your program, twenty copies of the function will be grafted into your object code.

An inline Function Example

Our final sample program features a single inline function that returns the value achieved when its first argument is raised to its second argument's power. As an example, the following call will return the value $2^5 = 2*2*2*2*2 = 32$:

```
power( 2, 5 );
```

Use cd to move back up to the projects directory and then into the directory named chap4_8. The source code for this example is in the file named inline.cpp. Compile and link the source code by typing this line at the DOS prompt:

```
sc inline.cpp
```

The compiler will compile your source code, and the linker will link it into an executable file named inline.exe. Run your newly created executable by typing

```
inline
```

at the DOS prompt. Here's what you'll see:

```
power( 2, 3 ): 8
power( 3, 6 ): 729
power( 5, 0 ): 1
power( -3, 4 ): 81
```

Let's take a look at the source code.

The inline Source Code

inline.cpp starts with the standard include file, followed by a function prototype that features the keyword inline:

```
#include <iostream.h>

inline  long power( short base, short exponent );
```

main() calls power() four times and prints the result of each call:

```
int main()
{
  cout << "power( 2, 3 ): " <<
      power( 2, 3 ) << "\n";

  cout << "power( 3, 6 ): " <<
      power( 3, 6 ) << "\n";

  cout << "power( 5, 0 ): " <<
```

```
        power( 5, 0 ) << "\n";

    cout << "power( -3, 4 ): " <<
        power( -3, 4 ) << "\n";

    return 0;
}
```

By preceding `power()`'s declaration by the `inline` keyword, we've asked the compiler to replace each of the four function calls in `main()` with the code in `power()`. Note that this replacement affects the object code and has no impact on the source code:

```
inline  long power( short base, short exponent )
{
  long  product = 1;
  short i;

  if ( exponent < 0 )
    return( 0 );

  for ( i=1; i<=exponent; i++ )
    product *= base;

  return( product );
}
```

The two clear benefits of using inline code instead of a #define macro are type-safety and side-effects protection.
    Consider this #define macro:

```
#define square(a) ( (a) * (a) )
```

Compare that macro to this inline function:

```
inline int square( int a )
{
    return( a * a );
}
```

The inline version restricts its parameter to an integral value, while the `#define` performs a simple-minded text substitution.

Now suppose you call `square()` with a prefix operator:

```
xSquared = square( ++x );
```

The `#define` version expands this as follows:

```
xSquared = ( (++x) * (++x) );
```

which has the unwanted side effect of incrementing x twice. The inline version doesn't do this.

The upshot here is that both `#defines` and `inlines` offer an inline performance advantage, but the `inline` does its job a little more carefully.

Summary Congratulations! You've reached the first summit in your quest for C++ mastery. You've moved well beyond the boundaries of C and covered most of the syntax you'll need to build your own C++ programs. Your next goal is to move on to Chapter 5 and explore the world of object programming.

Object Programming Basics

This chapter introduces you to the basics of object programming, the heart and soul of C++. You'll learn all about C++ structures, see what sets them apart from their C brethren, and learn how to use C++ to create objects of your very own.

This Chapter at a Glance

BEFORE WE GET INTO THE MAIN THRUST OF THIS CHAPTER, let's take a moment and talk about **objects**.

There is nothing mysterious about the concept of an object. In C++, an object is any instance of a data type. For example, this line of code

```
int myInt;
```

declares an `int` object. This chapter will teach you how to use C++ to create, destroy, and manipulate objects in very powerful ways.

The first object we'll take a look at is the structure.

The Organizational Power of the Structure

One of the most valuable features shared by C and C++ is the structure. Without the structure, you'd have no way to group data that belonged together. For example, suppose you wanted to implement an employee data base that tracked an employee's name, employee ID, and salary. You might design a structure that looks like this:

```
const short kMaxNameSize = 20;

struct Employee
{
  char    name[ kMaxNameSize ];
  long    id;
  float   salary;
};
```

The great advantage of this structure is that it lets you bundle several pieces of information together under a single name. This concept is known as encapsulation.

For example, if you wrote a routine to print an employee's data, you *could* write

```
Employee  newHire;
  .
  .
  .

PrintEmployee( newHire.name, newHire.id,
  newHire.salary );
```

Did you notice anything unusual about the declaration of newHire in the preceding code sample? In C, this code would not have compiled. Instead, the declaration would have looked like this:

```
struct Employee newHire; /* The C version */
```

When the C++ compiler sees a structure declaration, it uses the structure name to create a new data type, making it available for future structure declarations.

On the other hand, it would be so much more convenient to pass the data in its encapsulated form:

```
PrintEmployee( &newHire );
```

Encapsulation allows you to represent complex information in a more natural, easily accessible form. In the C language, the `struct` is the most sophisticated encapsulation mechanism available. As you'll soon see, C++ takes encapsulation to a new level.

Encapsulating Data and Functions

While C structures are limited strictly to data, C++ supports structures composed of both data and functions.

Here's an example of a C++ structure declaration:

```
const short kMaxNameSize = 20;

struct Employee
{
//      Data members...
    char        employeeName[ kMaxNameSize ];
    long        employeeID;
    float       employeeSalary;

//      Member functions...
    void        PrintEmployee();
};
```

This example declares a new type named `Employee`. You can use the `Employee` type to declare individual `Employee` objects. Each `Employee` object is said to be a member of the `Employee` **class**.

The `Employee` class consists of three data fields as well as a function named `PrintEmployee()`. In C++, a class's data fields are known as **data members** and its functions are known as **member functions**.

Each `Employee` object you create gets its own copy of the `Employee` class data members. All `Employee` objects share a single set of `Employee` member functions.

Later in the chapter, you'll see how to access an object's data members and member functions. For now, let's take a look at the mechanisms C++ provides to create and destroy objects.

Creating an Object

There are two ways to create a new object. The simplest method is to define the object directly, just as you would a local variable:

```
Employee  employee1;
```

This definition creates an `Employee` object whose name is `employee1`. `employee1` consists of a block of memory large enough to accommodate each of the three `Employee` data members.

When you create an object by defining it directly, as we did above, memory for the object is allocated when the definition moves into scope. That same memory is freed up when the object drops out of scope.

For example, you might define an object at the beginning of a function:

```
void  CreateEmployee()
{
   Employee  employee1;

      .
      .
      .

}
```

When the function is called, memory for the object is allocated, right along with the function's other local objects. When the function exits, the object's memory is deallocated.

---

def'ə nish' ən

When the memory for an object is deallocated, the object is said to be *destroyed*.

If you want a little more control over when your object is destroyed, take advantage of C++'s new operator (introduced in Chapter 4).

First, define an object pointer, then call new to allocate the memory for your object. new returns a pointer to the newly created object. Here's some code that creates an Employee object:

```
Employee  *employeePtr;

employeePtr = new Employee;
```

The first line of code defines a pointer designed to point to an Employee object. The second line uses new to create an Employee object. new returns a pointer to the newly created Employee.

Accessing an Object's Members

Once you've created an object, you can modify its data members and call its member functions. If you've defined the object directly, you'll refer to its data members using the . operator:

```
Employee  employee1;

employee1.employeeSalary = 200.0;
```

If you're referencing the object through a pointer, use the -> operator:

```
Employee  *employeePtr;

employeePtr = new Employee;

employeePtr->employeeSalary = 200.0;
```

To call a member function, use the same technique. If the object was defined directly, you'll use the . operator:

```
Employee  employee1;

employee1.PrintEmployee();
```

If you're referencing the object through a pointer, you'll use the `->` operator:

```
Employee  *employeePtr;

employeePtr = new Employee;

employeePtr->PrintEmployee();
```

The Current Object

In the previous examples, each reference to a data member or member function started with an object or object pointer. Inside a member function, however, the object or object pointer isn't necessary to refer to the object for which the member function is executing.

For example, inside the `PrintEmployee()` function, you can refer to the data member `employeeSalary` directly, without referring to an object or object pointer:

```
if ( employeeSalary <= 200 )
  cout << "Give this person a raise!!!";
```

This code is a bit puzzling. What object does `employeeSalary` belong to? After all, you're used to writing

```
myObject->employeeSalary
```

instead of just plain

```
employeeSalary
```

The key to this puzzle lies in knowing which object spawned the call of `PrintEmployee()` in the first place. Although this may not be obvious, a call to a nonstatic member function *must* originate with a single object.

As you'll see later in the book, class members may be declared as static. A static data member holds a value that is global to a class and not specific to a single object of that class. A static member function is usually designed to work with a class's static data members.

Suppose you called `PrintEmployee()` from a nonEmployee function (such as `main()`). You *must* precede this call with a reference to an object:

```
employeePtr->PrintEmployee();
```

Whenever a member function is called, C++ keeps track of the object used to call the function. This object is known as the **current object**.

In the call of `PrintEmployee()` above, the object pointed to by `employeePtr` is the current object. Whenever this call of `PrintEmployee()` refers to an `Employee` data member or function *without* using an object reference, the current object (in this case, the object pointed to by `employeePtr`) is assumed.

Suppose `PrintEmployee()` then called another `Employee` function. The object pointed to by `employeePtr` is still considered the current object. A reference to `employeeSalary` would still refer to the current object's copy of `employeeSalary`.

The point to remember is that a nonstatic member function always starts with a single object in mind.

The "this" Object Pointer

C++ provides a generic object pointer, available inside any member function, that points to the current object. The generic pointer has the name "`this`." For example, inside every `Employee` function, the line

```
this->employeeSalary = 400;
```

is equivalent to this line:

```
employeeSalary = 400;
```

    `this` is useful when a member function wants to return a pointer to the current object, pass the address of the current object on to another function, or just store the address somewhere. This line of code

```
return this;
```

returns the address of the current object.

Deleting an Object

When you create an object using `new`, you have to take responsibility for destroying the object at the appropriate time. Just as a C programmer balances a call to `malloc()` with a call to `free()`, a C++ programmer balances each use of the `new` operator with an eventual use of the `delete` operator. Here's the syntax:

```
Employee  *employeePtr;

employeePtr = new Employee;

delete employeePtr;
```

    As you'd expect, `delete` destroys the specified object, freeing up any memory allocated for the object. Note that this freed-up memory includes memory for the actual object only and does not include any extra memory you may have allocated.

    For example, suppose the object is a structure and one of its data members is a pointer to another structure. When you `delete` the first structure, the second structure is not `deleted`.

If `delete` is used with a pointer having a value of 0, `delete` does nothing. If the pointer has *any other value*, `delete` will try to destroy the specified object.

Writing Member Functions

Once your structure is declared, you're ready to write your member functions. Member functions behave in much the same way as ordinary functions, with a few small differences. One difference, pointed out earlier, is that a member function has access to the data members and member functions of the object used to call it.

Another difference lies in the function implementation's title line. Here's a sample:

```
void  Employee::PrintEmployee()
{
  cout << "Employee Name:   " << employeeName << "\n";
}
```

Notice that the function name is preceded by the class name and two colons. This notation is mandatory and tells the compiler that this function is a member of the specified class.

The Constructor Function

Typically, when you create an object, you'll want to perform some sort of initialization on the object. For instance, you might want to provide initial values for your object's data members. The **constructor function** is C++'s built-in initialization mechanism.

The constructor function (or just plain constructor) is a member function that has the same name as the object's class. For example, the constructor for the `Employee` class is named `Employee()`. When an object is created, the constructor for that class is called.

Consider this code:

```
Employee  *employeePtr;

employeePtr = new Employee;
```

In the second line, the `new` operator allocates a new `Employee` object, then immediately calls the object's constructor. Once the constructor returns, the address of the new object is assigned to `employeePtr`.

This same scenario holds true in this declaration:

```
Employee  employee1;
```

As soon as the object is created, its constructor is called.

Here's our `Employee struct` declaration with the constructor declaration added in:

```
const short kMaxNameSize = 20;

struct Employee
{
//      Data members...
    char        employeeName[ kMaxNameSize ];
    long        employeeID;
    float       employeeSalary;

//      Member functions...
                Employee();
    void        PrintEmployee();
};
```

Notice that the constructor is declared without a return value. Constructors *never* return a value.

Here's a sample constructor:

```
Employee::Employee()
{
  employeeSalary = 200.0;
}
```

As mentioned earlier, the constructor is declared without a return value. This is proper form.

Constructors are optional. If you don't have any initialization to perform, don't define one.

Adding Parameters to Your Constructor

If you like, you can add parameters to your constructor. Constructor parameters are typically used to provide initial values for the object's data members. Here's a new version of the `Employee()` constructor:

```
Employee::Employee( char *name, long id,
                    float salary )
{
  strncpy( employeeName, name, kMaxNameSize );

  employeeName[ kMaxNameSize - 1 ] = '\0';

  employeeID = id;
  employeeSalary = salary;
}
```

The constructor copies the three parameter values into the corresponding data members.

Notice that `strncpy()` was used, ensuring that the copy will work, even if the source string was not properly terminated. A null terminator is provided at the end of the string for just such an emergency.

The object that was just created is always the constructor's current object. In other words, when the constructor refers to an `Employee` data member, such as `employeeName` or `employeeSalary`, it is referring to the copy of that data member in the newly created object.

This line of code supplies the new operator with a set of parameters to pass on to the constructor:

```
employeePtr = new Employee( "Dave Mark", 1000, 200.0 );
```

This line of code does the same thing without using **new**:

```
Employee  employee1( "Dave Mark", 1000, 200.0 );
```

As you'd expect, this code creates an object named `employee1` by calling the `Employee` constructor, passing it the three specified parameters.

Just for completeness, here's the class declaration again, showing the new constructor:

```
struct Employee
{
//      Data members...
    char        employeeName[ kMaxNameSize ];
    long        employeeID;
    float       employeeSalary;

//      Member functions...
                Employee( char *name, long id,
                    float salary );
    void        PrintEmployee();
};
```

The Destructor Function

The **destructor function** is called for you, just as the constructor is. Unlike the constructor, however, the destructor is called when an object in its class is `deleted` or goes out of scope. Use the destructor to clean up after your object before it goes away. For instance, you might use the destructor to deallocate any additional memory your object may have allocated.

The destructor function is named by a tilde character (~) followed by the class name. The destructor for the `Employee` class is named `~Employee()`. The destructor has *no* return value and *no* parameters.

Technically, the name of the `Employee` constructor is `Employee::Employee()` and the name of its destructor is `Employee::~Employee()`. Just thought you'd like to know.

Here's a sample destructor:

```
Employee::~Employee()
{
    cout << "Deleting employee #" << employeeID << "\n";
}
```

If you created your object using new, the destructor is called when you use `delete`:

```
Employee  *employeePtr;

employeePtr = new Employee;

delete employeePtr;
```

If your object was defined directly, the destructor is called just before the object is destroyed. For example, if the object was declared at the beginning of a function, the destructor is called when the function exits.

If your object was declared as a global or static variable, its constructor will be called at the beginning of the program and its destructor will be called just before the program exits. Yes, global objects have scope, just as local objects do.

Here's an updated `Employee` class declaration showing the constructor and destructor:

```
struct Employee
{
//      Data members...
    char        employeeName[ kMaxNameSize ];
    long        employeeID;
    float       employeeSalary;

//      Member functions...
                Employee( char *name, long id,
                  float salary );
                ~Employee();
    void        PrintEmployee();
};
```

Access Privileges

When you declare a class, you need to decide which data members and functions you'd like to make available to the rest of your program. C++ gives you the power to hide a class's functions and data from all the other functions in your program or allow access to a select few.

For example, consider the `Employee` class we've been working with throughout the chapter. In the current model, an `Employee`'s name is stored in a single array of `chars`. Suppose you wrote some code that created a new `Employee`, specifying the name, id, and salary, then later in your program you decided to modify the `Employee`'s name, perhaps adding a middle name provided while your program was running.

With the current design, you could access and modify the `Employee`'s `employeeName` data member from anywhere in your program. As time passes and your program becomes more complex, you might find yourself accessing `employeeName` from several places in your code.

Now imagine what happens when you decide to change the implementation of `employeeName`. For example, you might decide to break the single `employeeName` into three separate data members, one each for the first, middle, and last names.

Imagine the hassle of having to pore through your code finding and modifying every single reference to `employeeName`, making sure you adhere to the brand-new model.

C++ allows you to hide the **implementation** details of a class (the specific type of each data member, for example), funneling all access to the implementation through a specific set of interface routines. By hiding the implementation details, the rest of your program is forced to go through the interface routines your class provides. That way, when you change the implementation, all you have to do is make whatever changes are necessary to the class's interface, without having to modify the rest of your program.

The mechanism C++ provides to control access to your class's implementation is called the **access specifier**.

Access Specifiers

C++ allows you to assign an access specifier to any of a class's data members and member functions. The access specifier defines which of your program's functions have access to the specified data member or function. The access specifier must be one of `public`, `private`, or `protected`.

If a data member or function is marked as `private`, access to it is limited to member functions of the same class (or, as you'll see later in the chapter, to classes or member functions marked as a `friend` of the class).

On the flip side, the `public` specifier gives complete access to the member function or data member, limited only by scope.

The third C++ access code is `protected`. The `protected` access code offers the same protection as `private`, with one exception. A `protected` data member or function can also be accessed by a class *derived* from the current class. Since we won't get to derived classes until later in the book, we'll put off discussion of the `protected` access code till then.

By default, the data members and member functions of a class declared using the struct keyword are all public. By adding the private keyword to our class declaration, we can limit access to the Employee data members, forcing the outside world to go through the provided member functions:

```
struct Employee
{
//      Data members...
  private:
    char       employeeName[ kMaxNameSize ];
    long       employeeID;
    float      employeeSalary;

//      Member functions...
  public:
             Employee( char *name, long id,
               float salary );
             ~Employee();
    void     PrintEmployee();
};
```

Once the compiler encounters an access specifier, all data members and functions that follow are marked with that code, at least until another code is encountered. In this example, the three data members are marked as private and the three member functions are marked as public.

Note the : after the access specifier. Without it, your code won't compile!

The class Keyword

So far, all of our classes have been created using the struct keyword. You can also create classes, using the exact same syntax, substituting the keyword `class` for `struct`. The only difference is, that the members of a `struct` are all `public` by default and the members of a `class` are all `private` by default.

Why use `class` instead of `struct`? If you start with a `struct`, you give the world complete access to your class members unless you intentionally limit access using the appropriate access specifiers. If you start with a `class`, access to your class members is limited right from the start. You have to intentionally allow access by using the appropriate access specifiers.

For the remainder of this book, we'll use the `class` keyword to declare our classes. Here's the new version of the `Employee` class:

```
class Employee
{
//      Data members...
  private:
    char        employeeName[ kMaxNameSize ];
    long        employeeID;
    float       employeeSalary;

//      Member functions...
  public:
                Employee( char *name, long id,
                  float salary );
                ~Employee();
    void        PrintEmployee();
};
```

Notice that the `private` access specifier is still in place. Since the members of a `class`-based class are `private` by default, the `private` access specifier is not needed here, but it does make the code a little easier to read. The `public` access specifier is necessary, however, to give the rest of the program access to the `Employee` member functions.

**Bringing It
All Together**

With all that we've covered so far, we're ready for our next sample program. `employee.cpp` brings these concepts together.

An Object Programming Example

Use `cd` to move into the `projects` directory and then into the directory named `chap5_1`. The source code for this example is in the file named `employee.cpp`. Compile and link the source code by typing this line at the DOS prompt:

```
sc employee.cpp
```

The compiler will compile your source code, and the linker will link it into an executable file named `employee.exe`. Run your newly created executable by typing

```
employee
```

at the DOS prompt. Here's what you'll see:

```
Creating employee #1
Creating employee #2
-----
Name:   Dave Mark
ID:     1
Salary: 200
-----
-----
Name:   Steve Baker
ID:     2
Salary: 300
-----
Destroying employee #2
Destroying employee #1
```

Let's take a look at the source code.

The employee Source Code

As you look through `employee.cpp`, you should see some familiar sights. This program takes the `Employee` class described throughout this chapter through its paces.

The first thing you'll notice is the additional include file `<string.h>`, which is needed for the call to `strncpy()` later in the program:

```
#include <iostream.h>
#include <string.h>
```

The `const kMaxNameSize` and the `Employee` class declaration are identical to those presented earlier in the chapter. Notice that the data members are all marked as `private` (unnecessary, but it does make the code easier to read) while the member functions are marked as `public`:

```
const short kMaxNameSize = 20;

class Employee
{
//      Data members...
  private:
    char   employeeName[ kMaxNameSize ];
    long   employeeID;
    float  employeeSalary;

//      Member functions...
  public:
          Employee( char *name, long id,
            float salary );
          ~Employee();
    void  PrintEmployee();
};
```

The `Employee` class has three member functions: a constructor, a destructor, and a utility routine named `PrintEmployee()`. The constructor, `Employee()`, uses its three parameters to initialize each of the `Employee` data members:

```
Employee::Employee( char *name, long id,
  float salary )
{
```

To avoid a possible nonterminated string in the name parameter, we'll use strncpy() to copy all the bytes from name into employeeName. strncpy() copies kMaxNameSize characters from name to employeeName. If the name string is less than kMaxNameSize characters long, strncpy() will also copy over the null terminator:

```
strncpy( employeeName, name, kMaxNameSize );
```

If name is not null-terminated or is kMaxNameSize bytes long or longer, we'll stick a null terminator at the very end of employeeName to ensure that one exists:

```
employeeName[ kMaxNameSize - 1 ] = '\0';
```

Finally, we'll copy the remaining two parameters into their respective data members:

```
employeeID = id;
employeeSalary = salary;
```

Once the data members are initialized, the constructor sends a message to the console, telling us which Employee object was just created:

```
  cout << "Creating employee #" << employeeID << "\n";
}
```

Since no extra memory was allocated, there's not a whole lot for the destructor to do. Just like the constructor, the destructor sends a message to the console, telling us which Employee object was just deleted:

```
Employee::~Employee()
{
  cout << "Deleting employee #" << employeeID << "\n";
}
```

`PrintEmployee()` displays the contents of the three data members of the current object:

```
void  Employee::PrintEmployee()
{
  cout << "-----\n";
  cout << "Name:    " << employeeName << "\n";
  cout << "ID:      " << employeeID << "\n";
  cout << "Salary: " << employeeSalary << "\n";
  cout << "-----\n";
}
```

`main()` is the control center where all the action is. First, we define an `Employee` object, passing three parameters to the constructor:

```
int main()
{
  Employee  employee1( "Dave Mark", 1, 200.0 );
```

As the `Employee` constructor is called, it displays the following line on the console:

```
Creating employee #1
```

Next, an `Employee` object pointer is defined:

```
Employee  *employee2;
```

This time, `new` is used to create a second `Employee` object:

```
employee2 = new Employee( "Steve Baker", 2, 300.0 );
```

Once again, the `Employee` constructor is called, sending another line to the console:

```
Creating employee #2
```

Now, both objects are used to call the `PrintEmployee()` member function. `employee1` is an object and uses the `.` operator to access its member function; `employee2` is a pointer and uses the `->` operator to access the `PrintEmployee()` function:

```
employee1.PrintEmployee();
employee2->PrintEmployee();
```

These two calls result in the following output:

```
-----
Name:   Dave Mark
ID:     1
Salary: 200
-----
-----
Name:   Steve Baker
ID:     2
Salary: 300
-----
```

Next, the object pointed to by `employee2` is deleted:

```
  delete employee2;
}
```

This causes `employee2`'s destructor to be called, resulting in this line of output:

```
Destroying employee #2
```

Finally, `main()` exits and all of `main()`'s local variables (including `employee1`) are deallocated. As soon as `employee1` is deallocated, its destructor is called, sending a final line of output to the console:

```
Destroying employee #1
```

Notice that `employee1`'s destructor isn't called until `main()` has exited.

BY THE WAY

Before you move on to the next section, take another look at your program's output. If you like, run the program again. Notice that every single line of output was produced by an object's member function. Although you did call `PrintEmployee()` directly, the constructor and destructor functions were called for you when you created and deleted an object.

Consider the line of code used to delete an `Employee` object:

```
delete employee1;
```

This line of code does not contain a function call. It does not contain code that prints information to the console. Even so, a function call *was* made (the destructor function, called for you). A line of output *was* sent to the console.

The point here is that there's action going on behind the scenes. Stuff happens automatically. You delete an object, and the destructor is called for you. This might seem like a minor point, but it gives you your first peek at the power of object programming.

Friends

In the preceding program, the `Employee` class marked its data members as `private` and its member functions as `public`. As we discussed earlier, the idea behind this strategy is to hide the implementation details of a class from the rest of the program, funneling all access to the class's data members through a set of interface routines.

For example, suppose we wanted to provide access to the `Employee` class's `employeeSalary` data member. Since `employeeSalary` is marked as `private`, there's no way to access this data member outside the `Employee` class. If we wanted to, we could provide a pair of `public` member functions that a user of the `Employee` class could use to retrieve (`GetEmployeeSalary()`) and modify (`ChangeEmployeeSalary()`) the value of `employeeSalary`.

Sometimes this strategy just doesn't cut it. For example, suppose you created a `Payroll` class to generate paychecks for your `Employees`. Clearly, the `Payroll` class is going to need access to an `Employee`'s salary. But if you create a `public` `GetEmployeeSalary()` member function (or you mark `employeeSalary` as `public`), you make `employeeSalary` available to the entire program, something you might not want to do.

The solution to this problem is provided by C++'s `friend` mechanism. C++ allows you to designate a class or a single member function as a `friend` to a specific class. In the previous example, we could designate the `Payroll` class as a `friend` to the `Employee` class:

```
class Employee
{
  friend class Payroll;

//      Data members...
  private:
    char   employeeName[ kMaxNameSize ];
    long   employeeID;
    float  employeeSalary;

//      Member functions...
  public:
         Employee( char *name, long id,
           float salary );
         ~Employee();
    void  PrintEmployee();
};


class Payroll
{
//      Data members...
  private:

//      Member functions...
  public:
         Payroll();
         ~Payroll();
    void  PrintCheck( Employee *payee );
};
```

The friend statement (see the first line of the Employee class declaration) is always placed in the class whose data members and functions are being shared. In this case, the Employee class is willing to share its private data members and functions with its new friend, the Payroll class. Once the Payroll class has friend access to the Employee class, it can access private data members and functions like employeeSalary.

Three Types of Friends

There are three ways to designate a friend. As we've already seen, you can designate an entire class as a friend to a second class. You can also designate a specific class function as a friend to a class. For example, the Payroll class we just declared contains a function named PrintCheck(). We might want to designate the PrintCheck() function as a friend of the Employee class, rather than the entire Payroll class:

```
class Employee
{
  friend void Payroll::PrintCheck( Employee *payee );

//        Data members...
  private:
    char   employeeName[ kMaxNameSize ];
    long   employeeID;
    float  employeeSalary;

//        Member functions...
  public:
         Employee( char *name, long id,
           float salary );
         ~Employee();
    void  PrintEmployee();
};
```

In this code, the friend definition specifies the Payroll member function Payroll::PrintCheck() instead of the entire Payroll class. Since the friend statement refers to a member function of another class, the full name of the function (including the class name and the two colons) is included.

You can also designate a nonmember function as a `friend`. For example, you could designate `main()` as a `friend` to the `Employee` class:

```
class Employee
{
  friend int  main();

//      Data members...
  private:
    char   employeeName[ kMaxNameSize ];
    long   employeeID;
    float employeeSalary;

//      Member functions...
  public:
          Employee( char *name, long id,
            float salary );
          ~Employee();
    void  PrintEmployee();
};
```

This arrangement gives `main()` access to all `Employee` data members and functions, even those marked as `private`. Just because `main()` is a `friend` doesn't give any special privileges to any other functions, however. Choose your `friends` carefully!

A Friendly Example

Our next example combines the `Employee` class created earlier with the `Payroll` class described in this section. Use `cd` to move back up to the `projects` directory and then into the directory named `chap5_2`. The source code for this example is in the file named `friends.cpp`. Compile and link the source code by typing this line at the DOS prompt:

```
sc friends.cpp
```

The compiler will compile your source code, and the linker will link it into an executable file named `friends.exe`. Run your newly created executable by typing

```
friends
```

at the DOS prompt. Here's what you'll see:

```
Creating payroll object
Creating employee #1000
-----
Name:    Carlos Derr
ID:      1000
Salary: 500
-----
Pay $500 to the order of Carlos Derr...

Destroying employee #1000
Destroying payroll object
```

Let's take a look at the source code.

The friends Source Code

`friends.cpp` starts just like `employee.cpp`, with the same two `#include`s and the same `const` definition:

```
#include <iostream.h>
#include <string.h>

const short kMaxNameSize = 20;
```

Since the `Payroll` class declaration refers to the `Employee` class (check out the parameter to `PrintCheck()`) and its declaration comes first, we'll need a forward declaration of the `Employee` class:

```
class Employee;
```

Next comes the declaration of the `Payroll` class:

```
//-------------------------------------- Payroll
```

```
class Payroll
{
//      Data members...
  private:

//      Member functions...
  public:
          Payroll();
          ~Payroll();
    void  PrintCheck( Employee *payee );
};
```

To keep this example as simple as possible, we've stripped Payroll down to its bones: no data members, a constructor, a destructor, and a PrintCheck() function. Further down in the source, the Employee class will mark the PrintCheck() function as a friend.

Next comes the Employee class declaration. You may have noticed that we didn't list the Payroll member functions right after the Payroll class declaration. Our reason was that Payroll::PrintCheck() refers to the Employee data member employeeSalary, which hasn't been declared yet:

```
//------------------------------------- Employee

class Employee
{
  friend void Payroll::PrintCheck( Employee *payee );

//      Data members...
  private:
    char   employeeName[ kMaxNameSize ];
    long   employeeID;
    float  employeeSalary;

//      Member functions...
  public:
          Employee( char *name, long id,
            float salary );
          ~Employee();
    void  PrintEmployee();
};
```

Take a look at the `friend` declaration inside the `Employee` class declaration. Notice that we've opted to make `Payroll::PrintCheck()` a friend of the `Employee` class. Now, `PrintCheck()` is the only `Payroll` function with access to the `private Employee` data members.

> Interestingly, if you leave `PrintCheck()`'s parameter out of the `friend` statement, the code won't compile. Since you can have more than one function with the same name (remember overloaded functions from Chapter 4?), if the parameter is left out, the compiler tries to match the `friend` statement with a version of `PrintCheck()` with no parameters. When it doesn't find one, the compiler reports an error.

Next come the `Payroll` member functions. The constructor and destructor print messages letting you know they were called, while `PrintCheck()` prints a simulated check using the `private Employee` data members `employeeSalary` and `employeeName`:

```
//------------------- Payroll Member Functions

Payroll::Payroll()
{
  cout << "Creating payroll object\n";
}

Payroll::~Payroll()
{
  cout << "Destroying payroll object\n";
}

void  Payroll::PrintCheck( Employee *payee )
{
  cout << "Pay $" << payee->employeeSalary
     << " to the order of "
     << payee->employeeName << "...\n\n";
}
```

The `Employee` member functions are the same as they were in `employee.cpp`:

```
//------------------- Employee Member Functions

Employee::Employee( char *name, long id,
  float salary )
{
  strncpy( employeeName, name, kMaxNameSize );

  employeeName[ kMaxNameSize - 1 ] = '\0';

  employeeID = id;
  employeeSalary = salary;

  cout << "Creating employee #" << employeeID << "\n";
}

Employee::~Employee()
{
  cout << "Destroying employee #" << employeeID << "\n";
}

void  Employee::PrintEmployee()
{
  cout << "-----\n";
  cout << "Name:    " << employeeName << "\n";
  cout << "ID:      " << employeeID << "\n";
  cout << "Salary: " << employeeSalary << "\n";
  cout << "-----\n";
}
```

Once again, `main()` is where the action is. We start by defining a couple of pointers, one to an `Employee` object and one to a `Payroll` object:

```
//------------------------------------- main

int main()
{
  Employee  *employee1Ptr;
  Payroll   *payroll1Ptr;
```

Next, we use new to create a new `Payroll` object and a new `Employee` object:

```
payroll1Ptr = new Payroll;

employee1Ptr = new Employee( "Carlos Derr", 1000,
    500.0 );
```

The two constructors are called, generating these two lines of output:

```
Creating payroll object
Creating employee #1000
```

Next, `PrintEmployee()` is called:

```
employee1Ptr->PrintEmployee();
```

The `PrintEmployee()` call generates five lines of output:

```
-----
Name:    Carlos Derr
ID:      1000
Salary: 500
-----
```

Next, `PrintCheck()` is called. `PrintCheck()` takes a pointer to the `Employee` object as a parameter:

```
payroll1Ptr->PrintCheck( employee1Ptr );
```

A check is printed to the specified `Employee` using `employeeName` and `employeeSalary`:

```
Pay $500 to the order of Carlos Derr...
```

Finally, both objects are deleted:

```
delete employee1Ptr;
delete payroll1Ptr;
```

The two destructors print their respective messages:

```
Destroying employee #1000
Destroying payroll object
```

Summary

So far, you've gotten a taste of object programming. You've learned how to create a class and how to define objects of that class either directly or by using `new`. You've learned about constructors and destructors, and you've seen how these routines are called when an object is created or destroyed.

You've learned the difference between `private` and `public` data members and functions. You've also learned how to establish a `friend` relationship between a class and another class or function.

Perhaps most important of all, you've started down a new programming path. You are now well on your way to becoming an object programmer. In Chapter 6, you'll move further down that path, exploring some of fundamental techniques you'll want to develop as your C++ programs become more and more sophisticated.

Chapter 6

Derived
Classes

C++ allows you to create classes that are based on other classes. These derived classes retain access to all the data members and member functions of their base class. This feature, known as inheritance, plays a critical role in object programming.

This Chapter at a Glance

C++ ALLOWS YOU TO USE ONE CLASS DECLARATION, known as a **base class**, as the basis for the declaration of a second class, known as a **derived class**. For example, you might declare an Employee class that describes your company's employees. Next, you might declare a Sales class, based on the Employee class, that describes employees in the sales department.

This chapter is filled with examples that emphasize the advantages of classes derived from other classes. As you read through the chapter, focus on the syntax and techniques demonstrated by each example. The mechanics and philosophy presented here form the body and soul of that part of object programming known as **class derivation**.

Inheritance   One of the most important features of class derivation is **inheritance**. Just like the cherished heirlooms you hope to inherit from your granduncle Morty, a derived class inherits all of the data members and member functions from its base class.

As an example, consider the following class declaration:

```
class Base
{
  public:
    short    baseMember;

    void     SetBaseMember( short baseValue );
};
```

This class, `Base`, has two members, a data member named `baseMember` and a member function named `SetBaseMember()`. Both of these members will be inherited by any classes derived from this class. Figure 6.1 shows how an object of the `Base` class might look from a graphic perspective.

FIGURE 6.1
An object of the
Base *class.*

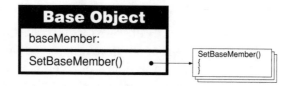

Here's another class declaration:

```
class Derived : Base
{
  public:
    short    derivedMember;

    void     SetDerivedMember( short derivedValue );
}
```

This class is a derived class named, appropriately enough, `Derived`. The ": Base" at the end of the title tells you that this class is derived from the class named `Base`. Figure 6.2 shows what a `Derived` object might look like from a graphic perspective. As you'd expect, this object has its own copy of the data member `derivedMember` as well as access to the member function `SetDerivedMember()`.

FIGURE 6.2

An object of the `Derived` *class.*

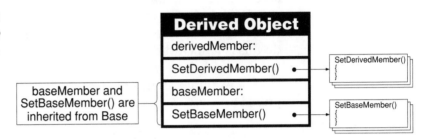

What you might not have expected are the members *inherited* by this object, that is, the `Base` class data member `baseMember` as well as the `Base` class member function `SetBaseMember()`.

Here's some code that allocates a `Derived` object, then accesses various data members and functions:

```
Derived *derivedPtr;

derivedPtr = new Derived;

derivedPtr->SetDerivedMember( 20 );

cout << "derivedMember = " << derivedPtr->derivedMember;

derivedPtr->SetBaseMember( 20 );

cout << "\nbaseMember = " << derivedPtr->baseMember;
```

Notice that the object pointer `derivedPtr` is used to access its own data members and functions as well as its inherited data members and functions. Notice also that the example does not create a `Base` object. This is important. When an object inherits data members and functions from its base class, the compiler allocates the extra memory needed for all inherited members right along with memory for the object's own members.

Access and Inheritance

Although a derived class inherits all of the data members and member functions from its base class, it doesn't necessarily retain access to each member.

Here's how this works. When you declare a derived class, you declare its base class as either `public` or `private`. One way to do this is to include either `public` or `private` in the title line of the declared class.

For example, in this declaration, the class `Base` is marked as `public`:

```
class Derived : public Base
{
  public:
    short    derivedMember;

    void    SetDerivedMember( short derivedValue );
}
```

In this declaration, `Base` is marked as `private`:

```
class Derived : private Base
{
  public:
    short    derivedMember;

    void    SetDerivedMember( short derivedValue );
}
```

You can also mark a base class as `public` or `private` by leaving off the access specifier. If you use the `class` keyword to declare the derived class, the base class defaults to `private`. If you use the `struct` keyword to declare the derived class, the base class defaults to `public`.

Once you know whether the base class is `public` or `private`, you can determine the access of each of its inherited members by following these three rules:

1. The derived class does not have access to `private` members inherited from the base class. This is true regardless of whether the base class is `public` or `private`.

2. If the base class is `public`, the members inherited from the base class retain their access level (providing the inherited member is not `private`, of course). This means that an inherited `public` member remains `public` and an inherited `protected` member remains `protected`.

3. If the base class is `private`, the members inherited from the base class are marked as `private` in the derived class.

> If these rules seem a bit confusing, don't worry. As you go through each of the chapter's sample programs, things should become clearer. For the moment, just mark this page so that you can refer back to it later.

In Chapter 5, we adopted the strategy of declaring our data members as `private` and our member functions as `public`. This approach works well if the class will never be used as a base class for later derivation. If you ever plan on using a class as the basis for other classes, declare your data members as `protected` and your member functions as `public`.

A `protected` member can be accessed only by members of its class or by members of any classes derived from its class. In a base class, `protected` is just like `private`. The advantage of `protected` is that it allows a derived class to access the member, while protecting it from the outside world. We'll get back to this strategy in a bit. For now, let's take a look at an example of class derivation.

A Class Derivation Example

So far in this chapter, you've learned how to derive one class from another and you've been introduced to the **protected** access specifier. Our first sample program brings these lessons to life. Use **cd** to move into the **projects** directory and then into the directory named **chap6_1**. The source code for this example is in the file named **derived.cpp**. Compile and link the source code by typing this line at the DOS prompt:

```
sc derived.cpp
```

The compiler will compile your source code, and the linker will link it into an executable file named **derived.exe**. Run your newly created executable by typing

```
derived
```

at the DOS prompt. Here's what you'll see:

```
baseMember was set to 10
derivedMember was set to 20
```

Let's take a look at the source code.

The derived Source Code

As usual, **derived.cpp** starts by including **<iostream.h>**:

```
#include <iostream.h>
```

Next, we declare a class named **Base**, which we'll use later as the basis for a second class named **Derived**:

```
//-------------------------------------- Base

class Base
{
```

Base has a single data member, a **short** named **baseMember**, which is marked as **private**:

```
//      Data members...
  private:
    short baseMember;
```

Base also includes two member functions, each marked as protected. SetBaseMember() sets baseMember to the specified value, while GetBaseMember() returns the current value of baseMember:

```
//      Member functions...
  protected:
    void  SetBaseMember( short baseValue );
    short GetBaseMember();
};

void  Base::SetBaseMember( short baseValue )
{
  baseMember = baseValue;
}

short Base::GetBaseMember()
{
  return baseMember;
}
```

Since baseMember is private, it cannot be accessed by any function outside the Base class. Since SetBaseMember() and GetBaseMember() are protected, they can only be accessed by Base member functions and from within any classes derived from Base. Note that main() cannot access either of these functions.

Our second class, Derived, is derived from Base:

```
//--------------------------------- Base:Derived

class Derived : public Base
{
```

The public keyword following the colon in the class title line marks Base as a public base class.

As mentioned earlier, if a base class is declared as public, all inherited public members remain public and inherited protected members remain `protected`. Inherited `private` members are not accessible by the derived class.

> If you marked `Base` as `private` instead of `public`, all inherited members would be marked as `private` and would not be accessible by any classes derived from `Derived`. The point here is this: If you mark the base class as `private`, you effectively end the inheritance chain.

As a general rule, you should declare your derived classes using `public` inheritance:

```
class Derived : public Base
```

It's rare that you'd want to reduce the amount of information inherited by a derived class. Most of the time, a derived class is created to *extend* the reach of the base class by adding new data members and functions. As you go through the examples in this and later chapters, the idea of derived classes as extenders will appear again and again.

`Derived` has a single data member, a `short` named `derivedMember`, which is declared as `private`:

```
//      Data members...
  private:
    short derivedMember;
```

`derivedMember` can only be accessed by a `Derived` member function. That's it. `Derived` contains two member functions, `SetMembers()` and `PrintDataMembers()`:

```
//      Member functions...
  public:
    void  SetMembers( short baseValue,
                      short derivedValue );
    void  PrintDataMembers();
};
```

SetMembers() takes two shorts, assigns the first to derivedMember, and passes the second to SetBaseMember(). SetBaseMember() was used because Derived does not have direct access to baseMember:

```
void  Derived::SetMembers( short baseValue,
                           short derivedValue )
{
  derivedMember = derivedValue;
  SetBaseMember( baseValue );
}
```

PrintDataMembers() prints the values of baseMember and derivedMember. Since Derived doesn't have direct access to baseMember, GetBaseMember() is called to retrieve the value:

```
void  Derived::PrintDataMembers()
{
  cout << "baseMember was set to "
    << GetBaseMember() << '\n';

  cout << "derivedMember was set to "
    << derivedMember << '\n';
}
```

main() starts by declaring a Derived pointer and then using new to create a new Derived object (since we didn't include a constructor for either of our classes, nothing exciting has happened yet):

```
//---------------------------------- main()

int main()
{
  Derived   *derivedPtr;

  derivedPtr = new Derived;
```

It's important to understand that when the Derived object is created, it receives its own copy of baseMember, even though it doesn't have access to baseMember. If the Derived object wants to modify its copy of baseMember, it will have to do so via a call to Base::SetBaseMember(), which it also inherited.

Now things start to get interesting. main() uses the pointer to the Derived object to call SetMembers(), setting its copy of baseMember to 10 and derivedMember to 20:

```
derivedPtr->SetMembers( 10, 20 );
```

Next, we call the Derived member function PrintDataMembers():

```
derivedPtr->PrintDataMembers();

return 0;
}
```

As you saw when you ran the program, the values of the two data members are successfully set:

```
baseMember was set to 10
derivedMember was set to 20
```

Just as the Derived object pointer is able to take advantage of inheritance to call SetBaseMember(), PrintDataMembers() is able to print the value of the inherited data member baseMember by calling GetBaseMember().

For the moment, don't worry too much about the advantages of inheritance. Instead, concentrate on the mechanics and syntax of inheritance. Once you master the *how*, the *why* will come naturally.

Derivation, Constructors, and Destructors

When an object is created, its constructor is called to initialize the object's data members. When the object is destroyed, its destructor is called to perform any necessary cleanup.

Suppose the object belongs to a derived class, and suppose it inherits a few data members from its base class. How do these inherited data members get initialized? When the object is destroyed, who does the cleanup for the inherited data members?

As it turns out, C++ solves this tricky issue for you. Before the compiler calls an object's constructor, it first checks to see whether the object belongs to a derived class. If so, the constructor belonging to the base class is called and then the object's own constructor is called. The base class constructor initializes the object's inherited members, while the object's own constructor initializes the members belonging to the object's class (Figure 6.3).

FIGURE 6.3
The base class constructor is called before the derived class constructor.

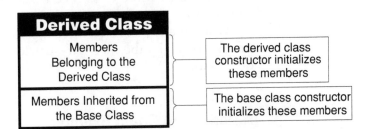

The *reverse* holds true for the destructor. When an object of a derived class is destroyed, the derived class's destructor is called and then the base class's destructor is called.

The Derivation Chain

There will frequently be times when you derive a class from a base class that is, itself, derived from some other class. Each of these classes acts like a link in a **derivation chain**. The constructor/destructor calling sequence just described still holds, no matter how long the derivation chain.

Suppose you declare three classes, A, B, and C, where class B is derived from A and C is derived from B. Take a look at Figure 6.4.

FIGURE 6.4
Three classes in a single derivation chain where class B is derived from A and C is derived from B.

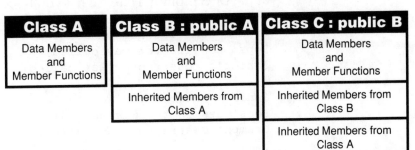

When you create an object of class B, it will inherit the members from class A. When you create an object of class C, it will inherit the members from class B, which includes the inherited members from class A.

When an object from class C is created, the compiler follows the derivation chain from C to B to A and discovers that A is the ultimate base class in this chain. The compiler calls the class A constructor, then the class B constructor, and finally the class C constructor.

When the object is destroyed, the class C destructor is called first, followed by the class B destructor and, finally, by the class A destructor.

A Derivation Chain Example

Our second sample program demonstrates the order of constructor and destructor calls in a three-class derivation chain. Use `cd` to move back up to the `projects` directory and then into the directory named `chap6_2`. The source code for this example is in the file named `gramps.cpp`. Compile and link the source code by typing this line at the DOS prompt:

```
sc gramps.cpp
```

The compiler will compile your source code, and the linker will link it into an executable file named `gramps.exe`. Run your newly created executable by typing

```
gramps
```

at the DOS prompt. Here's what you'll see:

```
Gramps' constructor was called!
Pops' constructor was called!
Junior's constructor was called!
----
Junior's destructor was called!
Pops' destructor was called!
Gramps' destructor was called!
```

As you can see by the output, each class constructor was called once, then each class destructor was called once in reverse order. Let's take a look at the source code.

The gramps Source Code

`gramps.cpp` starts with the usual `#include`:

```
#include <iostream.h>
```

Next, the `Gramps` class is declared:

```
//------------------------------------- Gramps


class Gramps
{
//      Data members...
```

Notice that none of the classes in this program have any data members. For the moment, we're interested only in the order of constructor and destructor calls.

Both the constructor and the destructor are declared `public`:

```
//      Member functions...
  public:
        Gramps();
        ~Gramps();
};
```

The `Gramps` constructor and destructor are pretty simple; each prints an appropriate message to the console:

```
Gramps::Gramps()
{
  cout << "Gramps' constructor was called!\n";
}

Gramps::~Gramps()
{
  cout << "Gramps' destructor was called!\n";
}
```

Our next class is derived from the `Gramps` class:

```
//-------------------------------- Pops:Gramps

class Pops : public Gramps
{
//        Data members...
```

Notice that we use the `public` keyword in the class title line. This ensures that the constructor and the destructor inherited from `Gramps` are marked as `public` inside the `Pops` class.

Once again, this class has no data members. Both the constructor and the destructor are marked as `public`. They'll be inherited by any class derived from `Pops`:

```
//        Member functions...
  public:
        Pops();
        ~Pops();
};
```

Just like those of `Gramps`, the `Pops` constructor and destructor are simple and to the point; each sends an appropriate message to the console:

```
Pops::Pops()
{
  cout << "Pops' constructor was called!\n";
}

Pops::~Pops()
{
  cout << "Pops' destructor was called!\n";
}
```

`Junior` is to `Pops` what `Pops` is to `Gramps`. `Junior` inherits not only the `Pops` members but the `Gramps` members as well (as you'll see in a minute, when you create and then delete a `Junior` object, both the `Gramps` and the `Pops` constructor and destructor will be called):

```
//-------------------------------   Junior:Pops

class Junior : public Pops
{
//      Data members...

//      Member functions...
  public:
        Junior();
        ~Junior();
};
```

The `Junior` constructor and destructor are just like those of `Gramps` and `Pops`; each sends an appropriate message to the console:

```
Junior::Junior()
{
  cout << "Junior's constructor was called!\n";
}

Junior::~Junior()
{
  cout << "Junior's destructor was called!\n";
}
```

`main()`'s job is to create and delete a single `Junior` object. Watch what happens:

```
//------------------------------------   main()

int main()
{
  Junior    *juniorPtr;
```

When the `Junior` object is created, the derivation chain is followed backward until the ultimate base class, `Gramps`, is reached:

```
  juniorPtr = new Junior;
```

The `Gramps` constructor is called, giving the `Gramps` class a chance to initialize its data members. Next, the `Pops` constructor is called, and, finally, the `Junior` constructor is called:

```
Gramps' constructor was called!
Pops' constructor was called!
Junior's constructor was called!
```

Then, a dividing line is printed, just for looks:

```
cout << "----\n";
```

Next, the `Junior` object is deleted, and, this time, the derivation chain is followed in the reverse order. The `Junior` destructor is called, then the `Pops` destructor, and, finally, the `Gramps` destructor:

```
delete juniorPtr;

return 0;
}
```

Here's the output produced by these destructor calls:

```
Junior's destructor was called!
Pops' destructor was called!
Gramps' destructor was called!
```

Some Food for Thought

Before we move on to our next program, take a minute to look back over the `gramps` source code. Notice that each of the three classes marked their constructor and destructor as `public`. What would happen if you changed the `Gramps` constructor to `private`? Go try it. I'll wait.

Your code didn't compile because `Junior` no longer has access to the `Gramps` constructor. Now go change the `Gramps` constructor from `private` to `protected` and compile your program.

This time, your program compiled. Why? When `Junior` inherited the `Gramps` constructor, it had access to the `Gramps` constructor. Remember, when a derived class inherits a `protected` member from a `public` base class, the inherited member is marked as `protected`.

Now go and change the `Junior` constructor from `public` to `protected` and recompile. What happened?

This time, the compiler complained that the `Junior` constructor was not accessible. Since the `Junior` constructor was declared `protected`, it is accessible by classes derived from `Junior`, but not by outside functions like `main()`. When `main()` creates a new `Junior` object, it *must* have access to the `Junior` constructor.

On the other hand, you've seen that `main()` does *not* need access to the `Gramps` and `Pops` constructors to create a `Junior` object. When you changed the `Gramps` constructor to `protected`, `Junior` had access to the `Gramps` constructor and `main()` didn't, yet the program still compiled.

Think about these issues. Go back to the previous program, `derived`, and make similar changes to it. Get to know the rules for inheritance and access.

Base Classes and Constructors with Parameters

Our first program in this chapter, `derived`, declared two classes, `Base` and `Derived`. Neither of these classes included a constructor. Our second program, `gramps`, featured three classes. Though all three classes declared a constructor, none of the constructors declared any parameters.

Our next example enters uncharted waters by declaring classes whose constructors contain parameters. What's the big deal about constructor parameters? In a world without class derivation, not much. When you add derived classes into the picture, however, things get a bit more complex. Here's why.

Imagine a base class whose constructor sports a single parameter:

```
class Base
{
  public:
    Base( short baseParam );
};
```

Now, add a derived class based on this base class:

```
class Derived : public Base
{
  public:
    Derived();
};
```

Notice that the derived class constructor is declared without a parameter. When a `Derived` object is created, the `Base` constructor is called. What parameter is passed to this constructor?

The secret lies in the definition of the derived class constructor. When a base class constructor has parameters, you have to provide some extra information in the derived class constructor's title line. This information tells the compiler how to map data from the derived class constructor to the base class constructor's parameter list.

For example, we might define the derived class constructor this way:

```
Derived::Derived() : Base( 20 )
{
  cout << "Inside the Derived constructor";
}
```

Notice the "`: Base( 20 )`" at the end of the title line. This code tells the compiler to pass the number 20 as a parameter when the `Base` constructor is called.

This technique is useful when your derived class constructor also has parameters. Check out the following piece of code:

```
Derived::Derived( short derivedParam ) : Base(
  derivedParam )
{
}
```

This constructor takes a single parameter, `derivedParam`, and maps it to the single parameter in its base class constructor. When a `Derived` object is created, as follows,

```
Derived *derivedPtr;
```

```
derivedPtr = new Derived( 20 );
```

the parameter is passed to the `Base` constructor. Once the `Base` constructor returns, the same parameter is passed to the `Derived` constructor.

In the preceding example, the `Derived` constructor does nothing but pass along a parameter to the `Base` constructor. Though it may take some getting used to, this technique is quite legitimate. It is perfectly fine to define an empty function whose sole purpose is to map a parameter to a base class constructor.

Another Classy Example

Our next example combines the class derivation techniques from our first two programs with the constructor parameter-mapping mechanism described in the previous section. Use `cd` to move back up to the `projects` directory and then into the directory named `chap6_3`. The source code for this example is in the file named `square.cpp`. Compile and link the source code by typing this line at the DOS prompt:

```
sc square.cpp
```

The compiler will compile your source code, and the linker will link it into an executable file named `square.exe`. Run your newly created executable by typing

```
square
```

at the DOS prompt. Here's what you'll see:

```
Area is: 100
Area is: 150
```

Let's take a look at the source code.

The square Source Code

`square.cpp` starts in the usual way, by including `<iostream.h>`:

```
#include <iostream.h>
```

Next, the first of two classes is declared. `Rectangle` will act as a base class:

```
//------------------------------------- Rectangle

class Rectangle
{
```

The data members of our base class are declared as `protected`; the member functions, `public`. `height` and `width` hold the height and width of a `Rectangle` object:

```
//      Data members...
  protected:
    short height;
    short width;
```

The `Rectangle()` constructor takes two parameters, `heightParam` and `widthParam`, that are used to initialize the `Rectangle` data members. The member function `DisplayArea()` displays the area of the current object:

```
//      Member functions...
  public:
        Rectangle( short heightParam, short
          widthParam );
    void  DisplayArea();
};
```

`Rectangle()` uses its two parameters to initialize the `Rectangle` data members:

```
Rectangle::Rectangle( short heightParam, short
  widthParam )
{
```

```
   height = heightParam;
   width = widthParam;
}

void  Rectangle::DisplayArea( void )
{
  cout << "Area is: " <<
    height * width << '\n';
}
```

The Square class is derived from the Rectangle class. Just as a square is a specialized form of rectangle (a rectangle whose sides are all equal), a Square object is a specialized Rectangle object. The Square class has no data members, just a single member function, the Square() constructor:

```
//----------------------------- Rectangle:Square

class Square : public Rectangle
{
//      Data members...
```

The Square() constructor takes a single parameter, a short named side:

```
//      Member functions...
  public:
        Square( short side );
};
```

The Square() constructor has one purpose in life. It maps the single Square() parameter to the two parameters required by the Rectangle() constructor. A square whose side has a length of side is equivalent to a rectangle with a height of side and a width of side:

```
Square::Square( short side ) : Rectangle( side, side )
{
}
```

`main()` starts by declaring a `Square` pointer and a `Rectangle` pointer:

```
//----------------------------------- main()

int main()
{
  Square    *mySquare;
  Rectangle *myRectangle;
```

The `Square` pointer is used to create a new `Square` object with a side of 10:

```
  mySquare = new Square( 10 );
```

As specified by the `Square()` constructor's title line, the compiler calls `Rectangle()`, passing 10 as both `heightParam` and `widthParam`. The `Rectangle()` constructor initializes the `Square` object's inherited data members `height` and `width` to 10, just as if you'd created a `Rectangle` with a height of 10 and a width of 10.

Next, the `Square` object's inherited member function, `DisplayArea()`, is called:

```
  mySquare->DisplayArea();
```

`DisplayArea()` uses the inherited data members `height` and `width` to calculate the area of the `Square`:

```
Area is: 100
```

As far as `DisplayArea()` is concerned, the object whose area it just calculated was a `Rectangle`. It had no idea it was working with data members *inherited* from a `Rectangle`. That's part of the power of object programming.

Finally, the `Rectangle` pointer is used to create a new `Rectangle` object with a height of 10 and a width of 15:

```
myRectangle = new Rectangle( 10, 15 );
myRectangle->DisplayArea();

return 0;
}
```

When we call `DisplayArea()`, it displays the appropriate area:

```
Area is: 150
```

An Important Lesson

This program demonstrates a very important point. With just a few lines of code, we can add a new dimension to an existing class *without modifying the existing class.*

The `Square` class takes advantage of what's already in place, building on the data members and member functions of its base class. Essentially, `Square` added a shortcut to the `Rectangle` class, a quicker way to create a `Rectangle` when the height and width are the same.

This may not seem like a significant gain to you, but there's an important lesson behind this example. C++ makes it easy to build upon existing models, to add functionality to your software by deriving from existing classes.

As you gain experience in object programming, you'll build up a library of classes that you'll use again and again. Sometimes, you'll use the classes "as is." At other times, you'll extend an existing class by deriving a new class from it. By deriving new classes from existing classes, you get the best of both worlds. Code that depends on the base classes will continue to work quite well without modification. Code that takes advantage of the new, derived classes will work just as well, allowing these classes to live in harmony with their base classes.

In my mind, this is what object programming is all about.

Overriding Member Functions

In the preceding example, the derived class, Square, inherited the member function, DisplayArea(), from its base class, Rectangle. Sometimes, it's useful to override a member function from the base class with a more appropriate function in the derived class. For example, you could have provided Square with its own version of DisplayArea() that based its area calculation on the fact that the height and width of a square are equal.

Here's another example. Suppose you create a base class named Shape and a series of derived classes such as Rectangle, Circle, and Triangle. You can create a DisplayArea() function for the Shape class, then override DisplayArea() in each of the derived classes.

Suppose you want to create a linked list of Shapes. To simplify matters for the software that manages the linked list, you can treat the derived objects as Shapes, no matter what their actual type. Then, when you call the Shape's DisplayArea() function, their true identity will emerge. A Triangle will override the Shape DisplayArea() function with a Triangle DisplayArea() function. The Rectangle and Circle will have their own versions as well. The trick is to get C++ to call the proper overriding function, if one exists.

Creating a Virtual Function

The linked list model just presented has a slight problem. Suppose the linked list contains a pointer to a Shape that is actually one of Rectangle, Triangle, or Circle. Now suppose that Shape pointer is used to call the member function DisplayArea():

```
myShapePtr->DisplayArea();
```

As it is now, this code will call the function Shape::DisplayArea() even if the Shape pointed to by myShapePtr is a Rectangle, Triangle, or Circle.

The solution to this problem? Declare `Shape::DisplayArea()` as a `virtual` function. By declaring a base member function that we intend to override using the `virtual` keyword, we are asking the compiler to call the overriding function instead of the base function, even if the object used to call the function belongs to the base class.

A Virtual Function Example

Our final program in this chapter provides a simple example of virtual function overriding by using a base class named `Shape` and two derived classes, `Rectangle` and `Triangle`. Use `cd` to move back up to the `projects` directory and then into the directory named `chap6_4`. The source code for this example is in the file named `whatami.cpp`. Compile and link the source code by typing this line at the DOS prompt:

```
sc whatami.cpp
```

The compiler will compile your source code, and the linker will link it into an executable file named `whatami.exe`. Run your newly created executable by typing

```
whatami
```

at the DOS prompt. Here's what you'll see:

```
I'm a rectangle!
I'm a triangle!
I don't know what kind of shape I am!
```

Let's take a look at the source code.

The whatami Source Code

`whatami.cpp` also starts in the usual way, by including `<iostream.h>`:

```
#include <iostream.h>
```

Next, the base class `Shape` is declared. `Shape` contains a single member function, `WhatAmI()`. When it is called, `WhatAmI()` tells you what kind of shape it belongs to. Notice that it is declared using the `virtual` keyword, which tells the compiler that you'd like any overriding function to be called, if one exists:

```
//------------------------------------- Shape

class Shape
{
//       Data members...

//       Member functions...
  public:
    virtual void  WhatAmI();
};
```

Here's the definition of `Shape::WhatAmI()`:

```
void  Shape::WhatAmI()
{
  cout << "I don't know what kind of shape I am!\n";
}
```

Notice that the `virtual` keyword isn't used here. The `virtual` keyword is only allowed in the function declaration inside the class declaration.

Our next class, `Rectangle`, is derived from the `Shape` class. `Rectangle` also has a single member function named `WhatAmI()`:

```
//------------------------------- Shape:Rectangle

class Rectangle : public Shape
{
//       Data members...

//       Member functions...
  public:
    void  WhatAmI();
};
```

Rectangle's version of WhatAmI() is called when the object doing the calling is a Rectangle:

```
void  Rectangle::WhatAmI()
{
  cout << "I'm a rectangle!\n";
}
```

Our next class, Triangle, is also derived from Shape:

```
//--------------------------------- Shape:Triangle

class Triangle : public Shape
{
//      Data members...

//      Member functions...
  public:
    void  WhatAmI();
};
```

Once again, Triangle has its own version of WhatAmI():

```
void  Triangle::WhatAmI()
{
  cout << "I'm a triangle!\n";
}
```

Now comes the fun part. main() declares three Shape pointers, s1, s2, and s3:

```
//------------------------------------- main()

int main()
{
  Shape *s1, *s2, *s3;
```

Each of these pointers is used to create a new object, a Rectangle, a Triangle, and a Shape:

```
  s1 = new Rectangle;
  s2 = new Triangle;
  s3 = new Shape;
```

You may be wondering why the three pointers are all declared as Shapes while the objects assigned to the pointers are of three different types. This is done intentionally. If you're building a linked list of shapes, you can store a pointer to each object in the list as a Shape pointer rather than as a Rectangle pointer or Triangle pointer. In this way, your list management software doesn't have to know what type of shape it is dealing with. If you want to call WhatAmI() (or some other, more useful function) for each object in the list, you just step through the list, one object at a time, treating each object as if it were a Shape. If the object belongs to a derived class that overrides the function, C++ will make sure the correct function is called.

Once our three objects are created, we try using each object to call WhatAmI():

```
s1->WhatAmI();
s2->WhatAmI();
s3->WhatAmI();
```

When the Rectangle object is used to call WhatAmI(), we get this result:

```
I'm a rectangle!
```

When the Triangle object is used to call WhatAmI(), we get this result:

```
I'm a triangle!
```

Finally, when the Shape object is used to call WhatAmI(), we get this result:

```
I don't know what kind of shape I am!
```

In this example, the Shape class exists just so that we can create useful, derived classes from it. Creating a Shape object is not particularly useful.

Summary   Congratulations! You've made it through the hardest part of object programming with C++. You've mastered most of the skills you'll need to write your own object-oriented programs.

The remainder of this book is dedicated to filling in the gaps. Though there's still a major topic or two to cover, you'll find that most of the toughest aspects of C++ are behind you. Once again, congratulations, and welcome to the world of object programming!

Chapter 7

Operator Overloading

C++ allows you to overload its built-in operators, customizing them to work with objects you define. This chapter provides examples that show you how to take full advantage of this powerful and creative technique.

This Chapter at a Glance

THE C++ FEATURE UP FOR DISCUSSION IN THIS CHAPTER is **operator overloading**. In C++, you can overload any of the built-in operators, such as + or *, giving each one your own personal twist.

For instance, imagine that you're running a restaurant and you want to write some software to handle your billing, print your menus, and so on. Your program might create a `MenuItem` class that looks something like this:

```
class MenuItem
{
  private:
    float   price;
    char    name[ 40 ];

  public:
            MenuItem( float itemPrice,
              char *itemName );
    float   GetPrice();
};
```

Your software would define a `MenuItem` object for each item on the menu. When someone orders, you'd calculate the bill by adding together the `price` of each `MenuItem`. Here's an example:

```
MenuItem chicken( 8.99, "Chicken Kiev with salad" );
MenuItem houseWine( 2.99, "Riesling by the glass" );
float    total;

total = chicken->GetPrice()
      + houseWine->GetPrice();
```

This particular diner had the chicken and a glass of the house wine. The total is calculated using the member function `GetPrice()`. Nothing new here.

The Operator Overloading Alternative

Operator overloading provides an alternative way of figuring up the bill. If things are set up properly, the compiler will interpret the statement

```
total = chicken + houseWine;
```

by adding the `price` of `chicken` to the `price` of `houseWine`. Ordinarily, the compiler would complain if you tried to use a nonintegral type with the + operator. You can get around this limitation by giving the + operator a new meaning.

To do this, create a function to overload the + operator:

```
float operator+( MenuItem item1, MenuItem item2 )
{
  return( item1.GetPrice() + item2.GetPrice() );
}
```

Notice the name of this new function. Any function whose name follows the form

```
operator<C++ operator>
```

is said to *overload the specified operator*. When you overload an operator, you're asking the compiler to call your function instead of interpreting the operator as it normally would.

Calling an Operator Overloading Function

When the compiler calls an overloading function, it maps the operator's operands to the function's parameters. For example, suppose the function

```
float operator+( MenuItem item1, MenuItem item2 )
{
  return( item1.GetPrice() + item2.GetPrice() );
}
```

is used to overload the + operator. When the compiler encounters the expression

```
chicken + houseWine
```

it calls `operator+()`, passing `chicken` as the first parameter and `houseWine` as the second parameter. `operator+()`'s return value is used as the result of the expression.

The number of operands taken by an operator determines the number of parameters passed to its overloading function. For example, a function designed to overload a unary operator takes a single parameter; a function designed to overload a binary operator takes two parameters.

Operator Overloading Using a Member Function

You can also use a member function to overload an operator. For example, the function

```
float MenuItem::operator+( MenuItem item )
{
  return( GetPrice() + item.GetPrice() );
}
```

overloads the + operator and performs pretty much the same function as the earlier example. The difference lies in the way a member function is called by the compiler.

When the compiler calls an overloading member function, it uses the first operand to call the function and passes the remainder of the operands as parameters. So with the function just given in place, the compiler handles the expression

```
chicken + houseWine
```

by calling `chicken.operator+()`, passing `houseWine` as a parameter, as if you had made the following call:

```
chicken.operator+( houseWine )
```

Again, the value returned by the function is used as the result of the expression.

Multiple Overloading Functions

The previous example brings up an interesting point. What will the compiler do when it encounters several functions that overload the same operator? For example, both of the following functions overload the + operator:

```
float operator+( MenuItem item1, MenuItem item2 )

float MenuItem::operator+( MenuItem item )
```

If both are present, which one is called?

The answer to this question is, neither! The compiler will not allow you to create an ambiguous overloading situation. You *can* create several functions that overload the same operator, however. You might create one version of `operator+()` that handles `MenuItems` and another that allows you to add two arrays together. The compiler chooses the proper overloading function based on the types of the operands.

An Operator Overloading Example

Here's an example that brings some of these concepts to life. First, we'll declare a `Time` class and use it to store a length of time specified in hours, minutes, and seconds. Then, we'll overload the + and *= operators and use them to add two times together and to multiply a time by a specified value. Use cd to move into the `projects` directory and then into the directory named `chap7_1`. The source code for this example is in the file named `addtime.cpp`. Compile and link the source code by typing this line at the DOS prompt:

```
sc addtime.cpp
```

The compiler will compile your source code, and the linker will link it into an executable file named `addtime.exe`. Run your newly created executable by typing

```
addtime
```

at the DOS prompt. Here's what you'll see:

```
(1:10:50)
(2:24:20)
--------
(3:35:10)
*       2
--------
(7:10:20)
```

Let's take a look at the source code.

The addtime Source Code

As usual, `addtime.cpp` starts by including `<iostream.h>`:

```
#include <iostream.h>
```

Next, we declare the `Time` class, which is used to store time in hours, minutes, and seconds:

```
class Time
{
//       Data members...
  private:
    short hours;
    short minutes;
    short seconds;
```

Next come the member functions. The first, `NormalizeTime()`, converts any overflow in the `seconds` and `minutes` data members; for example, 70 seconds is converted to 1 minute and 10 seconds. `NormalizeTime()` will only be used from within the `Time` class. Since we're not planning on deriving any classes from `Time`, we've left it as `private`. The rest of the member functions will be `public`:

```
//       Member functions...
    void  NormalizeTime();
  public:
```

The `Time` class sports two constructors. The first takes no parameters and is used to create a `Time` object with all three data

members set to 0 (you'll see why later on in the code). The second
`Time` constructor uses its three parameters to initialize the three
`Time` data members:

```
Time();
Time( short h, short m, short s );
```

`Display()` displays the time stored in the current object,
`operator+()` overloads the + operator, and `operator*=()`
overloads the *= operator:

```
    void  Display();
    Time  operator+( Time &aTime );
    void  operator*=( short num );
};
```

Next come the two overloaded constructors. The first one
initializes all three data members to 0. The second initializes the
data members and then calls `NormalizeTime()` to resolve any
overflow:

```
Time::Time()
{
   seconds = 0;
   minutes = 0;
   hours = 0;
}

Time::Time( short h, short m, short s )
{
   seconds = s;
   minutes = m;
   hours = h;

   NormalizeTime();
}
```

`NormalizeTime()` starts by adding the `seconds` overflow
to `minutes`, and then it adds the `minutes` overflow to `hours`:

```
void  Time::NormalizeTime()
{
   hours += ((minutes + (seconds/60)) / 60);
```

Next, the same calculation is performed to calculate a new value for `minutes` and then for `seconds`:

```
minutes = (minutes + (seconds/60)) % 60;

seconds %= 60;
}
```

`Display()` is self-explanatory:

```
void  Time::Display()
{
  cout << "(" << hours << ":" << minutes
       << ":" << seconds << ")\n";
}
```

`operator+()` is called when the + operator is used to add two `Time` objects together. The first operand is used as the current object, and the second operand corresponds to the parameter `aTime`:

```
Time  Time::operator+( Time &aTime )
{
  short h;
  short m;
  short s;
```

Notice that `aTime` is declared as a reference parameter. Why? This code would also work if `aTime` were declared without the `&`.

Without the `&`, the compiler would create a copy of the parameter to pass in to `operator+()`. Since C++ passes its parameters on the stack, this could cause a problem if the parameter was big enough. With the `&`, `aTime` is a reference to the object passed in as a parameter.

Next, the `hours`, `minutes`, and `seconds` data members of the two objects are added together and stored in the local variables h, m, and s:

```
h = hours + aTime.hours;
m = minutes + aTime.minutes;
s = seconds + aTime.seconds;
```

Next, a new `Time` object is created using h, m, and s. Since the `Time` constructor calls `NormalizeTime()`, there's no need to do that here:

```
Time  tempTime( h, m, s );
```

It is perfectly OK to declare an object in the middle of your code. In this case, we wanted to initialize h, m, and s before we created `tempTime`.

Finally, we return the newly created object. Since we are not using a reference, the compiler will make a copy of `tempTime`, then return the copy. The compiler is responsible for destroying this copy, so you don't have to worry about it:

```
    return tempTime;
}
```

`operator*=()` is called when the `*=` operator is used to multiply a `Time` object by a constant. Notice that `operator*=()` does not return a value because the multiplication is performed inside the `Time` object that appears as the first operand:

```
void  Time::operator*=( short num )
{
```

Each of the `Time` object's data members is multiplied by the specified `short`:

```
    hours *= num;
    minutes *= num;
    seconds *= num;
```

Since we won't be creating a new `Time` object, we call
`NormalizeTime()` to fix any overflow problems that may have
just been caused:

```
NormalizeTime();
}
```

> In general, your overloading functions return a value if it
> makes sense for the operator being overloaded. If the
> operator includes an =, chances are you'll make your
> changes in place and won't return a value, as we did
> with `operator*=()`. If the operator doesn't include an
> =, you'll most likely return a value, as we did with
> `operator+()`.
>
> Before you make the decision, build a few expres-
> sions using the operator under consideration. Do the
> expressions resolve to a single value? If so, then you
> want your overloading function to return a value.

`main()` starts by defining two `Time` objects (the values in parentheses represent `hours`, `minutes`, and `seconds`, respectively):

```
int main()
{
  Time   firstTime( 1, 10, 50 );
  Time   secondTime( 2, 24, 20 );
```

Next, a third `Time` object is created, this time via a call to the
`Time` constructor that doesn't take any parameters:

```
Time   sumTime;
```

`Display()` is called to display the data members of the two
`Time` objects, and then a line is drawn under the two `Time`s:

```
firstTime.Display();
secondTime.Display();

cout << "--------\n";
```

Here are the results:

```
(1:10:50)
(2:24:20)
--------
```

Next, the + operator is used to add the two `Times` together, and the resulting object is displayed:

```
sumTime = firstTime + secondTime;
sumTime.Display();
```

Here's what this result looks like:

```
(3:35:10)
```

Now, two more lines are sent to the console:

```
cout << "*        2\n";
cout << "--------\n";
```

Here's what they look like:

```
*        2
--------
```

These lines indicate that we'll be multiplying our previous result by 2.

We accomplish this multiplication by using the `*=` operator and then display the results:

```
sumTime *= 2;
sumTime.Display();

    return 0;
}
```

Here's the final time:

```
(7:10:20)
```

If you like, try substituting your own numbers and run the program again.

A Few Restrictions

Now that you've mastered the basics of operator overloading, you need to be aware of a few restrictions. First, you can only overload C++'s built-in operators (see Figure 7.1). This means that you can't create any new operators. You can't suddenly assign a new meaning to the letter *z*, for example.

FIGURE 7.1

You can overload these operators.

Overloadable Operators				
+	-	*	/	%
^	&	|	~	!
,	=	<	>	<=
>=	++	--	<<	>>
==	!=	&&	||	+=
-=	/=	%=	^=	&=
|=	*=	<<=	>>=	[]
()	->	->*	new	delete

Second, it may not be obvious from Figure 7.1, but there are a few built-in operators that you can't overload (see Figure 7.2).

FIGURE 7.2

You can't overload these operators.

Nonoverloadable Operators				
.	.*	::	?:	sizeof()

Third, you can't change the way an operator works with a predefined type. For example, you can't write your own `operator()` function to add two `int`s together.

DETAIL

Here's a rule of thumb for you. If you want the compiler to even consider calling your overloading function, either make the function a class member function, or else make one of its parameters an object. Remember, the compiler will complain if you write an `operator()` function designed to work solely with C++'s built-in types.

Fourth, when you overload the ++ and -- operators, you'll have to provide two versions of the `operator` function, one to support prefix notation and one to support postfix notation. The compiler distinguishes between the two by checking for a dummy `int` parameter. The prefix version of your `operator` function should not have any parameters; the postfix version takes a single `int`.

Here's an example of a prefix and postfix ++ overloading operator for the `Time` class from our last program. First, the prefix `operator` function:

```
Time operator++()
{
   *this = *this + 1;
   return *this;
}
```

Now here's a version of the postfix `operator` function:

```
Time operator++( int )
{
   Time aTime = *this;

   *this = *this + 1;
   return aTime;
}
```

Notice the unused `int` parameter in the postfix `operator++()` function. That's how the compiler identifies this function as postfix. Finally, you'll want to add a new version of `operator+()` to handle adding 1 to a `Time` object (as we do in the two functions above):

```
Time Time::operator+( int num )
{
   hours += 1;

   return *this;
}
```

Go ahead and add this code to your program. Don't forget to add the function declarations to your `Time` class declaration.

Fifth, you can't change an operator's precedence by overloading it. If you want to force an expression to be evaluated in a specific order, use parentheses.

Sixth, overloading functions cannot specify default parameters. This restriction makes sense since a function with default parameters can be called with a variable number of arguments. For example, you could call the function

```
MyFunc( short a=0, short b=0, short c=0 )
```

using anywhere from zero to three arguments. If an `operator()` function allowed default parameters, you'd be able to use an operator without any operands! If you did that, how would the compiler know which overloading function to call? You get the idea.

Seventh, you can't change the number of operands handled by an operator. For example, you couldn't make a binary operator unary.

Covering All the Bases

Earlier in the chapter, we looked at a function that overloaded the + operator and was designed to add the `price` of two `MenuItem`s together:

```
float operator+( MenuItem item1, MenuItem item2 )
{
  return( item1.GetPrice() + item2.GetPrice() );
}
```

When the compiler encountered an expression like

```
chicken + houseWine
```

where both `chicken` and `houseWine` were declared as `MenuItem`s, it called `operator+()`, which passed the two operands as parameters. The `float` produced by adding both `price`s together was returned as the result of the expression.

What happens when the compiler evaluates an expression like

```
chicken + houseWine + applePie
```

This expression seems innocent enough, but look at it from the compiler's viewpoint. First, the subexpression

```
chicken + houseWine
```

is evaluated, resolving to a `float`. Next, this `float` is combined with `applePie` in the expression

```
<float> + applePie
```

Hmmm...what does the compiler do with this expression? We designed an overloading function that handles the + operator when its operands are both `MenuItems`, but we don't have one that handles a `float` as the first operand and a `MenuItem` as the second operand.

Now take a look at the following expression:

```
chicken + (houseWine + applePie)
```

First, the compiler evaluates the subexpression

```
(houseWine + applePie)
```

resolving it to a `float`. That leaves us with the expression

```
chicken + <float>
```

Once again, we designed an `operator+()` function that handles + and two `MenuItems`, but we don't have one that handles a `MenuItem` as the first operand and a `float` as the second operand.

Overloading an Overloading Function

As you can see, you frequently need more than one version of the same `operator()` function. To accomplish this task, you use a technique introduced back in Chapter 4, function overloading. Just as with any other function, you can overload an `operator()` function by providing more than one version, each with its own unique signature.

Remember, a function's signature is based on its parameter list and not on its return value.

How Many Versions Are Needed?

Figuring out how many versions of an `operator()` function to provide is actually pretty straightforward. Start by making a list of the number of possible types you want to allow for each of the operator's operands. Don't forget to include the type returned by your `operator()` function.

In the previous example, we wanted `operator+()` to handle a `float` or a `MenuItem` as either operand, which yields the possibilities shown in Figure 7.3. The left column shows the possibilities for the left operand; the right column shows the possibilities for the right operand. Your list will have `left * right` entries in it, where `left` is the number of types allowed for the left operand and `right` is the number of types allowed for the `right` operand.

FIGURE 7.3

Possible operands for the + operator, given that each operand can be either a `float` *or a* `MenuItem`.

Left	+	Right
float		float
float		MenuItem
MenuItem		float
MenuItem		MenuItem

Figure 7.3 lists four possible operand combinations. The first case involves an expression of the form

```
<float> + <float>
```

As pointed out earlier, you can't create an `operator()` function based solely on built-in types. Fortunately, the compiler does a perfectly fine job of adding two `float`s together.

With this first case taken care of by the compiler, we're left to construct the remaining three `operator+()` functions. Our next program, menu, uses function overloading to do just that.

An Overloader Overloading Example

Use `cd` to move back up to the `projects` directory and then into the directory named `chap7_2`. The source code for this example is in the file named `menu.cpp`. Compile and link the source code by typing this line at the DOS prompt:

```
sc menu.cpp
```

The compiler will compile your source code, and the linker will link it into an executable file named `menu.exe`. Run your newly created executable by typing

```
menu
```

at the DOS prompt. Here's what you'll see:

```
MenuItem::operator+( MenuItem item )
operator+( float subtotal, MenuItem item )

Total: 15.969999

MenuItem::operator+( MenuItem item )
MenuItem::operator+( float subtotal )

Total: 15.969999
```

Let's take a look at the source code.

The menu Source Code

`menu.cpp` starts with two include files and a single constant:

```
#include <iostream.h>
#include <string.h>

const short kMaxNameLength = 40;
```

Next, the `MenuItem` class is declared. The `MenuItem` class contains two data members. `price` lists the price of the item while `name` contains the item's name as it might appear on a menu:

```
//------------------------------------- MenuItem

class MenuItem
{
  private:
    float    price;
    char     name[ kMaxNameLength ];
```

Notice that both data members are marked as `private`, which shouldn't be a problem since we won't be deriving any new classes from `MenuItem`.

The `MenuItem` class features four member functions. The constructor, `MenuItem()`, initializes the `MenuItem` data members; the `GetPrice()` function returns the value of the `price` data member:

```
  public:
            MenuItem( float itemPrice,
              char *itemName );
    float   GetPrice();
```

The two `operator+()` functions handle the cases where a `MenuItem` object appears as the first operand to the + operator. If the second operand is also a `MenuItem`, the first of the two functions is called; if the second operand is a `float`, the second function is called:

```
    float   operator+( MenuItem item );
    float   operator+( float subtotal );
};
```

The `MenuItem()` constructor copies its first parameter into the `price` data member, and then it uses `strcpy()` to copy the second parameter into the `name` data member:

```
MenuItem::MenuItem( float itemPrice, char *itemName )
{
```

```
    price = itemPrice;
    strcpy( name, itemName );
}
```

For the sake of simplicity, we used `strcpy()` to copy the parameter into `name`. The `Employee` constructor in Chapter 5's first sample program provides a safer alternative. Check it out.

`GetPrice()` returns the value stored in the data member `price`:

```
float MenuItem::GetPrice()
{
    return( price );
}
```

The first version of `operator+()` handles expressions of the form

```
<MenuItem> + <MenuItem>
```

First, it prints out a message showing which `operator+()` function is called:

```
float MenuItem::operator+( MenuItem item )
{
    cout << "MenuItem::operator+( MenuItem item )\n";
```

Next, it adds together the two versions of `price` representing the left and the right operands. `GetPrice()` retrieves the `price` of the left operand (the `MenuItem` acting as the current object), and `item.GetPrice()` retrieves the `price` of the right operand (the `MenuItem` passed as a parameter). The sum of these two prices is returned as a `float`:

```
    return( GetPrice() + item.GetPrice() );
}
```

The second version of `operator+()` handles expressions of the form

```
<MenuItem> + <float>
```

First, it prints out a message showing which `operator+()` function is called:

```
float MenuItem::operator+( float subtotal )
{
  cout << "MenuItem::operator+( float subtotal )\n";
```

Next, it adds together the `price` of the current object, retrieved by calling `GetPrice()`, and the `float` passed as a parameter. The sum is returned as a `float`:

```
  return( GetPrice() + subtotal );
}
```

The third version of `operator+()` is, by necessity, not a member function of any class. To understand why this is so, take a look at the expressions this version of `operator+()` is designed to handle:

```
<float> + <MenuItem>
```

As mentioned earlier, the compiler uses the first operand to determine how the overloading `operator()` function is called. If the first parameter is an object, that object is used to call the `operator()` function and all other operands are passed to the function as parameters. If the first parameter is not an object, the compiler's list of candidate overloading functions is reduced to the program's nonclass `operator()` functions. Once a matching function is located, the compiler calls it, passing *all* of the operands as parameters.

Just like its compatriots, the third version of `operator+()` starts by printing a message showing which `operator+()` function is called:

```
//------------------------------------ operator+()
```

```
float operator+( float subtotal, MenuItem item )
{
  cout <<
  "operator+( float subtotal, MenuItem item )\n";
```

Next, the float and the MenuItem's price, retrieved by calling GetPrice(), are added together and returned as a float:

```
  return( subtotal + item.GetPrice() );
}
```

OK, here comes the good stuff! main() declares three MenuItem objects, initializing each with a price and a name:

```
//----------------------------------- main()

int main()
{
  MenuItem   chicken( 8.99, "Chicken Kiev with salad" );
  MenuItem   houseWine( 2.99, "Riesling by the glass" );
  MenuItem   applePie( 3.99, "Apple Pie a la Mode" );
```

main() also declares a float used to hold the result of our MenuItem addition:

```
  float    total;
```

Next, the three MenuItems are added together, the result is stored in total, and the total is printed:

```
  total = chicken + houseWine + applePie;

  cout << "\nTotal: " << total
    << "\n\n";
```

When the compiler encounters the expression

```
chicken + houseWine + applePie
```

it first processes the subexpression

```
chicken + houseWine
```

Since we're adding two `MenuItems` together, the compiler calls the first of our three `operator+()` functions, as shown by the first line of output:

```
MenuItem::operator+( MenuItem item )
```

Next, this subtotal is used to process the remainder of the expression:

```
<subtotal> + applePie
```

Since we're now adding a `float` to a `MenuItem`, the compiler calls the third `operator+()` function, as shown by the next line of output:

```
operator+( float subtotal, MenuItem item )
```

Once the calculations are complete, the total is printed:

```
Total: 15.969999
```

Why 15.969999 instead of 15.97? Since we are using the default settings of the `iostream` library, we don't have much control over the precision used to print `floats`. In our next chapter, we'll explore the mechanisms you can use to fine-tune your `iostream` output.

Then, the three `MenuItems` are added together again, this time with a slight wrinkle—the addition of parentheses wrapped around the last two operands:

```
    total = chicken + (houseWine + applePie);
```

These parentheses force the compiler to start by evaluating the subexpression

```
(houseWine + applePie)
```

Once again, we're adding two `MenuItem`s together, as shown by the next line of output:

```
MenuItem::operator+( MenuItem item )
```

Next, this subtotal is used to process the remainder of the expression:

```
chicken + <subtotal>
```

Since we're now adding a `MenuItem` to a `float`, the compiler calls the second `operator+()` function, as shown by the following line of output:

```
MenuItem::operator+( float subtotal )
```

Finally, the total is printed a second time:

```
    cout << "\nTotal: " << total

    return 0;
}
```

As expected, this matches the earlier total:

```
Total: 15.969999
```

Special Cases   The remainder of this chapter is dedicated to a few special cases. Specifically, we'll focus on writing `operator()` functions that overload the new, `delete`, `()`, `[ ]`, `->`, and `=` operators.

> One characteristic shared by each of these operators is that they can only be overloaded by a nonstatic class member function. Basically, this means that you won't be using the nonclass `operator()` function strategy from our previous example for any of the operators in this section.

Overloading new and delete

There are two ways you can overload new and delete. You can create two member functions named operator new() and operator delete() as part of your class design. You might do this if you wanted to implement your own memory management scheme for a specific class.

Another way to overload new and delete is to overload the global new and delete operators by providing operator new() and operator delete() functions that are not members of a class. You might do this if you wanted new and delete to always initialize newly allocated memory.

> Whatever your reasons for overloading new and delete, proceed with caution. No matter how you do it, once you overload new and delete, you are taking on a big responsibility, one that can get you in deep trouble if you don't handle things properly.

An operator new Example

Here's a small example you can use as the basis for your own new and delete operator() functions. Use cd to move back up to the projects directory and then into the directory named chap7_3. The source code for this example is in the file named new.cpp. Compile and link the source code by typing this line at the DOS prompt:

```
sc new.cpp
```

The compiler will compile your source code, and the linker will link it into an executable file named new.exe. Run your newly created executable by typing

```
new
```

at the DOS prompt. Here's what you'll see:

```
new: 1 byte(s).
delete: 1 byte(s).
```

Let's take a look at the source code.

The new Source Code

new.cpp starts with a #include you've seen before:

```
#include <iostream.h>
```

new defines a class named Blob, which doesn't do much, but it does contain overloading functions for new and delete:

```
//----------------------------------- Blob

class Blob
{
  public:
    void  *operator new( size_t blobSize );
    void   operator delete( void *blobPtr,
          size_t blobSize );
};
```

There are lots of details worth noting in the new and delete operator() functions. First, notice the space between the words operator and new and between operator and delete. Without the space, the compiler might think you were creating a function called operatornew(), a perfectly legal C++ function name.

Next, note that operator new() returns a void *. This is required. In general, your version of new will return a pointer to the newly allocated object or block of memory. If your memory management scheme calls for relocatable blocks, you might want to return a handle (pointer to a pointer) instead. The choice is yours:

```
void  *Blob::operator new( size_t blobSize )
{
  cout << "new: " << blobSize << " byte(s).\n";
```

```
    return new char[ blobSize ];
}
```

The `operator new` function must take at least one parameter of type `size_t`. The value for this parameter is provided automatically by the compiler and specifies the size of the object to be allocated. Any parameters passed to `new` will follow the `size_t` in the parameter list.

The `operator delete` function never returns a value and *must* be declared to return a `void`. `delete` always takes at least one parameter, a pointer to the block to be deleted. The second parameter, a `size_t`, is optional. If you provide it, it will be filled with the size, in bytes, of the block pointed to by the first parameter:

```
void  Blob::operator delete( void *blobPtr, size_t
            blobSize )
{
  cout << "delete: " << blobSize << " byte(s).\n";

  delete [] blobPtr;
}
```

Sometimes the size passed as the second parameter to `operator delete()` isn't quite what you expected. If the pointer being `deleted` is a pointer to a base class yet the object pointed to belongs to a class derived from the base class, the second parameter to `operator delete()` will be the size of the base class.

There is an exception to this rule. If the base class's destructor is `virtual`, the `size` parameter will hold the proper value, the size of the object actually being `deleted`.

Overloading `delete` and `new` is tricky work. If you plan on writing your own `operator()` functions for `new` and `delete`, check out section 12.5 in the *Annotated C++ Reference Manual*.

main() creates a new Blob and then deletes it:

```
//----------------------------------- main()

int main()
{
  Blob  *blobPtr;

  blobPtr = new Blob;
  delete blobPtr;

  return 0;
}
```

When the Blob is created, the overriding new is called, and the following line of output appears:

```
new: 1 byte(s).
```

Where did the value 1 come from? This value is actually compiler dependent. THIN C++ allocates a minimum of 1 byte for an object, regardless of whether the object has any data members or not.

When the object is deleted, the overloaded version of delete is called, and the next line of output is generated:

```
delete: 1 byte(s).
```

Overloading ( )

The next special case is the function that overrloads the ( ) operator, also known as the *function call operator*. One reason to overload the function call operator is to provide a shorthand notation for accessing an object's critical data members. As mentioned earlier, ( ) can only be overloaded by a nonstatic class member function. Here's an example.

An operator( ) Example

Use cd to move back up to the projects directory and then into
the directory named chap7_4. The source code for this example
is in the file named caller.cpp. Compile and link the source
code by typing this line at the DOS prompt:

```
sc caller.cpp
```

The compiler will compile your source code, and the linker will
link it into an executable file named caller.exe. Run your
newly created executable by typing

```
caller
```

at the DOS prompt. Here's what you'll see:

```
Price of Stimpy doll: $36.990002
Price with 4.5% tax:  $38.654552
```

Let's take a look at the source code.

The caller Source Code

caller.cpp starts with the standard #include:

```
#include <iostream.h>
```

Next, caller defines an Item class. An Item object represents an item for sale at Uncle Ren's Toy-o-rama. For the purpose
of this example, I've kept things pretty simple. Item features a
single data member, price, and two member functions, the
Item( ) constructor and a function designed to overload the call
operator:

```
//------------------------------------- Item

class Item
{
  private:
    float    price;
```

```
    public:
            Item( float itemPrice );
      float operator()( float taxRate = 0 );
};
```

The `Item()` constructor copies its parameter into the `price` data member:

```
Item::Item( float itemPrice )
{
  price = itemPrice;
}
```

The `operator()()` function may look odd, but the syntax using two pairs of parentheses is correct:

```
float Item::operator()( float taxRate )
{
```

The first pair of parentheses designates the operator being overloaded; the second pair surrounds any parameters being passed to the function. In this case, one parameter, `taxRate`, is specified. Notice that `taxRate` has a default value of 0. You'll see why in a minute.

The `operator()()` function takes the specified `taxRate` and applies it to the `Item`'s `price`, returning the `Item`'s total price:

```
  return( ((taxRate * .01) + 1) * price );
}
```

Since the function call operator can only be overloaded by a class member function, the previous reference to `price` refers to the data member of the object used in combination with the call operator.

main() starts by creating an Item object. The Stimpy doll was Uncle Ren's biggest seller last year (although Log came in a close second):

```
//------------------------------------  main()

int main()
{
  Item  stimpyDoll( 36.99 );
```

Here's where the call overload comes into play:

```
  cout << "Price of Stimpy doll: $" << stimpyDoll();
```

By taking advantage of the default parameter, the function call

```
stimpyDoll()
```

returns stimpyDoll's price. We could have accomplished the same thing by coding

```
stimpyDoll.price
```

or

```
stimpyDoll( 0 )
```

Next, we use the same function to calculate the cost of the doll with 4.5% tax included:

```
  cout << "\nPrice with 4.5% tax:  $"
       << stimpyDoll( 4.5 );

  return 0;
}
```

Once again, we take advantage of the overloaded function call operator. This time, we provide a parameter. Notice that the same overloading function is used for two different (though closely related) purposes.

You may have noticed the Stimpy doll's price (including tax) printed as

```
Price with 4.5% tax:   $38.654552
```

Wouldn't it be nice if you could trim the price to $38.65 (who needs those extra digits, anyway)? Well, stick around until Chapter 8, where you'll learn how to customize iostream in all sorts of ways.

The key to properly overloading the function call operator is to use it to provide access to a key data member. If your object represents a character string, you might overload ( ) to provide access to a substring, using a pair of parameters to provide the starting position and length of the substring.

Another strategy uses ( ) as an iterator function for accessing data kept in a sequence or list. Each call to ( ) bumps a master pointer to the next element in the list and returns the new data element. No question about it, the function call operator is a useful operator to overload.

Overloading [ ]

Another useful operator to overload is [ ], also known as the *subscript operator*. Although it can be used for other things, [ ] is frequently overloaded to provide range checking for arrays. You'll see how to do this in a moment.

The subscript overloading syntax is similar to that of the function call operator. In the statement

```
myChar = myObject[ 10 ];
```

the [ ] overloading function belonging to the same class as myObject is called with a single parameter, 10. The value that is returned by the function is assigned to the variable myChar.

On the flip side of the coin, the [ ] overloading function *must* support a [ ] expression on the left side of the assignment statement, like so:

```
myObject[ 10 ] = myChar;
```

The next example shows you how to properly overload [ ].

An operator[ ] Example

Use **cd** to move back up to the **projects** directory and then into the directory named **chap7_5**. The source code for this example is in the file named **subscrpt.cpp**. Compile and link the source code by typing this line at the DOS prompt:

```
sc subscrpt.cpp
```

The compiler will compile your source code, and the linker will link it into an executable file named **subscrpt.exe**. Run your newly created executable by typing

```
subscrpt
```

at the DOS prompt. Here's what you'll see:

```
B. X. Clinton
index out of bounds!!!
Z. X. Clinton
```

Let's take a look at the source code.

The subscrpt Source Code

subscrpt.cpp starts with some familiar #includes and a constant that is used to declare a string data member:

```
#include <iostream.h>
#include <string.h>

const short kMaxNameLength = 40;
```

The Name class is fairly simple. It is designed to hold a null-terminated string containing a person's name as well as a short containing the length of the string:

```
//------------------------------------ Name

class Name
{
  private:
    char     nameString[ kMaxNameLength ];
    short    nameLength;
```

The member functions include a constructor as well as two operator overloading functions. One function overloads [ ]; the other overloads ( ):

```
  public:
             Name( char *name );
    void     operator()();
    char     &operator[]( short index );
};
```

The constructor copies the provided string to the nameString data member and places the length of the string in the nameLength data member:

```
Name::Name( char *name )
{
  strcpy( nameString, name );
  nameLength = strlen( name );
}
```

The ( ) operator overloading function simply prints the character string in nameString:

```
void  Name::operator()()
{
  cout << nameString << "\n";
}
```

The [ ] operator overloading function takes a single parameter, an index into the character string. Notice the unusual return type. By specifying a char reference as a return type, the function ensures that the [ ] operator can appear on either side of an assignment statement. Essentially, an expression such as

```
myObject[ 0 ]
```

is turned into a char variable containing the character returned by the [ ] overloading function:

```
char& Name::operator[]( short index )
{
```

Here's the real advantage to overloading the [ ] operator. Before you access the specified character, you can first do some bounds checking, making sure the character is actually *in* the character string! If the specified index is out-of-bounds, we print a message and point to the first character in the string. In real life, you'd probably want to jump to some error-handling code, but I've decided to keep things simple here:

```
  if ( ( index < 0 ) || ( index >= nameLength ) )
  {
    cout << "index out of bounds!!!\n";
    return( nameString[ 0 ] );
  }
```

If the index is in bounds, the specified character is returned:

```
  else
    return( nameString[ index ] );
}
```

main() contains the proof of the pudding. First, a Name object is created, bearing a presidential tag:

```
//------------------------------------- main()

int main()
{
  Name  pres( "B. J. Clinton" );
```

Next, the fourth character in the string is replaced by the character 'X':

```
pres[ 3 ] = 'X';
pres();
```

When `pres()` is called, the modified string is displayed:

```
B. X. Clinton
```

Then, the character 'Z' is placed well out-of-bounds and the string is displayed again:

```
pres[ 25 ] = 'Z';
pres();

    return 0;
}
```

The `[ ]` overloading function lets you know that the specified index is out-of-bounds and the assignment is performed on the first character of the string instead:

```
index out of bounds!!!
Z. X. Clinton
```

Overloading ->

Next on the special cases list is the `->` operator, also known as the *member access operator*. Like the other operators presented in this section, overloading `->` provides a shorthand notation that can save you code and add an elegant twist to your program.

When the compiler encounters the `->` operator, it checks the type of the left-hand operand. If the operand is a pointer, `->` is evaluated normally. If the operand is an object or object reference, the compiler checks to see whether the object's class provides an `->` overloading function.

If no `->` overloading function is provided, then the compiler reports an error, since the `->` operator requires a pointer, not an object. If the -> overloading function *is* present, the left operand is used to call the overloading function. When the overloading function returns, its return value is substituted for the original left operand, and the evaluation process is repeated. When used this way, the -> operator is known as a **smart pointer**.

If these rules sound confusing, hold on. The next example should make them loud and clear.

An operator-> Example

Use cd to move back up to the projects directory and then into the directory named chap7_6. The source code for this example is in the file named smartptr.cpp. Compile and link the source code by typing this line at the DOS prompt:

```
sc smartptr.cpp
```

The compiler will compile your source code, and the linker will link it into an executable file named smartptr.exe. Run your newly created executable by typing

```
smartptr
```

at the DOS prompt. Here's what you'll see:

```
Name: Bill Clinton
```

Let's take a look at the source code.

The smartptr Source Code

smartptr.cpp starts with some #includes and a constant that you know and love:

```
#include <iostream.h>
#include <string.h>

const short kMaxNameLength = 40;
```

smartptr defines two classes. The Name class holds two null-terminated strings containing a person's first and last names. The member function DisplayName() displays the name in the console window:

```
//------------------------------------- Name

class Name
{
  private:
    char   first[ kMaxNameLength ];
    char   last[ kMaxNameLength ];

  public:
          Name( char *lastName, char *firstName );
    void  DisplayName();
};

Name::Name( char *lastName, char *firstName )
{
  strcpy( last, lastName );
  strcpy( first, firstName );
}

void  Name::DisplayName()
{
  cout << "Name: " << first << " " << last;
}
```

The Politician class represents a politician. To keep things simple, the info is limited to the politician's age and a pointer to a Name object containing the politician's name:

```
//------------------------------------- Politician

class Politician
{
  private:
    Name    *namePtr;
    short   age;

  public:
          Politician( Name *namePtr, short age );
```

The Politician class also contains a member function designed to overload the -> operator. The function returns a pointer to the politician's Name object (the fact that it returns a pointer is key, as you'll see):

```
    Name      *operator->();
};

Politician::Politician( Name *namePtr, short age )
{
  this->namePtr = namePtr;
  this->age = age;
}

Name   *Politician::operator->()
{
  return( namePtr );
}
```

main() embeds a last and first name into a Name object and then uses that object to create a new Politician object (so far, no big deal):

```
//------------------------------------- main()

int main()
{
  Name        myName( "Clinton", "Bill" );
  Politician  billClinton( &myName, 46 );
```

Next, the Politician object is combined with the smart pointer to call DisplayName():

```
  billClinton->DisplayName();

  return 0;
}
```

There are several problems here. First, billClinton is an object and not a pointer, yet it is used with the -> operator. Second, the member function DisplayName() is not a member of the

`Politician` class. How can it be called directly from a `Politician` object?

Basically, the -> overloading function is doing its thing as a smart pointer by bridging the gap between a `Politician` object and a `Name` member function. When the compiler encounters the -> operator, it checks the type of the left operand. Since `billClinton` is not a pointer, the compiler checks for an -> overloading function in the `Politician` class. When the overloading function is found, it is called, using `billClinton` as the current object. The function returns a pointer to a `Name` object. The compiler substitutes this return value for the original, yielding

```
namePtr->DisplayName();
```

The compiler again checks the type of the left operand. This time, the operand is a pointer and the -> operator is evaluated normally. The `namePtr` is used to call the `Name` function `DisplayName()`, resulting in the following line of output:

```
Name: Bill Clinton
```

As you can see, overloading the -> operator provides a shortcut that allows you to run a direct line between two different classes.

You can take this model one step further by supposing that the -> overloading function returns a `Name` object rather than a pointer to a `Name` object. The compiler then substitutes the `Name` object in the original expression and reevaluates:

```
myName->DisplayName();
```

Once again, since the left operand is an object and not a pointer, the left operand's class is examined in search of another -> overloading function. This substitution and call of -> overloading functions is repeated until a pointer is returned (the end of the chain is reached). Only then is the -> operator evaluated in its traditional form.

> You can use this technique to walk along a chain of objects. Each -> overloading function evaluates some criteria, returning an object if the search should continue or a pointer if the end condition has been met. C++ is cool, eh?

Overloading =

And now, finally, we've reached the last of the special cases, the operator=() function. Why overload the = operator? To best understand why, take a look at what happens when you assign one object to another.

Suppose you define a `String` class, like this:

```
class String
{
  private:
    char     *s;
    short    stringLength;

  public:
             String( char *theString );
};
```

The data member `s` points to a null-terminated string. The data member `stringLength` contains the length of the string. The constructor `String()` initializes both data members. Notice that no memory has been allocated for `s`. This is done inside the constructor.

Now suppose you create a pair of `Strings`, like this:

```
String  source( "from" );
String  destination( "to" );
```

And then, you assign one of the `String` objects to the other, like this:

```
destination = source;
```

What happens?

As it turns out, the = operator copies one object to another by a process called **memberwise assignment**. Basically, this means that each data member within one object is copied, one at a time, to the corresponding data member in the receiving object.

The trouble with memberwise assignment is in the way it deals with allocated memory, such as you'd find with a null-terminated character string. When one (`char *`) is copied to another, the address stored in the (`char *`) is copied, not the data pointed to by the address. Once the statement

```
destination = source;
```

executes, both `String`s point to the same null-terminated string in memory. The default = operator isn't smart enough to allocate the appropriate amount of new memory and then use `strcpy()` to make a copy of the string. That's where `operator=()` comes in.

If you want the ability to assign the contents of one object to another, and the objects contain allocated memory, you'll have to write a smart = overloading function that knows how to do it right. Here's an example.

An operator= Example

Use `cd` to move back up to the `projects` directory and then into the directory named `chap7_7`. The source code for this example is in the file named `equals.cpp`. Compile and link the source code by typing this line at the DOS prompt:

```
sc equals.cpp
```

The compiler will compile your source code, and the linker will link it into an executable file named `equals.exe`. Run your newly created executable by typing

```
equals
```

at the DOS prompt. Here's what you'll see:

```
String address: 120333490
String address: 120333500
----
String address: 120333490
String address: 120335560
```

Let's take a look at the source code.

The equals Source Code

`equals.cpp` starts with the same old `#includes`:

```
#include <iostream.h>
#include <string.h>
```

The `String` class described earlier is defined next, with a few additions:

```
//-------------------------------------- String

class String
{
  private:
    char    *s;
    short   stringLength;
```

The constructor still allocates the memory for the specified string, but now several new functions are added:

```
  public:
            String( char *theString );
            ~String();
    void    DisplayAddress();
    String  &operator=( const String &fromString );
};
```

The constructor starts by calculating the length of the specified string, storing the result in `stringLength`. Next, new is used to allocate the proper amount of memory (the extra byte is for the null terminator at the end of the string). Finally, `strcpy()` is called to copy the source string to the data member s:

```
String::String( char *theString )
{
  stringLength = strlen( theString );
  s = new char[ stringLength + 1 ];

  strcpy( s, theString );
}
```

If s is declared as an array of fixed size, instead of as a dynamic string pointer, memberwise assignment works just fine since the memory for the array is part of the object itself. Since s points to a block of memory outside the object, memberwise assignment passes it by.

The `String` destructor uses `delete` to destroy the array of chars pointed to by s:

```
String::~String()
{
  delete [] s;
}
```

The member function `String::DisplayAddress()` provides a shorthand way of displaying the address of the first byte of a string:

```
void  String::DisplayAddress()
{
  cout << "String address: " << (unsigned long)s
    << "\n";
}
```

Here's the = overloading function. Just like `operator[]()`, this function must return an l-value. In this case, we return a reference to a `String` object. We also take a `String` reference as a parameter. Use the following sample code as a template for all your `operator=()` functions:

```
String  &String::operator=( const String &fromString )
{
```

> Since you can only assign an object to another object of the same class, the type of the return value will always agree with the type of the parameter. `const` in the parameter declaration just marks the parameter as read-only.

`operator=()` starts by freeing up the memory occupied by the old string. Next, the new value for the data member `stringLength` is copied from the source `String`. After that, `new` is used to allocate a block for the new string, and `strcpy()` is used to copy the source string into s:

```
delete [] s;

stringLength = fromString.stringLength;

s = new char[ stringLength + 1 ];

strcpy( s, fromString.s );
```

Since `this` is a pointer to the current object, `*this` is the object itself. We return `*this` to satisfy our need to return an l-value:

```
return( *this );
}
```

`main()` puts everything to the test. First, two `String` objects are created and initialized:

```
//--------------------------------------- main()
```

```
int main()
{
  String     captain( "Picard" );
  String     doctor( "Crusher" );
```

Next, the address of each String's string is displayed:

```
  captain.DisplayAddress();
  doctor.DisplayAddress();
```

The result is the following two lines of output:

```
String address: 120333490
String address: 120333500
```

Notice that the addresses of the two strings are different.
    Now, a separator line is printed:

```
  cout << "----\n";
```

Here's the result:

```
----
```

Then, the object captain is assigned to the object doctor, and the addresses of the two text strings are again displayed:

```
  doctor = captain;

  captain.DisplayAddress();
  doctor.DisplayAddress();

  return 0;
}
```

Again, notice that the addresses are different:

```
String address: 120333490
String address: 120335560
```

If the = operator is not overloaded, the address of the captain string simply copies into the doctor object's s data member and both addresses are the same. Want to prove this? Easy. Comment out the `operator=()` function (every single line, not just the insides) as well as its declaration inside the `String` class declaration, and run the program again. Without the `operator=()` function, the `String` destructor would try to `delete` the same block of memory twice!

Summary

Congratulations are definitely in order here! Personally, I think that operator overloading is the most difficult part of C++ to understand but provides the most fun in experimentation.

Well, the fun isn't over yet. In Chapter 8, you're going to dive into `iostream`. You'll find out how to overload the << and >> operators, giving you more control over your output, and you'll learn the difference between file handling in C and file handling in C++. Let's go!

Chapter 8

Inside iostream

Every sample program in this book has taken advantage of C++'s iostream library. This chapter takes a closer look at iostream's rich feature set.

This Chapter at a Glance

THROUGHOUT THIS BOOK, WE'VE DEPENDED ON `iostream`'s insertion operator (`<<`) for all of our output and `iostream`'s extraction operator (`>>`) for all of our input. While these operators serve us well, there's much more to `iostream` than has been demonstrated so far.

For example, you can easily customize `iostream` so that the `>>` and `<<` operators recognize your own personally designed data structures and classes. You can also use `iostream` to write to and read from files or even character arrays. As you'll see, `iostream` is a powerful extension of the C++ language.

The Character-Based Interface

`iostream`'s basic unit of currency is the character. Before a number is written to a file, it is converted to a series of `chars`. When a number is read from the console, it is read as a series of `chars` and then, if necessary, converted to the appropriate numerical form and stored in a variable.

`iostream` was designed to support a character-based user interface. As characters are typed on the user's keyboard, they appear on the console. When your program has something to say to the user, it uses `iostream` to send a stream of characters to the console.

If you plan to write programs for environments such as Windows, the Macintosh, or perhaps even a graphical version of Unix (Motif, X-windows, whatever), you'll probably do all your user-interface development using class libraries that come with your development environment. `iostream` doesn't know a thing about drop-down menus, windows, or even a mouse, but as you'll see, it's more than a library of user-interface routines.

Even if your user interface isn't character-based, `iostream` still has a lot to offer. You can use the same mechanisms you'd use to manage your console I/O to manage your program's file I/O. The same methods you'd use to write a stream of characters to a file can be used to write those same characters to an array in memory. What links these disparate techniques is their common ancestry.

The iostream Classes

The `iostream` library is built upon a set of powerful classes. The `iostream` base class is named `ios`. While you might not work directly with an `ios` object, you'll definitely work with `ios`' members as well as with classes derived from `ios`.

istream and ostream

You've already started to work with two classes derived from ios. The istream class is designed to handle input from the keyboard. cin is an istream object that C++ automatically creates for you. The ostream class is designed to handle output to the console. cout, cerr, and clog are ostream objects that are also automatically created for you. As you've already seen, cout is used for standard output. cerr and clog are used in the same way as cout. They provide a mechanism for directing error messages.

Usually cerr is tied to the console, although some operating systems (such as Unix) allow you to redirect cerr, perhaps sending the error output to a file or to another console. cerr is *unbuffered*, which means that output sent to cerr appears immediately on the cerr device. clog is a *buffered* version of cerr and is not supported by all C++ development environments. To decide which error output vehicle to use (clog or cerr), consult your operating system manual.

Working with istream and ostream

Up to this point, your experience with iostream has centered on the extraction (>>) and insertion (<<) operators. For example, the following code reads in a number, stores it in a variable, and then prints out the value of the number:

```
short    myNum;

cout << "Type a number: ";

cin >> myNum;

cout << "Your number was: " << myNum;
```

There are a couple of things worth noting in this example. First, the `iostream` input and output are buffered. Just as in C, all input and all output are accumulated in buffers until either the buffers are filled or the buffers are flushed. On the input side, the buffer is traditionally flushed when a carriage return is entered. On the output side, the buffer is usually flushed either when input is requested or when the program ends. Later in the chapter, you'll learn how to flush your own buffers (how exciting!).

The second feature worth noting is that >> eats up white space. In other words, >> ignores spaces and tabs in the input stream. To >>, the line

    123

is the same as this line:

123

If you're reading in a series of numbers, this works out pretty well. But if you're trying to read in a stream of text, you might want to preserve the white space interspersed throughout your input. Fortunately, `istream` offers some member functions that are white-space savvy.

get( )

The `istream` member function `get()` reads a single character from the input stream. `get()` comes in three different flavors.

The first version of `get()` takes a `char` reference as a parameter and returns a reference to an `istream` object:

```
istream &get(char &destination);
```

Since `get()` is an `istream` member function, you can use `cin` to call it (after all, `cin` is just an `istream` object):

```
char   c;

cin.get( c );
```

This version of `get()` reads a single character from the input stream, writes the `char` into its `char` parameter (c), and then returns the input stream reference (`cin`). Since `get()` returns the input stream, it can be used in a sequence, as in the following example:

```
char   c;
short myShort;

cout << "Type a char and a short: ";

cin.get( c ) >> myShort;
```

This code grabs the first character from the input stream and stores it in `c`. Next, the input stream is parsed for a `short`, and the `short` is placed in `myShort`. If the input to this example were

```
123
```

then `c` would end up with the character `1`, while `myShort` would end up with the value `23`.

The second version of `get()` is declared as follows:

```
istream &get(char *buffer, int length, char
          delimiter = '\n');
```

This version of `get()` extracts up to `length` – 1 characters and stores them in the memory pointed to by `buffer`. If the `char` `delimiter` is encountered in the input stream, the `char` is pushed back into the stream and the extraction stops. For example, the code

```
char   buffer[ 10 ];

cin.get( buffer, 10, '*' );
```

starts to read characters from the input stream. If a `*` is encountered, the extraction stops, the `*` is pushed back into the stream, and a null terminator is placed at the end of the string just read into `buffer`.

If no `*` is encountered, nine characters are read into `buffer`, and, again, `buffer` is null-terminated. Notice that `get()` reads only $n-1$ characters, where n is specified as the second parameter; `get()` is smart enough to save one byte for the null terminator.

If the third parameter is left out, this version of `get()` uses `'\n'` as the terminating character. This allows you to use `get()` to extract a full line of characters without overflowing your input buffer. For example, the code

```
char  buffer[ 50 ];

cin.get( buffer, 50 );
```

reads up to 49 characters or one line from the input stream, whichever is shorter. Either way, the string stored in `buffer` gets null-terminated.

The third version of `get()` is declared as follows:

```
int get();
```

This version of `get()` reads a single character from the input stream and returns the character, cast as an `int`, as in the following example:

```
int   c;

while ( (c = cin.get()) != 'q' )
  cout << (char)c;
```

This code reads the input stream, one character at a time, until a q is read. Each character is echoed to the console as it is read.

The third version of `get()` returns an `int` and not a `char` to allow it to return the end-of-file character. Typically, `EOF` has a value of –1. By returning an `int`, `get()` allows for 256 possible `char` values as well as for the end-of-file character. Although `EOF` isn't particularly useful when reading from the console, we'll use this version of `get()` later in the chapter to read the contents of a file.

getline( )

Another `istream` member function that you might find useful is `getline()`:

```
istream &getline(char *buffer, int length,
  char delimiter = '\n');
```

getline() behaves just like the second version of get(), but it returns the delimiter character instead of pushing it back into the input stream.

ignore( )

ignore() is used to discard characters from the input stream:

```
istream &ignore(int length = 1, int delimiter = EOF);
```

ignore() follows the same basic algorithm as getline(). It reads up to length characters from the input stream and discards them. This extraction stops if the specified delimiter is encountered. Notice that each of these parameters has a default value, which allows you to call ignore() without parameters.

Here's an example:

```
char  buffer[ 100 ];

cin.ignore( 3 ).getline( buffer, 100 );

cout << buffer;
```

This code drops the first three characters from the input stream and then reads the remainder of the first line of input into buffer. Next, the string stored in buffer is sent to the console. Notice that the value returned by ignore() is used to call getline(). This is equivalent to the following sequence of code:

```
cin.ignore( 3 );
cin.getline( buffer, 100 );
```

Once again, pick a style you're comfortable with and stick with it.

peek( )

peek() allows you to sneak a peek at the next character in the input stream without removing the character from the stream:

```
int peek();
```

Just like the third version of get(), peek() returns an int rather than a char. This allows peek() to return the end-of-file character, if appropriate, which makes `peek()` perfect for peeking at the next byte in a file.

put( )

The `ostream` member function `put()` provides an alternative to the << operator for writing data to the output stream:

```
ostream &put(char c);
```

`put()` writes the specified character to the output stream. It then returns a reference to the stream, so `put()` can be used in a sequence. Here's an example:

```
cout.put( 'H' ).put( 'i' ).put( '!' );
```

As you might have guessed, the preceding line of code produces this friendly message:

```
Hi!
```

putback( )

`putback()` puts the specified `char` back into the input stream, making it the next character to be returned by the next input operation:

```
istream &putback(char c);
```

Note that c must be the last character extracted from the stream. Since `putback()` returns an `istream` reference, it can be used in a sequence, similar to the example combining `ignore()` and `getline()` shown earlier.

seekg( ) and seekp( )

The `istream` member function `seekg()` gives you random access to an input stream:

```
istream &seekg(streampos p);
```

Call `seekg()` to position a stream's `get` pointer exactly where you want it. A second version of `seekg()` allows you to position the get pointer relative to the beginning or end of a stream or relative to the current get position:

```
istream &seekg( streamoff offset, relative_to
  direction );
```

In this second version of seekg(), the second parameter is one of ios::beg, ios::cur, or ios::end.

The ostream member function seekp() gives you random access to an output stream:

```
ostream &seekp(streampos p);
```

Just like seekg(), seekp() allows you to position a stream's put pointer exactly where you want it. seekp() also comes in a second flavor:

```
ostream &seekp( streamoff offset, relative_to
  direction );
```

For more detail on seekg(), seekp(), and their miscellaneous support routines, browse through <iostream.h>.

Some Useful Utilities

To aid you with your stream input and output operations, C++ provides a set of standard utilities that you may find useful (plain old ANSI C also provides these routines). To use any of the utilities described in this section, you must include the header file <ctype.h>.

Each of the thirteen functions takes an int as a parameter. The int represents an ASCII character. Two of the functions, tolower() and toupper(), map this character either to its lowercase or its uppercase ASCII equivalent. For example, tolower('A') would return 'a', while toupper('x') would return 'X'.

The remaining eleven functions return either 1 or 0, depending on the nature of the character passed in. The function isalpha() returns 1 if its argument is a character in the range 'a' through 'z' or in the range 'A' through 'Z'. The function isdigit() returns 1 if its argument is a character in the range '0' through '9'. The function isalnum() returns 1 if its argument causes either isalpha() or isdigit() to return 1.

> The constants TRUE and FALSE (whether in upper or lower case) are not part of the C++ language. Logical boolean operators such as == and != return an integer value of 1 if the comparison is true and 0 otherwise. Rather than using 1 and 0 in my source code, I prefer to use the following consts instead:
>
> ```
> const short   true = 1;
> const short   false = 0;
> ```

The function ispunct() returns 1 if the character is a punctuation character. The punctuation characters are ASCII characters in the ranges 33–47, 58–64, 91–96, and 123–126 (consult your nearest ASCII chart). The function isgraph() returns 1 if its argument causes isalpha(), isdigit(), or ispunct() to return 1.

islower() returns 1 if the character is in the range 'a' through 'z'. isupper() returns 1 if the character is in the range 'A' through 'Z'. isprint() returns 1 if the character is a printable ASCII character. iscntrl() returns 1 if the character is a control character. isspace() returns 1 if the character has an ASCII value in the range 9–13 or if it has a value of 32 (space). Finally, isxdigit() returns 1 if the character is a legal hex digit (0–9, a–f, or A–F).

The thirteen functions just described are summarized in the table in Figure 8.1.

Working with Files

iostream contains two classes created especially for working with files. The ifstream class is derived from istream and is designed to read data from a file. Since ifstream inherits

FIGURE 8.1

*Some useful utilities.
Don't forget to include
the file* <ctype.h>.

Some Useful Utilities	
int isalnum(int);	True if char isalpha() or isdigit().
int isalpha(int);	Is char in range a–z or A–Z?
int iscntrl(int);	Is char control character?
int isdigit(int);	Is char in range 0–9?
int isgraph(int);	True if char isalpha() or isdigit() or ispunct().
int islower(int);	Is char in range a–z?
int isprint(int);	Is char printable ASCII character?
int ispunct(int);	Is char in ASCII range 33–47, 58–64, 91–96, 123–126?
int isspace(int);	Is char in ASCII range 9–13 or 32?
int isupper(int);	Is char in range A–Z?
int isxdigit(int);	Is char in ASCII range 0–9, a–f, A–F?
int tolower(int);	Maps upper case to lower case.
int toupper(int);	Maps lower case to upper case.

istream's member functions, you can use an ifstream object to take advantage of istream functions like get().

The ofstream class is derived from ostream and is designed to write data to a file. Since ofstream inherits ostream's member functions, you can use an ofstream object to take advantage of ostream functions like put().

Reading Data from a File

The ifstream constructor comes in several varieties. The most widely used of these takes two parameters:

```
ifstream(const char* name, int mode=ios::in );
```

The first parameter is a null-terminated string containing the name of a file to be opened. The second describes the mode used to open the file. The legal modes are described in the table in Figure 8.2. They are declared as part of the ios class (check out <iostream.h>). The default mode is ios::in, which opens the file for reading.

FIGURE 8.2

These file-opening modes are declared as part of the ios *class.*

File-Opening Modes	
ios::in	Input allowed
ios::out	Output allowed
ios::ate	Seek to EOF at open
ios::app	Output allowed, append only
ios::trunc	Output allowed, discard existing contents
ios::nocreate	Open fails if file *doesn't* exist
ios::noreplace	Open fails if file *does* exist

Some operating systems (such as Unix) support a third, optional parameter for ifstream (and for ofstream as well). The third parameter specifies the protection level used to open the file. In general, the protection parameter is used only with multiple-user operating systems where more than one person has access to the same set of files. Read your development environment manual to see whether this extra parameter is supported.

Since you'll most likely want to use the default mode of ios::in when you open a file for reading, you can leave off the last parameter when you create an ifstream object:

```
ifstream    readMe( "myfile.txt" );
```

This definition creates an ifstream object named readMe. Next, it opens a file named myfile.txt for reading, attaching the open file to readMe.

ifstream objects have data members that track whether a file is attached to the stream and, if so, whether the file is open for reading. If a file is attached and open for reading, a get pointer is maintained that marks how far you've read into the file. Normally, the get pointer starts life at the very beginning of the file.

Once your file is opened for reading, you can use all of the iostream input functions described earlier to read data from the file. For example, the following code opens a file and then reads a single character from it:

```
char        c;
ifstream    readMe( "myfile.txt" );

readMe.get( c );
```

A File-Reading Example

Our first sample program uses this technique to read a file and display the contents in the console window. Use **cd** to move into the **projects** directory and then into the directory named **chap8_1**. The source code for this example is in the file named **readme.cpp**. Compile and link the source code by typing this line at the DOS prompt:

```
sc readme.cpp
```

The compiler will compile your source code, and the linker will link it into an executable file named **readme.exe**. Before you run **readme**, be sure the file **myfile.txt** is in the **chap8_1** directory. Run your newly created executable by typing

```
readme
```

at the DOS prompt. Here's what you'll see:

```
The Darlan-Ferengi wars raged on
for centuries before the final battle,
known as the "Dawn of Arcturus", was fought.
```

Let's take a look at the source code.

The readme Source Code
As usual, **readme.cpp** starts by including **<iostream.h>**. Next, you'll encounter a new include file, **<fstream.h>**, which contains the declarations of the **ifstream** and **ofstream** classes

(take some time and look through this include file; you'll learn a lot about the nooks and crannies of `iostream` file management):

```
#include <iostream.h>
#include <fstream.h>
```

`main()` starts by defining an `ifstream` object named `readMe`, asking the constructor to open the file named `myfile.txt` with the default mode of `ios::in`:

```
int main()
{
  ifstream  readMe( "myfile.txt" );
```

We're now ready to read the contents of the file.

The variable `c` is used to hold each character read from the file:

```
  char    c;
```

Next comes a `while` loop that reads the contents from the file associated with `readMe`, one character at a time. Each time a character is successfully read, it is written out to the console. Notice that the `ifstream` object `readMe` is used just like the `istream` object `cin` when it comes to calling `get()`, which is true for all of the other `istream` member functions as well:

```
  while ( readMe.get( c ) )
    cout << c;

  return 0;
}
```

You may be wondering how this loop ever terminates. Since `get()` returns an `istream` reference, how will `readMe.get( c )` ever evaluate to 0? The answer to this question lies in understanding the `iostream` state bits.

The iostream State Bits

Every stream, whether an `istream` or an `ostream`, has a series of four **state bits** associated with it:

```
enum io_state
{
  goodbit=0,
  eofbit=1,
  failbit=2,
  badbit=4
};
```

`iostream` uses these bits to indicate the relative health of their associated stream. You can poke and prod these bits yourself, but there are four functions that reflect each bit's setting.

For example, the function

```
int good();
```

returns nonzero if the stream used to call it is ready for I/O. Basically, if `good()` returns 1, you can assume that all is right with your stream and expect that your next I/O operation will succeed.

The function

```
int eof();
```

returns 1 if the last I/O operation puts you at end-of-file.

The function

```
int fail();
```

returns 1 if the last operation fails for some reason. As an example, an input operation might fail if you try to read a `short` but encounter a text string instead.

The function

```
int bad();
```

returns 1 if the last operation fails *and* the stream appears to be corrupted. When `bad()` returns 1, you're in deep guacamole.

Finally, the function

```
void    clear( int newState=0 );
```

is used to reset the state bits to the state specified as a parameter. In general, you should call `clear()` without specifying a parameter. `clear()`'s default parameter sets the state bits back to the pristine, `good` setting. If you don't clear the state bits after a failure, you won't be able to continue reading data from the stream. (You'll see an example of this in a moment.)

For the most part, you should focus on the value returned by `good()`. As long as `good()` returns 1, there's no need to check any of the other functions. Once `good()` returns 0, you can find out why by querying the other three state functions.

The Coolness of good( )

Now comes the cool part. In the program `readme`, we encountered a `while` loop that used an `iostream` function as its conditional expression:

```
while ( readMe.get( c ) )
    cout << c;
```

What caused this `while` loop to exit? `readme.get( c )` returns a reference to `readMe`, correct? Actually, this is where the C++ compiler displays a little sleight of hand. When the compiler detects an `iostream` I/O function used where an `int` is expected, it uses the current value of `good()` as the return value for the function. The previous `while` loop exits when `readMe.get( c )` either fails or hits an end-of-file.

A good( ) Example

Our second sample program demonstrates the basics of working with the `iostream` state bits and state bit functions. Use `cd` to move back up to the `projects` directory and then into the directory named `chap8_2`. The source code for this example is in the file named `statebts.cpp`. Compile and link the source code by typing this line at the DOS prompt:

```
sc statebts.cpp
```

The compiler will compile your source code, and the linker will link it into an executable file named `statebts.exe`. Run your newly created executable by typing

```
statebts
```

at the DOS prompt. Here's what you'll see:

```
Type a number:
```

Type a number small enough to fit inside a `short`, like 256:

```
Type a number: 256
```

When you hit a return, `statebts` will tell you what your number is and then ask you to type another:

```
Your number is: 256

Type a number:
```

This time, type the letter *x* and hit a return. `statebts` will tell you that the *x* is not a number and then ask you for another number:

```
Type a number: x
x is not a number...Type 0 to exit

Type a number:
```

Now type the number 0, which tells `statebts` to drop out of its main loop:

```
Type a number: 0
Goodbye...
```

Let's take a look at the source code.

The statebts Source Code

statebts.cpp starts with the usual #include (since we won't be doing any file I/O, there's no need to include <fstream.h>):

```
#include <iostream.h>
```

Next, statebts declares values for true and false:

```
const short true = 1;
const short false = 0;
```

statebts creates a loop that reads in a number and then prints the number in the console window. If the number entered is 0, the program exits. Things start to get interesting when a letter is entered instead of a number:

```
int main()
{
  char  done = false;
  char  c;
  short number;
```

Note that done acts as a Boolean logic operator. When it is set to true, the loop exits. c and number are used to hold data read from the console.

We enter the main loop, are prompted for a number, and then use >> to read the number from the console:

```
  while ( ! done )
  {
    cout << "Type a number: ";
    cin >> number;
```

If a number appropriate for a short is typed at the prompt, cin.good() returns 1:

```
    if ( cin.good() )
```

If the number typed is 0, we say goodbye and drop out of the loop; otherwise, we display the number and start all over again:

```
{
  if ( number == 0 )
  {
    cout << "Goodbye...";
    done = true;
  }
  else
    cout << "Your number is: " << number
            << "\n\n";
}
```

If the input is of the wrong type (the letter *x* or 1.34, for instance) or is a number that is too large (99999) or too small (–72999), the input operation fails and `cin.fail()` returns 1:

```
else if ( cin.fail() )
```

The first thing we must do is call `clear()` to reset the state bits (if we don't clear the state bits back to their supple, healthy state, we won't be able to continue reading data from the stream):

```
{
  cin.clear();
```

Once the state bits are reset, we read the character that caused the the stream to choke. Since we're not trying to interpret this character as a number, this read won't fail. Having read in the offending character, we display it, along with an appropriate message on the console:

```
cin.get( c );
cout << c << " is not a number...";
cout << "Type 0 to exit\n\n";
}
```

This example implements a rather simple-minded recovery algorithm. If you typed in something like *xxzzy*, the loop would fail five times since you knock out only a single character with each recovery. You might want to try your hand at a more sophisticated approach. For

> example, you might use `cin.ignore()` to suck in all
> the characters up to and including a carriage return.
> Better yet, you might use `cin.get()` to read in the
> remainder of the offending characters and then pack-
> age them in an appropriate error message.

The final possibility lies with a call to `bad()`. Since the `bad`
bit will likely never be set, you'll probably never see this message. No sense taking chances, though:

```
    else if ( cin.bad() )
    {
      cout << "\nYikes!!! Gotta go...";
      done = true;
    }
  }

  return 0;
}
```

More File Info

Earlier, the `ifstream` constructor was used to open a file for
reading:

```
ifstream  readMe( "myfile.txt" );
```

In the same way, the `ofstream` constructor can be used to open a
file for writing:

```
ofstream writeMe( "myfile.txt" );
```

Writing Data to a File

The `ofstream` constructor takes two parameters, with `ios::out`
used as the default `mode` parameter. Note that you can pass more
than one `mode` flag at a time. To open a file for writing if the file
already exists, try something like this:

```
ofstream writeMe( "myfile.txt", ios::out
  | ios::nocreate );
```

Refer back to the table in Figure 8.2 for the rest of the mode flags.

There is a way to open a file for both reading and writing. Use the `fstream` class and pass both the `ios::in` and `ios::out` mode flags, like this:

```
fstream  inAndOut( "rdandwrt.txt", ios::in
  | ios::out );
```

The `fstream` class is set up with two file position indicators, one for reading and one for writing. You really should read through the file `<fstream.h>`. You'll find all kinds of cool stuff in there. While you're at it, read through `<iostream.h>` as well. If you see a file named `<stream.h>`, beware! `<stream.h>` was written to support a library known as `streams`, a predecessor to `iostream`. `<stream.h>` is obsolete.

Once your file is open, you can close it by calling the `close()` member function:

```
writeMe.close();
```

In general, this call isn't really necessary since the `ifstream` and `ofstream` destructors automatically close the file attached to their associated stream.

You can also create an `ifstream` or `ofstream` without associating it with a file. Why would you want to do this? If you planned on opening a series of files, one at a time, you might want to do this by using a single stream, not by declaring one stream for each file. Using a single stream is more economical. Here's an example:

```
ifstream    readMe;
```

```
readMe.open( "file1.txt" );
// Read contents - be sure to include error
// checking!
readMe.close();

readMe.open( "file2.txt" );
// Read contents - be sure to include error
// checking!
readMe.close();

// Repeat this as necessary...
```

read( ), write( ), and Others

There are some `istream` member functions that are particularly useful when dealing with files. The member function `read()` reads a block of `size` bytes and stores the bytes in the buffer pointed to by `data`:

```
istream &read(void *data, int size);
```

As you'd expect, if an end-of-file is reached before the requested bytes are read, the `fail` bit is set. The member function `istream::gcount()` returns the number of bytes successfully read:

```
size_t gcount();
```

The member function `write()` inserts a block of `size` bytes from the buffer pointed to by `data`:

```
ostream &write(const void *data, size_t size);
```

The member function `ostream::pcount()` returns the number of bytes inserted by the preceding `write()` call:

```
size_t pcount();
```

Customizing iostream

There are times when the standard operators and member functions of `iostream` just don't cut it. For example, remember the `MenuItem` class we declared in Chapter 7:

```
class MenuItem
{
  private:
    float   price;
    char    name[ 40 ];

  public:
            MenuItem::MenuItem( float itemPrice,
              char *itemName );
    float   MenuItem::GetPrice();
};
```

Suppose you want to display the contents of a `MenuItem` using `iostream`. You can write a `DisplayMenuItem()` member function that takes advantage of `iostream`, but that is somewhat awkward. If you want to display a `MenuItem` in the middle of a `cout` sequence, you have to break the sequence up, sandwiching a call to `DisplayMenuItem()` in the middle:

```
cout << "Today's special is: ";
myItem.DisplayMenuItem();
cout << "...\n";
```

Wouldn't it be nice if `iostream` knew about `MenuItem`s so that you could do something more convenient, like this:

```
cout << "Today's special is: " << myItem << "...\n";
```

Why, there *is* a way to do this, after all! Using the techniques covered in Chapter 7, you create an `operator<<()` function that knows exactly how you want your `MenuItem` displayed. (You'll see an example of this in a moment.)

What's more, you can overload the `>>` operator, providing an `operator>>()` function that knows how to read in a `MenuItem`. The only restriction on both of these cases is that your `>>` and `<<`

overloading functions must return the appropriate stream reference so that you can use the >> and << operators in a sequence.

An >> and << Overloading Example

Our next sample program extends the `ostream` and `istream` classes by adding functions that overload both >> and <<. Use `cd` to move back up to the `projects` directory and then into the directory named `chap8_3`. The source code for this example is in the file named `overlod2.cpp`. Compile and link the source code by typing this line at the DOS prompt:

```
sc overlod2.cpp
```

The compiler will compile your source code, and the linker will link it into an executable file named `overlod2.exe`. Before you run `overlod2`, be sure the file `menuitms.txt` is in the `chap8_3` directory. Run your newly created executable by typing

```
overlod2
```

at the DOS prompt. Here's what you'll see:

```
Spring Rolls ($2.99)
Hot and Sour Soup ($3.99)
Hunan Chicken ($8.99)
General Tso's Shrimp ($9.99)
Spring Surprise ($15.99)
```

Let's take a look at the source code.

The overlod2 Source Code

`overlod2.cpp` starts with some familiar `#includes` and a `const` definition from Chapter 7's menu program:

```
#include <iostream.h>
#include <fstream.h>
#include <string.h>

const short kMaxNameLength = 40;
```

The `MenuItem` class is a slightly modified version of the one in Chapter 7. For one thing, the constructor is left out. Instead of initializing the data members when a `MenuItem` is created, `iostream` is used to read in a series of `MenuItem`s from a file and initialize each data member using the newly added `SetName()` and `SetPrice()` member functions:

```
//------------------------------------- MenuItem

class MenuItem
{
  private:
    float    price;
    char     name[ kMaxNameLength ];

  public:
    void     SetName( char *itemName );
    char     *GetName();
    void     SetPrice( float itemPrice );
    float    GetPrice();
};
```

`SetName()` is used to set the value of the name data member:

```
void  MenuItem::SetName( char *itemName )
{
  strcpy( name, itemName );
}
```

`GetName()` returns a pointer to the name data member. By giving the caller of this `public` function direct access to name, we're sort of defeating the purpose of marking name as `private`. A more appropriate approach might be to have `GetName()` return a copy of name. For the purposes of discussion, the version of `GetName()` shown next will do:

```
char  *MenuItem::GetName()
{
  return( name );
}
```

`SetPrice()` is used to set the value of the `price` data member:

```
void  MenuItem::SetPrice( float itemPrice )
{
   price = itemPrice;
}
```

`GetPrice()` returns the value of the `price` data member:

```
float MenuItem::GetPrice()
{
   return( price );
}
```

The `operator>>()` function is called by the compiler whenever the `>>` operator is encountered having an `istream` as its left operand and a `MenuItem` as its right operand. Since all `>>` sequences are resolved to `istream` references, the left operand is always an `istream` object. To make this a little clearer, imagine an `>>` sequence with several objects in it:

```
cin >> a >> b;
```

`iostream` starts by evaluating this expression from the left, as if it were written like this:

```
(cin >> a) >> b;
```

Since the `>>` operator resolves to an `istream` object, the expression `cin >> a` resolves to `cin`, leaving this:

```
cin >> b;
```

The same logic holds true for the `<<` operator:

```
cout << a << b;
```

As the compiler evaluates this expression from left to right, the left operand of the `<<` operator is always an `ostream` object.

The point is, whether `istream` or `ostream`, all an `operator()` function needs to do to support sequences is to return the stream reference passed in as the first parameter:

```
//------------------------- iostream operators


istream &operator>>( istream &is, MenuItem &item )
{
  float itemPrice;
  char  itemName[ kMaxNameLength ];
```

`operator>>()` reads a single `MenuItem` object from the specified input stream. First, `getline()` is used to read the item's name. Notice that the second parameter to `getline()` is used to limit the number of characters read in, ensuring that `itemName` doesn't exceed its bounds. `SetName()` is used to copy the entered name into the `name` data member:

```
  is.getline( itemName, kMaxNameLength );
  item.SetName( itemName );
```

Then, `>>` is used to read the item's price into `itemPrice`, and `SetPrice()` is used to copy `itemPrice` into the `price` data member:

```
  is >> itemPrice;
  item.SetPrice( itemPrice );
```

When the extraction operator reads the price from the input stream, it leaves the carriage return following the number unread. `ignore()` is used to grab the carriage return, leaving the stream set up to read the next `MenuItem`:

```
  is.ignore( 1, '\n' );
```

Finally, the stream passed in to the `operator>>()` function is returned, preserving the integrity of the sequence:

```
  return( is );
}
```

`operator<<()` is somewhat simpler. It uses `<<` to write the name and `price` data members:

```
ostream &operator<<( ostream &os, MenuItem &item )
{
  os << item.GetName() << " ($"
    << item.GetPrice() << ") ";
```

Once again, the stream passed in as the first parameter is returned:

```
  return( os );
}
```

`main()` declares an `ifstream` object and ties it to the file named `menuitms.txt`. This file contains a list of `MenuItems` with the name and price of each item appearing on its own line:

```
//------------------------------------- main()

int main()
{
  ifstream  readMe( "menuitms.txt" );
```

`main()` also declares a `MenuItem` object named `item`. Notice that no parameters are passed because there's no constructor to do anything with the parameters:

```
  MenuItem  item;
```

Next, a `while` loop is used to read in all the `MenuItems` that can be read from the input stream (which is, in this case, a file named `menuitms.txt`). The overloaded version of `>>` is used to read in a `MenuItem`, and the overloaded version of `<<` is used to display the `MenuItem` in the console window:

```
  while ( readMe >> item )
    cout << item << "\n";

  return 0;
}
```

Here's what appears on the console:

```
Spring Rolls ($2.99)
Hot and Sour Soup ($3.99)
Hunan Chicken ($8.99)
General Tso's Shrimp ($9.99)
Spring Surprise ($15.99)
```

It's important to note that `operator>>()` and `operator<<()` are designed to work with any input and output stream. In this case, the `MenuItems` are read from a file and displayed in the console window. By making a few changes to `main()`—and *not* changing the two `operator()` functions—you can easily change the program to read from standard input (you'd probably want to add in a prompt or two) and send the output to a file. That's the real beauty of `iostream`!

Formatting Your Output

In the preceding program, we overloaded the << operator so that we could display a `MenuItem` precisely the way we wanted it to appear. Unfortunately, there's no way to overload the << operator to customize the appearance of built-in data types such as `short` or `float`. Fortunately, `iostream` provides several mechanisms that allow you to customize your I/O operations.

In general, `iostream` follows some fairly simple rules when it comes to formatting output. If you insert a single `char` in a stream, exactly one character position is used. When some form of integral data is inserted, the insertion is exactly as wide as the number inserted, including space for a sign, if applicable. No padding characters are used.

When a `float` is inserted, room is made for up to six places of precision to the right of the decimal place. Trailing zeros are dropped. If the number is either very large or very small (how big or how small depends on the implementation), exponential notation is used. Again, room is made for a sign, if applicable. For example, the number 1.234000 takes up five character positions in the stream since the trailing zeros are dropped:

```
1.234
```

When a string is inserted, each character, not including any null-terminator, takes up one character position.

The Formatting Flags

The `ios` class maintains a set of **formatting flags** that control various formatting features. You can use the `ios` member functions `setf()` and `unsetf()` to turn these features on and off. Each feature corresponds to a bit in a bit field maintained by the `ios` class.

Some features are independent, while others are grouped together. For example, the flag `ios::skipws` determines whether white space is skipped during extraction operations. This feature is not linked to any other features, so it may be turned on and off without impacting any of the other formatting flags.

To turn an independent flag on and off, you use the `setf()` and `unsetf()` member functions as follows:

```
cin.setf( ios::skipws ); // Skip whitespace on input
cin.unsetf( ios::skipws ); // Don't skip whitespace
                           // on input
```

Alternatively, you can use the `flag()` member function to retrieve the current flag settings as a group, OR the new flag into the group, and then use `flag()` again to reset the flag settings with the newly modified bit field:

```
int myFlags;
```

```
myFlags = cout.flag();    // returns flag
                          //bitfield
myFlags |= ios::skipws;   // ORs in skipws
                          // flag
cout.flag( myFlags );     // resets flags
```

Unless you really need to work at this level, you're better off sticking with setf() and unsetf(). Just thought you'd like to see the whole picture.

Turning independent flags on and off individually is no problem, but things get interesting when flags are grouped. For example, the radix flags determine the default base used to represent numbers in output. The radix flags are dec, oct, and hex, representing decimal, octal, and hexadecimal formats, respectively. The problem here is that only one of these flags should be turned on at a time. If you use setf(), you could easily turn all three flags on, producing unpredictable results.

To handle grouped flags, setf() makes use of a second, optional parameter that indicates which group a flag belongs to. For example, the radix flags dec, oct, and hex belong to the group basefield. To set the hex flag, you make the following call:

```
cout.setf( ios::hex, ios::basefield );
```

This call ensures that when the specified flag is set, the remainder of the fields in the group get unset.

The grouped flags left, right, and internal are part of the adjustfield group. They are used in combination with the width() member function. width() determines the minimum number of characters used in the next numeric or string output operation. If the left flag is set, the next numeric or string output operation appears left-justified in the currently specified width(). The output is padded with the currently specified fill() character. You can use fill() to change this padding character. An example should make this formatting feature clearer.

A Formatting Example

Use cd to move back up to the projects directory and then into the directory named chap8_4. The source code for this example is in the file named formattr.cpp. Compile and link the source code by typing this line at the DOS prompt:

```
sc formattr.cpp
```

The compiler will compile your source code, and the linker will link it into an executable file named formattr.exe. Run your newly created executable by typing

```
formattr
```

at the DOS prompt. Here's what you'll see:

```
202
202xx
-======101
*****Hello
```

Let's take a look at the source code.

The formattr Source Code

formattr.cpp starts with the standard #include:

```
#include <iostream.h>
```

main() starts by displaying the number 202 in the console window:

```
//----------------------------------- main()

int main()
{
  cout << 202 << '\n';
```

As you'd expect, this code produces the following line of output:

202

Next, `width()` is used to set the current width to 5, and `fill()` is used to make x the padding character:

```
cout.width( 5 );
cout.fill( 'x' );
```

Remember, `width()` applies only to the very next string or numeric output operation, even if it is part of a sequence. The padding character lasts until the next call of `fill()` or until the program exits.

If your output operation produces more characters than the current width setting, don't worry. All your characters will be printed.

Now, the `left` flag is set, asking `iostream` to left-justify the output in the field specified by `width()`:

```
cout.setf( ios::left, ios::adjustfield );

cout << 202 << '\n';
```

When the number 202 is printed again, it appears like this:

```
202xx
```

Then, `width()` is pumped up to 10, `fill()` is changed to =, and the `internal` flag is set. The `internal` flag asks `iostream` to place padding in between a number and its sign, if appropriate, so that it fills the `width()` field:

```
cout.width( 10 );
cout.fill( '=' );
cout.setf( ios::internal, ios::adjustfield );

cout << -101 << '\n';
```

Printing the number –101 produces the following line of output:

```
-======101
```

Finally, `width()` is reset to 10 (otherwise, it would have dropped to its default of 0), `fill()` is set to *, and the `right` flag is set to right-justify the output:

```
cout.width( 10 );
cout.fill( '*' );
cout.setf( ios::right, ios::adjustfield );

cout << "Hello";

return 0;
}
```

When the string `"Hello"` is printed, this line of output appears:

```
*****Hello
```

More Flags and Methods

The `showbase` flag is independent. If it is set, octal numbers are displayed with a leading zero and hex output appears with the two leading characters `0x`. The `showpoint`, `uppercase`, and `showpos` flags are also independent. If `showpoint` is set, trailing zeros in floating-point output are displayed. If `uppercase` is set, E rather than e is used in scientific notation and X rather than x is used in displaying hex numbers. If `showpos` is set, positive numbers appear with a leading +.

The `scientific` and `fixed` flags belong to the `floatfield` group. If `scientific` is set, scientific notation is used to display floating-point output. If `fixed` is set, standard notation is used. If neither bit is set, the compiler uses its judgment and prints very large or very small numbers using scientific notation and all other numbers using standard notation. To turn off both bits, you pass a zero instead of `fixed` or `scientific`:

```
cout.setf( 0, ios::floatfield );
```

Both the `fixed` and the `scientific` flags are tied to the `precision()` member function. `precision()` determines the number of digits displayed after the decimal point in floating-point output:

```
cout.precision( 6 ); // The default for precision...
```

Finally, the `unitbuf` and `stdio` flags are related but not grouped. If `unitbuf` is set, the output buffer is flushed after each output operation. `stdio`, which is only for folks using C I/O, flushes `stdout` and `stderr` after every insertion.

Using Manipulators

`iostream` provides special functions known as **manipulators** that allow you to perform specific I/O operations while you're in the middle of an insertion or an extraction. For example, consider this line of code:

```
cout << "Enter a number: " << flush;
```

This code makes use of the `flush` manipulator. When its turn comes along in the output sequence, the `flush` manipulator flushes the buffer associated with `cout`, forcing the output to appear immediately as opposed to waiting for the buffer to get flushed naturally (sort of like a C++ version of prunes!).

Just as an I/O sequence can appear in different forms, a manipulator can be called in several different ways. Here are two more examples, each of which calls the `flush` manipulator:

```
cout.flush();  // Call as a stream member function
flush( cout ); // Call with the stream as a parameter
```

Use whichever form fits in with the I/O sequence you are currently building. If you plan on calling any manipulators that take parameters, be sure to include the file `<iomanip.h>`. In addition, some `iostream` implementations require you to link with the `math` library to use certain manipulators. Check your development environment manual to be sure.

The Manipulators

`dec()`, `oct()`, and `hex()` turn on the appropriate format flags, thus turning off the rest of the flags in the `basefield` group. `endl()` places a carriage return (`'\n'`) in its output stream and then flushes the stream. `ends()` places a `null` character in its output stream and then flushes the stream. `ws()` eats up all the white space in its input stream until it hits either an end-of-file or the first non-white-space character.

None of the manipulators presented so far take any parameters. The six remaining to be discussed all take a single parameter and require the included file `<iomanip.h>`.

`setbase(int b)` sets the current radix to either 8, 10, or 16. `setfill(int f)` is a manipulator version of the `fill()` member function. `setprecision(int p)` is the manipulator version of `precision()`. `setw(int w)` is the manipulator version of `width()`. `setiosflags(long f)` is the manipulator version of `setf()`. `resetiosflags(long f)` is the manipulator version of `unsetf()`.

Here are two manipulator examples. The line

```
cout << setbase( 16 ) << 256 << endl;
```

produces this line of output:

```
100
```

And, the line

```
cout << setprecision( 5 ) << 102.12345;
```

produces this line of output:

```
102.12
```

istrstream and ostrstream

If you've ever worked with the C `stdio` function `sprintf()`, you'll recognize a similar feature in C++. `sprintf()` allows you to perform all the standard I/O functions normally associated with `printf()` and `fprintf()` on an array of characters.

The `istrstream` and `ostrstream` classes offer all the power of their ancestor classes (`istream` and `ostream` and, ultimately, `ios`) and allow you to write formatted data to a buffer that you create in memory. Here's an example.

A strstream Example

Use `cd` to move back up to the `projects` directory and then into the directory named `chap8_5`. The source code for this example is in the file named `strstrea.cpp`. Compile and link the source code by typing this line at the DOS prompt:

```
sc strstrea.cpp
```

The compiler will compile your source code, and the linker will link it into an executable file named `strstrea.exe`. Run your newly created executable by typing

```
strstrea
```

at the DOS prompt. Here's what you'll see:

```
Number of characters written: 10
Buffer contents: abcdefghi
```

Let's take a look at the source code.

The strstrea Source Code

`strstrea.cpp` starts with two `#includes`, the standard `<iostream.h>` and the file required for the `istrstream` and `ostrstream` classes, `<strstrea.h>`:

```
#include <iostream.h>
#include <strstrea.h>
```

The constant `kBufferSize` is used to define the size of the buffer that makes up the `ostrstream` object:

```
const short kBufferSize = 10;
```

main() creates a buffer to hold the stream's characters. The ostrstream constructor takes two parameters, a pointer to the buffer and the size of the buffer. The variable i is used to keep track of the number of characters written to the ostrstream:

```
//------------------------------------  main()

int main()
{
    char        buffer[ kBufferSize ];
    ostrstream  ostr( buffer, kBufferSize );
    short       i = 0;
```

Next, a while loop uses ostr just as it would use cout, writing characters to the stream until an end-of-file causes the loop to terminate. iostream generates the end-of-file when the put() pointer points beyond the last character in the stream's buffer (just like its ifstream counterpart). When the loop exits, ten characters, from a to j, have been written to the stream's buffer:

```
while ( ostr << (char)('a' + i) )
    i++;
```

Now, the number of characters written to the stream is displayed:

```
cout << "Number of characters written: "
    << i << '\n';
```

Here's the output generated by the previous line of code:

```
Number of characters written: 10
```

Next, a null terminator is written on the last byte of the stream's buffer, creating a null-terminated string in buffer:

```
buffer[ kBufferSize - 1 ] = '\0';
```

Finally, the contents of the stream are printed:

```
cout << "Buffer contents: " << buffer;
```

```
return 0;
}
```

The previous line of code results in this line of output:

```
Buffer contents: abcdefghi
```

Just as an `ostrstream` object mirrors the behavior of `cout`, you can create a similar example, using an `istrstream` object, that mirrors the behavior of `istrstream`. The `istrstream` constructor takes the same two parameters as the `ostrstream` constructor.

Together, `istrstream` and `ostrstream` give you a powerful set of tools to use when you work with strings in memory.

Summary

`iostream` offers you a significant capability. You can use the classes and member functions provided to build an ample user interface for your programs. In the event that you're working with a class library that provides a more sophisticated, graphical user interface, you can still use `iostream` to manage your file I/O as well as to manage an in-core string manipulation facility.

Although I've made every effort to present a complete description of `iostream`, there's no substitution for a thorough reading of the `iostream` included files. You'll find complete listings of the four included files `<iostream.h>`, `<fstream.h>`, `<iomanip.h>`, and `<strstrea.h>` in appendices at the back of the book.

Chapter 9 starts off with a relatively new feature of C++ known as *templates* and then moves on to a potpourri of other topics. See you there!

Chapter 9

C++
Potpourri

This chapter takes you down the homestretch, exploring an array of miscellaneous C++ topics. Once you finish this chapter, you'll have completed the first phase of your C++ education.

This Chapter
at a Glance

CONGRATULATIONS! YOU'VE REALLY COME A LONG
way. By getting to this point in the book, you've built yourself a
strong C++ foundation. Now you're ready for a few of the more
advanced topics. We'll start off with one of the newest additions
to C++, a feature known as **templates**.

Templates
When you design a class, you're forced to make some decisions about the data types that make up that class. For example, if your class contains an array, the class declaration specifies the array's data type. In the following class declaration, an array of shorts is implemented:

```
class Array
{
  private:
    short    arraySize; // Number of array elements
    short    *arrayPtr; // Pointer to the array

  public:
        Array( short size ); // Allocate an array
                             // of size shorts
        ~Array(); // Delete the array
};
```

In this class, the constructor allocates an array of arraySize elements, each element of type short. The destructor deletes the array. The data member arrayPtr points to the beginning of the array. To make the class truly useful, you'd probably want to add a member function that gives access to the elements of the array. You might extend the class further by adding a bounds-checking feature.

This Array class works just fine as long as an array of shorts meets your needs. What happens when you decide that an Array of shorts doesn't quite cut it? Perhaps you need to implement an array of longs or, even better, an array of your own, home-brewed data type.

One approach you can use is to make a copy of the Array class (member functions and all) and change it slightly to implement an array of the appropriate type. For example, here's a version of the Array class designed to work with an array of longs:

```
class LongArray
{
  private:
```

```
    short    arraySize; // Number of array elements
    long    *arrayPtr; // Pointer to the array

  public:
    LongArray( short size );  // Allocate an array
                              // of size longs
    ~LongArray();    // Delete the array
};
```

There are definitely problems with this approach. You are creating a maintenance nightmare by duplicating the source code of one class to act as the basis for a second class. Suppose you add a new feature to your **Array** class. Are you going to make the same change to the **LongArray** class?

The Templates Approach

C++ templates allow you to parameterize the data types used by a class or function. Instead of embedding a specific type in a class declaration, you provide a template that defines the type used by that class. An example should make this a little clearer.

Here's a templated version of the **Array** class presented earlier:

```
template <class T>
class Array
{
  private:
    short    arraySize; // Number of array elements
    T        *arrayPtr; // Pointer to the array

  public:
         Array( short size );  // Allocate an array
                               // of size T's
         ~Array(); // Delete the array
};
```

The keyword **template** tells the compiler that what follows is not your usual, run-of-the-mill class declaration. Following the keyword **template** is a pair of angle brackets that surround the template's **template argument list**. This list consists of a series of comma-separated arguments (one argument is the minimum). Each argument is made up of the keyword `class` followed by the argument name. In this case, the template argument list contains a single argument, `T`. Throughout the body of the class declaration that follows, the template arguments may be used as if they were data types. In the `Array` class, `T` is used to declare the data member `arrayPtr`.

Defining an Object Using a Template

Once your class template is declared, you can use it to create an object. When you declare an object using a class template, you have to specify a template argument list along with the class name.

Here's an example:

```
Array<long>   longArray( 20 );
```

The compiler uses the single parameter, `long`, to convert the `Array` template into an actual class declaration. This declaration is known as a **template instantiation**. The instantiation is then used to create the `longArray` object.

A Template Argument List Containing More Than One Type

As mentioned earlier, a template's argument list may contain more than one type. The `class` keyword must precede each argument, and an argument name may not be repeated.

Here's an example:

```
template <class Able, class Baker>
class MyClass
{
  public:
            MyClass( Able param );
            ~MyClass();
    Baker   MemberFunction( Baker param );
};
```

This template takes two arguments. The first, `Able`, is used to declare the constructor's single parameter. The second, `Baker`, is used in the declaration of `MemberFunction()`, both as a return type and to declare the `MemberFunction()` parameter.

Here's a definition of a `MyClass` object:

```
MyClass<long, char *> myObject( 250L );
```

Take a look at the template arguments. The first, `long`, will be substituted for `Able`. The second, `char *`, will be substituted for `Baker`.

Function Templates

The template technique can also be applied to functions. Here's an example of a function template declaration:

```
template <class T, class U>
T MyFunc( T param1, U param2 )
{
  T var1;
  U var2;
     .
     .
     .

}
```

As you'd expect, the declaration starts with the `template` key-word, which is immediately followed by the template argument list. The types defined in the template argument list are then used freely throughout the remainder of the function declaration. Once again, a type may not be repeated in the template argument list, and the template argument list must contain at least one parameter.

There is one additional rule that applies to function templates. Each of the template arguments must appear at least once in the function's signature. Since a function's signature does *not* include the function's return type, you must use each of the template arguments in the function's parameter list.

If you use a template to define a function, you must also include the same template information in the function's prototype. Here's a prototype for `MyFunc()`:

```
template <class T, class U>
T MyFunc( T param1, U param2 );
```

Function Template Instantiation

When you call a function that has been templated, the compiler uses the parameters passed to the function to determine the types of the template arguments.

Here's a simple example:

```
template <class T>
void  MyFunc( T param1 );
```

Suppose this function template were called as follows:

```
char  *s;

MyFunc( s );
```

The compiler would match the type of the calling parameter (`char *`) with the type of the receiving parameter (`T`). In this case, an instantiation of the function is created, and the type `char *` is substituted for `T` everywhere it occurs.

Here's another example:

```
template <class T>
void  MyFunc( T *param1 );
```

Suppose this function template were called as follows:

```
char  *s;

MyFunc( s );
```

In this case, the type `char *` would be matched against the template argument type `T *`. Again, an instantiation is created, but this time the type `char` is substituted for `T`.

In the case where more than one parameter is used, the type-matching process always starts with the first parameter and moves to the right. Each occurrence of a template argument type is checked and a substitute type deduced. Once a substitute type is determined, any further occurrences of that template argument type must match the first occurrence *exactly*.

Consider this template:

```
template <class T>
void  MyFunc( T param1, T param2 );
```

This call of `MyFunc()` won't compile:

```
short    i;
int      j;

MyFunc( i, j );
```

First, the compiler matches the first parameter and determines that `T` is a `short`. When the compiler moves on to the second parameter, it finds that `T` should be an `int`. Even though an `int` and a `short` are kissin' cousins, since they are not an exact match, the compiler coughs politely and then spits out your code.

If you so desire, you can overload a function template just as you overload any other function. Just remember that every call to a template function must match one and only one of the overloaded functions.

You can also design a nontemplated version of a function to work alongside a templated version. When a function call occurs, the compiler tries to match the parameters against the nontemplated version first. If the parameters match up, the nontemplated function is called. If no match is found, the regular template-matching process is started.

A Template Example

Our first sample program provides a basic demonstration of class and function templates. Use cd to move into the projects directory and then into the directory named chap9_1. The source code for this example is in the file named template.cpp. Compile and link the source code by typing this line at the DOS prompt:

```
sc template.cpp
```

The compiler will compile your source code, and the linker will link it into an executable file named template.exe. Run your newly created executable by typing

```
template
```

at the DOS prompt. Here's what you'll see:

```
index out of bounds(10)
----
myRay[0]: 1
myRay[1]: 4
myRay[2]: 16
myRay[3]: 64
myRay[4]: 256
myRay[5]: 1024
myRay[6]: 4096
myRay[7]: 16384
myRay[8]: 0
myRay[9]: 0
----
myLongRay[0]: 1
myLongRay[1]: 4
myLongRay[2]: 16
myLongRay[3]: 64
myLongRay[4]: 256
myLongRay[5]: 1024
myLongRay[6]: 4096
myLongRay[7]: 16384
myLongRay[8]: 65536
myLongRay[9]: 262144
```

Let's take a look at the source code.

The template Source Code

As usual, `template.cpp` starts by including `<iostream.h>`. Next, a `const`, which is used at various points in the program, is declared:

```
#include <iostream.h>

const short kNumElements = 10;
```

`template` declares a class template named `Array`. `Array` implements an array of type `T`, where `T` is the template's single argument:

```
//----------------------------------- Array

template <class T>
class Array
```

`Array` features three data members, all of them `private`. `arraySize` is the number of elements in the array; `arrayPtr` points to the beginning of the array; `errorRetValue` is identical in type to one of the array elements and comes into play when you try to exceed the bounds of the array:

```
{
  private:
    short    arraySize;
    T        *arrayPtr;
    T        errorRetValue;
```

The `Array()` constructor allocates memory for the array, the destructor deletes the allocated memory, and `operator[]()` is used to implement bounds checking:

```
  public:
        Array( short size );
        ~Array();
    T    &operator[]( short index );
};
```

In the following code, notice the format used to define a class template member function. The function starts with the `template` keyword, followed by the template's argument list. Next comes the class name, followed by the argument types surrounded by angle brackets. Finally, the traditional :: is followed by the function's name and signature:

```
template <class T>
Array<T>::Array( short size )
```

The constructor uses its parameter, `size`, to initialize `arraySize`. Then, an array of `size` elements of type `T` is allocated. Finally, `errorRetValue` is initialized to zero:

```
{
  arraySize = size;
  arrayPtr = new T[ size ];
  errorRetValue = 0;
}
```

The destructor uses `delete` to delete the memory allocated for the array. This statement tells the compiler that the destructor should be applied to every element in the array pointed to by `arrayPtr` (without the [ ] operators, the destructor is called only for the first element of the array; while this is not particularly interesting in the case of an array of `shorts`, it is vital in working with an array of objects having a specific destructor):

```
template <class T>
Array<T>::~Array()
{
  delete [] arrayPtr;
}
```

`operator[]()` is called whenever an `Array` element is accessed via the [ ] operators. `operator[]()` first checks to see whether the index is out of bounds. If it is, an error message is printed and the pseudo-element, `errorRetValue`, is returned (by placing an unusual value in `errorRetValue`, you can clue the calling code to the fact that the array reference was illegal if printing an error message doesn't fit into your error-handling strategy):

```
template <class T>
T &Array<T>::operator[]( short index )
```

```
{
  if ( ( index < 0 ) || ( index >= arraySize ) )
  {
    cout << "index out of bounds(" << index << ")\n";
    return( errorRetValue );
  }
```

If the index is in bounds, the appropriate element of the array is returned:

```
  else
    return( arrayPtr[ index ] );
}
```

The next function in the source code is the templated function `Power()`. As you can see, `Power()` is declared using the `template` keyword and a single template type, `T`. `Power()` takes two parameters of type `T` and returns a value of type `T` (the key here is that the type of the two parameters must match *exactly*):

```
//------------------------------------- Power

template <class T>
T Power( T base, T exponent )
```

`Power()` raises the parameter `base` to the `exponent` power, and the final result is returned:

```
{
  T i, product = 1;

  for ( i=1; i<=exponent; i++ )
    product *= base;

  return( product );
}
```

main() starts by defining a `short` version of `Array` and a `long` version of `Array` (you could have declared a class named `EraserHead` and used `Array` to create an array of `EraserHead`s):

```
//------------------------------------- main()
```

```
int main()
{
  Array<short>   myRay( kNumElements );
  Array<long>    myLongRay( kNumElements );
  short          i, shortBase = 4;
  long           longBase = 4L;
```

This loop fills the short array with consecutive powers of 4:

```
for ( i=0; i<=kNumElements; i++ )
  myRay[ i ] = Power( shortBase, i );
```

When i is equal to kNumElements, the array runs out-of-bounds, causing an error message to be printed on the console:

```
index out of bounds(10)
```

Next, a separator line is sent to the console:

```
cout << "----\n";
```

This loop prints the value of each element in the short array:

```
for ( i=0; i<kNumElements; i++ )
  cout << "myRay[" << i << "]: " << myRay[ i ]
       << "\n";
```

Here's the output:

```
----
myRay[0]: 1
myRay[1]: 4
myRay[2]: 16
myRay[3]: 64
myRay[4]: 256
myRay[5]: 1024
myRay[6]: 4096
myRay[7]: 16384
myRay[8]: 0
myRay[9]: 0
```

By the time we get to `Power( 4, 8 )` we've reached the limits of a signed `short`. Our solution? Redo the whole thing using `longs`. Thank goodness for templates, eh?

This loop uses the same approach to fill the array of `longs`, but this time we won't let the array run out-of-bounds:

```
for ( i=0; i<kNumElements; i++ )
  myLongRay[ i ] = Power( longBase, (long)i );
```

We print a separator line and then print the elements of the `long` array:

```
cout << "----\n";

for ( i=0; i<kNumElements; i++ )
  cout << "myLongRay[" << i
    << "]: " << myLongRay[ i ] << "\n";

return 0;
}
```

Here's the output:

```
----
myLongRay[0]: 1
myLongRay[1]: 4
myLongRay[2]: 16
myLongRay[3]: 64
myLongRay[4]: 256
myLongRay[5]: 1024
myLongRay[6]: 4096
myLongRay[7]: 16384
myLongRay[8]: 65536
myLongRay[9]: 262144
```

Templates are an extremely powerful part of C++. You might not make use of them right away, but as you develop more and more C++ code, you'll use templates to build a set of parameterized utility classes. For example, you'll probably want to create a linked-list template that you can customize to link up objects of varying types.

Multiple Inheritance

Our next topic is a variation on an earlier theme, class derivation. In the examples presented in Chapter 6, each derived class was based on a single base class. That doesn't have to be the case, however. C++ allows you to derive a class from more than one base class, a technique known as **multiple inheritance**. As its name implies, multiple inheritance means that a class derived from more than one base class inherits the data members and member functions from each of its base classes.

Why would you want to inherit members from more than one class? Check out the derivation chain in Figure 9.1. The ultimate base class, known as the **root base class**, in this chain is Computer. The two classes ColorComputer and LaptopComputer are special types of Computers, each inheriting the members from Computer and adding members of their own as well.

FIGURE 9.1
Multiple inheritance (the boldfaced data members are inherited).

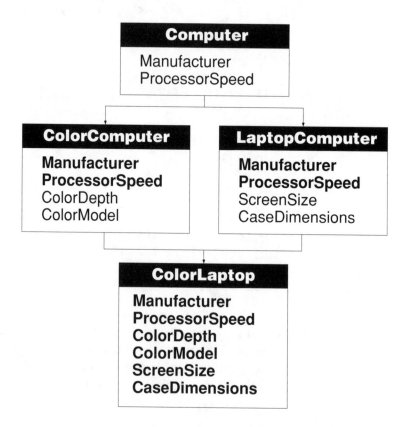

Here's where multiple inheritance comes into play. The class `ColorLaptop` is derived from both `ColorComputer` and `LaptopComputer` and inherits members from each class. Multiple inheritance allows you to take advantage of two different classes that work well together. If you want a program that models a color, laptop computer and you already have a `ColorComputer` class that manages color information and a `LaptopComputer` class that manages information about laptops, why reinvent the wheel? Think of the `ColorLaptop` class as the best of both worlds—the union of two already designed classes.

Just as with single inheritance, there are times when multiple inheritance makes sense and times when it is inappropriate. Use the "is a" rule to guide your design. If the derived class "is a" subset of the base class, derivation is appropriate. In our preceding example, a `ColorComputer` "is a" `Computer` and a `LaptopComputer` "is a" `Computer`. At the same time, a `ColorLaptop` is both a `ColorComputer` and a `LaptopComputer`. This model works just fine.

Let's look at another example. Imagine a `Date` class and a `Time` class. The `Date` class holds a date, like 07/27/94, while the `Time` class holds a time of day, like 10:24 A.M. Now suppose you wanted to create a `TimeStamp` class, derived from both the `Date` and `Time` classes. Would this make sense?

The answer is no! A `TimeStamp` is not a `Date` and it is not a `Time`. Instead, a `TimeStamp` "has a" `Date` and "has a" `Time`. When your derivation fits the "has a" model rather than the "is a" model, you should rethink your design. In this case, the `TimeStamp` class should include `Date` and `Time` objects as data members, rather than using multiple inheritance.

"is a" indicates inheritance. If "has a" describes the relationship between your derived and base classes, rethink your design.

A Multiple Inheritance Example

Our second sample program demonstrates multiple inheritance as well as a few additional C++ features that you should find interesting. Use `cd` to move back up to the `projects` directory and then into the directory named `chap9_2`. The source code for this example is in the file named `multiinh.cpp`. Compile and link the source code by typing this line at the DOS prompt:

```
sc multiinh.cpp
```

The compiler will compile your source code, and the linker will link it into an executable file named `multiinh.exe`. Run your newly created executable by typing

```
multiinh
```

at the DOS prompt. Here's what you'll see:

```
Favorite prey: Mice
Favorite toy: Ball of yarn
catID: 1
---------
Favorite prey: Crickets
Favorite toy: Bottle cap
catID: 2
---------
Favorite prey: Moths
Favorite toy: Spool of thread
catID: 3
---------
Cat destructor called: catID = 3...
Pet destructor was called!
Predator destructor was called!

Cat destructor called: catID = 2...
Pet destructor was called!
Predator destructor was called!

Cat destructor called: catID = 1...
Pet destructor was called!
Predator destructor was called!
```

Let's take a look at the source code.

The multiinh Source Code

`multiinh.cpp` starts with two `#include`s and a familiar `const`:

```
#include <iostream.h>
#include <string.h>

const short kMaxStringLength = 40;
```

Next, three classes are defined. The `Predator` class represents a predatory animal, while the `Pet` class represents a housepet. The `Cat` class is derived from both the `Predator` class and the `Pet` class. After all, a cat "is a" predator and a cat "is a" pet, right?

The `Predator` class is pretty simple. It features a single data member, a string containing the predator's favorite prey:

```
//-------------------------------------- Predator

class Predator
{
  private:
    char   favoritePrey[ kMaxStringLength ];
```

The `Predator` class also features a constructor as well as a destructor:

```
  public:
        Predator( char *prey );
        ~Predator();
};
```

The constructor initializes the `favoritePrey` data member and then prints its value:

```
Predator::Predator( char *prey )
{
  strcpy( favoritePrey, prey );

  cout << "Favorite prey: "
```

```
        << prey << "\n";
}
```

The destructor prints an appropriate message, just to let you know it was called:

```
Predator::~Predator()
{
  cout << "Predator destructor was called!\n\n";
}
```

The `Pet` class is almost identical to the `Predator` class, with a favorite toy substituted for a favorite prey:

```
//-------------------------------------- Pet

class Pet
{
  private:
    char  favoriteToy[ kMaxStringLength ];

  public:
        Pet( char *toy );
        ~Pet();
};

Pet::Pet( char *toy )
{
  strcpy( favoriteToy, toy );

  cout << "Favorite toy: "
    << toy << "\n";
}

Pet::~Pet()
{
  cout << "Pet destructor was called!\n";
}
```

The `Cat` class is derived from both the `Predator` and `Pet` classes. Notice that the keyword `public` precedes each of the base class names and that the list of base classes is separated by commas:

```
//------------------------- Cat:Predator,Pet

class Cat : public Predator, public Pet
```

Cat contains two data members. The first, catID, contains a unique ID for each Cat. While numbering your cats might not be that useful, if we were talking about Employees or Computers, a unique employee ID or serial number can be an important part of your class design.

Notice that the second data member, lastCatID is declared using the static keyword:

```
{
  private:
    short        catID;
    static short lastCatID;
```

Static Members

Let's discuss **static members** for a moment. When you declare a data member or member function as static, the compiler creates a single version of the member that is shared by all objects in that class.

Why do this? static members can be very useful. Since a static data member is shared by all objects, you can use it to share information between all objects in a class.

One way to think of a static member is as a global variable whose scope is limited to the class in which it is declared. This is especially true if the static member is declared as private or protected.

In this case, lastCatID is incremented every time a Cat object is created. Since lastCatID is not tied to a specific object, it always holds a unique serial number (which also happens to be the number of Cats created).

The declaration of a static data member is just that, a declaration. When you declare a static within a class declaration, you need to follow it up with a definition in the same scope. Typically, you'll follow your class declaration immediately with a definition of the static data member, like this:

```
short Object::lastObjectID;
```

If you like, you can use this definition to initialize the static member. static data member scope is limited to the file they are declared in.

> You'll typically stick your class declaration (along with the class's static member declarations) in a .h file. This is not the case for your static member *definition*. The definition should appear in the .cpp file where it will be used.

Along with your static data members, you can also declare a static member function. Again, the function is not bound to a particular object and is shared with the entire class. If the class MyClass included a static member function named MyFunc(), you could call the function using this syntax:

```
MyClass::MyFunc();
```

Since there is no current object when MyFunc() is called, you don't have the advantages of this and any references to other data members or member functions must be done through an object.

static member functions are usually written for the sole purpose of providing access to an associated static data member. To enhance your design, you might declare your static data member as private and provide an associated static member function marked as public or protected.

Back to multiinh

The `Cat` class has a constructor and a destructor:

```
public:
        Cat( char *prey, char *toy );
        ~Cat();
};
```

The `Cat` constructor uses a syntax first laid out in Chapter 6 to map its input parameters to the `Predator` and to the `Prey` constructors.

```
Cat::Cat( char *prey, char *toy ) :
  Predator( prey ), Pet( toy )
```

def'ə nish' ən

> The list that follows the constructor's parameter list is called the **member initialization list**. As you can see, a colon *always* precedes a constructor's member initialization list.

Next, `lastCatID` is incremented and the new value assigned to `catID`. Then, the new ID and a separator line are printed:

```
{
  catID = ++lastCatID;

  cout << "catID: " << catID
    << "\n---------\n";
}
```

The `Cat` destructor also prints a message containing the `catID`, just to make the program a little easier to follow:

```
Cat::~Cat()
{
  cout << "Cat destructor called: catID = "
    << catID << "...\n";
}
```

Next, the `static` member `lastCatID` is defined. Without this definition, the program wouldn't compile. Notice also that we take advantage of this definition to initialize `lastCatID`:

```
short Cat::lastCatID = 0;
```

> `static` data members, just like C++ globals, are automatically initialized to 0. To make the code a little more obvious, we kept the initialization in there, even though it is redundant.

Finally, `main()` creates three `Cat` objects. Compare the three `Cat` declarations with the program's output. Notice the order of constructor and destructor calls. Just as in Chapter 6's `gramps` program, the destructors are called in the reverse order of the constructors:

```
//------------------------------------- main()

int main()
{
  Cat TC( "Mice", "Ball of yarn" );
  Cat Benny( "Crickets", "Bottle cap" );
  Cat Meow( "Moths", "Spool of thread" );

  return 0;
}
```

Resolving Ambiguities

Deriving a class from more than one base class brings up an interesting problem. Suppose the two base classes from our previous example, `Predator` and `Pet`, each have a data member with the same name (which is perfectly legal, by the way). Let's call this data member `clone`. Now suppose that a `Cat` object is created, derived from both `Predator` and `Pet`. When this `Cat` refers to `clone`, which `clone` does it refer to, the one inherited from `Predator` or the one from `Pet`?

As it turns out, the compiler would complain if the `Cat` class referred to just plain `clone` because it can't resolve this ambiguity. To get around this problem, you can access each of the two `clones` by referring to

```
Predator::clone
```

or

```
Pet::clone
```

Here's another interesting problem brought on by multiple inheritance. Take a look at the derivation chain in Figure 9.2. Notice that the `Derived` class has two paths of inheritance back to its ultimate base class, `Root`.

FIGURE 9.2

Four classes in a derivation chain.

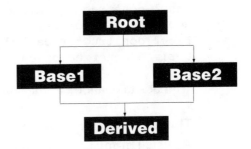

Since `Derived` is derived from both `Base1` and `Base2`, when a `Derived` object is created, `Base1` and `Base2` objects are created as well. When the `Base1` object is created, a `Root` object is created. When the `Base2` object is created, a second `Root` object is created.

Why is this a problem? Suppose `Root` contains a data member destined to be inherited by `Derived`. When `Derived` refers to the `Root` data member, which of the two `Root` objects contains the data member `Derived` is referring to? Sounds like another ambiguity to me.

A Multiple-Root Example

Before we resolve this latest ambiguity, here's an example that shows what happens when a derived class has two paths back to its root class. Use cd to move back up to the projects directory and then into the directory named chap9_3. The source code for this example is in the file named nonvirt.cpp. Compile and link the source code by typing this line at the DOS prompt:

```
sc nonvirt.cpp
```

The compiler will compile your source code, and the linker will link it into an executable file named nonvirt.exe. Run your newly created executable by typing

```
nonvirt
```

at the DOS prompt. Here's what you'll see:

```
Root constructor called
Base1 constructor called
Root constructor called
Base2 constructor called
Derived constructor called
```

Let's take a look at the source code.

The nonvirt Source Code

As usual, nonvirt.cpp starts by including <iostream.h>:

```
#include <iostream.h>
```

nonvirt declares the four classes shown in Figure 9.2. Root consists of a constructor that prints a message letting you know it was called:

```
//-------------------------------------- Root

class Root
{
  public:
    Root();
};

Root::Root()
{
```

```
   cout << "Root constructor called\n";
}
```

Base1 is derived from Root. Its constructor also prints a useful message:

```
//------------------------------------- Base1

class Base1 : public Root
{
  public:
    Base1();
};

Base1::Base1()
{
  cout << "Base1 constructor called\n";
}
```

Base2 is also derived from Root. Its constructor also prints a message in the console window:

```
//------------------------------------- Base2

class Base2 : public Root
{
  public:
    Base2();
};

Base2::Base2()
{
  cout << "Base2 constructor called\n";
}
```

Derived is derived from both Base1 and Base2. Just like all the other classes, Derived has its constructor print a message in the console window just to let you know it was called:

```
//------------------------------------- Derived

class Derived : public Base1, public Base2
{
```

```
    public:
      Derived();
};

Derived::Derived()
{
  cout << "Derived constructor called\n";
}
```

main() starts the constructor roller coaster by creating a Derived object:

```
//------------------------------------- main()

int main()
{
  Derived    myDerived;

  return 0;
}
```

Since Base1 is listed first in the Derived derivation list, a Base1 object is created first. Since Base1 is derived from Root, it causes a Root object to be created. The Root constructor is called and then the Base1 constructor is called, resulting in the following two lines of output:

```
Root constructor called
Base1 constructor called
```

Next, this process is repeated as a Base2 object is created. Since Base2 is also derived from Root, it causes a *second* Root object to be created. Once the Root constructor is called, control returns to Base2 and its constructor is called:

```
Root constructor called
Base2 constructor called
```

Once the Base2 object is created, control returns to the Derived class and the Derived constructor is called:

```
Derived constructor called
```

The Virtual Base Class Alternative

Once again, think about the problem raised by this last example. If the `Root` class contained a data member, how would the `Derived` object access the data member? Which of the two `Root` objects would contain the *real* copy of the data member?

The answer to this problem lies in the use of **virtual base classes**. Back in Chapter 6's `whatami` program, we declared a member function as `virtual` to allow a derived class to override the function. Basically, when a virtual function is called by dereferencing a pointer or reference to the base class, the compiler follows the derivation chain down from the root class to the most derived class and looks at each level for a function matching the virtual function. The lowest-level matching function is the one that is called.

Virtual functions are extremely useful. Here's why. Suppose you're writing a program that implements a window-based user interface. Let's say your standard window is broken into several areas (call them panes) and each pane is broken into subpanes. When the time comes to draw the contents of your window, your `Window` class's `Draw()` member function is called. If your `Pane` class also has a `Draw()` member function *and* if the `Window` version of `Draw()` is declared as `virtual`, the `Pane`'s `Draw()` is called instead.

This same logic applies to your `SubPane` class and its `Draw()` function. If it is derived from `Pane`, the `SubPane`'s `Draw()` is called instead of the `Pane`'s `Draw()`. This strategy allows you to derive from an existing class using a new class whose actions are more appropriate or more efficient.

A similar technique can be used to remove the ambiguity brought up when a derived class has two different paths back to one of its ancestor classes. In our earlier example, `Root` was the root class, and `Base1` and `Base2` were derived from `Root`. Finally,

`Derived` was derived from both `Base1` and `Base2`. When we created a `Derived` object, we ended up creating two `Root` objects. Thus the ambiguity.

By declaring `Root` as a virtual base class, we're asking the compiler to merge the two `Root` object creation requests into a single `Root` object (you'll see how to mark a class as `virtual` in a moment). The compiler gathers every reference to the virtual base class from the different constructor member initialization lists and picks the one that's tied to the deepest constructor. That reference is used, and all the others are discarded. This will become clearer as you walk through the next sample program.

To create a virtual base class, you must insert the `virtual` keyword in the member initialization lists between the virtual base class and the potentially ambiguous derived class. You don't need to mark every class between `Root` and `Derived` as long as the compiler has no path between `Root` and `Derived` that doesn't contain at least one `virtual` reference. The general strategy is to mark all *direct* descendants of the virtual base class. In this case, we'd need to place the `virtual` keyword in both the `Base1` and `Base2` member initialization lists.

Here's an example:

```
class Base1 : public virtual Root
{
  public:
    Base1();
};
```

The `virtual` keyword can appear either before or after the `public` keyword.

Once the `virtual` keywords are in place, the compiler ignores all member initialization list references to the `Root` class constructor except the deepest one. This sample `Derived` constructor includes a reference to the `Root` constructor:

```
Derived::Derived( short param ) : Root( param )
{
  cout << "Derived constructor called\n";
}
```

Even if the `Base1` and `Base2` constructors map parameters to the `Root` constructor, their mappings are superseded by the deeper, `Derived` constructor. By overriding the constructor mappings, the compiler makes sure that only a single object of the virtual base class (in this case, `Root`) is created.

A Virtual Base Class Example

This next example brings these techniques to life. Use `cd` to move back up to the `projects` directory and then into the directory named `chap9_4`. The source code for this example is in the file named `virtual.cpp`. Compile and link the source code by typing this line at the DOS prompt:

```
sc virtual.cpp
```

The compiler will compile your source code, and the linker will link it into an executable file named `virtual.exe`. Run your newly created executable by typing

```
virtual
```

at the DOS prompt. Here's what you'll see:

```
Root constructor called
Base1 constructor called
Base2 constructor called
Derived constructor called
------
num = 3
```

Let's take a look at the source code.

The virtual Source Code

As usual, `virtual.cpp` starts by including `<iostream.h>`:

```
#include <iostream.h>
```

This version of the Root class includes a data member named num:

```
//------------------------------------- Root

class Root
{
  protected:
    short num;

  public:
        Root( short numParam );
};
```

The Root() constructor takes a single parameter and uses it to initialize num (as you read through the code, try to figure out where the value for this parameter comes from):

```
Root::Root( short numParam )
{
  num = numParam;

  cout << "Root constructor called\n";
}
```

Base1 is derived from Root, but it treats Root as a virtual base class:

```
//------------------------------------- Base1

class Base1 : public virtual Root
{
  public:
    Base1();
};
```

Notice that the Base1() constructor asks the compiler to call the Root() constructor and passes it a value of 1. Will this call take place?

```
Base1::Base1() : Root( 1 )
{
```

```
    cout << "Base1 constructor called\n";
}
```

Base2 also declares **Root** as a virtual base class. Now there's no path down from **Root** that's not marked as `virtual`:

```
//------------------------------------ Base2

class Base2 : public virtual Root
{
  public:
    Base2();
};
```

The **Base2()** constructor asks the compiler to pass a value of 2 to the **Root()** constructor. Is this the value that is passed on to the **Root()** constructor?

```
Base2::Base2() : Root( 2 )
{
  cout << "Base2 constructor called\n";
}
```

The **Derived** class doesn't need the `virtual` keyword (although it wouldn't hurt if `virtual` were used here):

```
//------------------------------------ Derived

class Derived : public Base1, public Base2
{
  public:
          Derived();
    short GetNum();
};
```

The **Derived()** constructor also asks the compiler to pass a value on to the **Root()** constructor. Since **Derived** is the deepest class, this is the constructor mapping that takes precedence. The **Root** data member num should be initialized with a value of 3:

```
Derived::Derived() : Root( 3 )
{
```

```
    cout << "Derived constructor called\n";
}
```

This function makes the value of num available to main(). Why can't main() reference num directly? Derived inherits num and main() doesn't:

```
short Derived::GetNum()
{
  return( num );
}
```

main() creates a Derived object, causing a sequence of constructor calls:

```
//------------------------------------  main()

int main()
{
  Derived    myDerived;
```

Notice that the Root constructor is called only once:

```
Root constructor called
Base1 constructor called
Base2 constructor called
Derived constructor called
```

Finally, the value of num is printed (drum roll, please):

```
    cout << "------\n"
      << "num = " << myDerived.GetNum();

    return 0;
}
```

As you've already guessed, num has a value of 3, showing that the Base1 and Base2 constructor initializations are overridden by the deeper, Derived constructor initialization:

```
------
num = 3
```

Initialization Versus Assignment

When you think about initialization, you might think of a line of code like this, where the variable i is defined and *initialized* to a value of 21:

```
short    i = 21;
```

In the following code, i is defined and then a value of 21 is assigned to i:

```
short    i;

i = 21;
```

The point here is that the compiler thinks of initialization and assignment as two completely different operations. Every constructor is broken into two parts, the initialization part and the assignment part. The initialization part takes place in the *member initialization list*. The assignment part takes place in the *body* of the constructor. The remainder of this section discusses things you should know about initialization and assignment as they relate to object construction.

const and Reference Types

When a const is defined, a value is tied to it at initialization. In the strictest sense of the word, you can't *assign* a value to a const. This code will compile:

```
const short kMaxNameLength = 20;
```

This code won't compile:

```
const short kMaxNameLength;

kMaxNameLength = 20; // Aaack!
```

The same holds true for a reference type. A reference type must be given a value at initialization. This code compiles just fine:

```
short    number = 20;
short    &numberAlias = number;
```

This code, on the other hand, is destined for failure:

```
short    &numberAlias; // Error: Must be
                       // initialized!!
```

You can declare a class data member as a `const` or a reference type, but beware! You can't provide these data members their initial value via an assignment statement. Instead, you must use the member initialization list to do your dirty work for you. Here's an example:

```
class MyClass
{
  private:
    const short    kMaxNameLength;
    short          &numberAlias;
    short          number;

  public:
    MyClass( short  constValue );
};

MyClass::MyClass( short constValue ) :
  kMaxNameLength( constValue ), numberAlias( number )
{
  // kMaxNameLength is set to constValue
  // numberAlias references number
}
```

Up until this point, we've used the member initialization list to map parameters from the constructor to a base class. In this example, we use the member initialization list to initialize some members. How appropriate!

If you include a data member name in the member initialization list and follow the name by an expression surrounded by parentheses, the compiler uses the expression to initialize the data member. In the previous chunk of code, kMaxNameLength is initialized to the value in constValue and numberAlias is set to reference number. As you can see, the member initialization list is pretty useful.

A Member Initialization List Example

Here's a working version of the previous chunk of code. Use cd to move back up to the projects directory and then into the directory named chap9_5. The source code for this example is in the file named init.cpp. Compile and link the source code by typing this line at the DOS prompt:

```
sc init.cpp
```

The compiler will compile your source code, and the linker will link it into an executable file named init.exe. Run your newly created executable by typing

```
init
```

at the DOS prompt. Here's what you'll see:

```
Before: number = 10
After:  number = 20
```

Let's take a look at the source code.

The init Source Code

As usual, init.cpp starts by including <iostream.h>:

```
#include <iostream.h>
```

The declaration of MyClass is pretty much the same as the one you just saw. To simplify things, all the data members are declared as `public`. Also, the constructor is filled out to make things a little more interesting:

```
//------------------------------------ MyClass

class MyClass
{
  public:
    const short    kMaxNameLength;
    short          &numberAlias;
    short          number;

    MyClass( short  constValue );
};
```

The constructor takes a single parameter, a value used to initialize our `const` variable. The member initialization list is used to initialize `kMaxNameLength` and `numberAlias`:

```
MyClass::MyClass( short constValue ) :
  kMaxNameLength( constValue ), numberAlias( number )
```

We start off by assigning `number` the value stored in `kMaxNameLength`:

```
{
  number = kMaxNameLength;
```

To prove that `kMaxNameLength` is initialized properly, we print out the value in `number`:

```
cout << "Before: number = "
  << number << "\n";
```

This results in the following line of output:

```
Before: number = 10
```

Next, to prove that `numberAlias` references `number`, `numberAlias` is incremented by 10:

```
numberAlias += 10;
```

Now, we print out the value of number again:

```
cout << "After:  number = "
  << number << "\n";
}
```

Just as we'd hoped, number now has a value of 20:

```
After:  number = 20
```

main() has a pretty simple job—just to create a MyClass object and pass a value of 10 to its constructor:

```
//----------------------------------- main()

int main()
{
  MyClass   myObject( 10 );

  return 0;
}
```

Memberwise Initialization

In certain instances, a special form of initialization, known as **memberwise initialization**, is used to initialize a newly created object. Basically, memberwise initialization is the technique of copying the contents of one object, data member by data member, into another object.

Memberwise initialization is a convenient way to make a copy of an object. Here's one way to do this:

```
MyClass obj1( 20 );
MyClass obj2 = obj1;  // Uses memberwise
                      // initialization
```

The first line of code defines an object of class MyClass and passes the number 20 to its constructor. The second line creates another MyClass object, but instead of calling the constructor, the second object becomes an exact duplicate of the first object.

There are several other ways to achieve memberwise initialization. If you pass an object by value as a parameter, the compiler creates a local copy of your parameter, using memberwise initialization to initialize the copy. Also, if you write a function that returns an object, memberwise initialization is used to copy the returned object into the object receiving the returned object.

Memberwise initialization is easy to use and it *is* convenient, but there's a catch. Memberwise initialization makes an exact copy of an object, *including any and all pointers*. Suppose you declare a `Name` class that holds someone's first and last names:

```
class Name
{
  private:
    char  *last;
    char  *first;

  public:
    Name( char *firstParam, char *lastParam );
};
```

Suppose also that the `Name()` constructor allocates the memory for `last` and `first`, based on the size of the two constructor parameters. This being the case, you might define a `Name` like this:

```
Name  yourAuthor( "Dave", "Mark" );
```

What happens if you define a second `Name` by using the memberwise initialization syntax?

```
Name  aCopy = yourAuthor;
```

Now, `yourAuthor` and `aCopy` share some common memory. Both copies of `last` point to the same block of memory, and both copies of `first` point to the same block of memory. If you `delete` one of the objects, the other object is left with a dangling pointer. That can be a problem.

The Copy Constructor

You can provide a memberwise initialization function for any of your classes. Before the compiler does a memberwise copy, it first checks to see whether your class includes an overloaded version of your constructor having the form

```
MyClass( const MyClass &curObject )
```

where `MyClass` is the class being copied. This special constructor is known as a **copy constructor**.

If you provide a copy constructor, it is called whenever memberwise initialization is called for. Your copy constructor should copy the current object into the object passed by reference as a parameter. If the object to be copied contains any pointers, you may want to reallocate the necessary memory in the copy instead of blindly copying the pointers.

A Memberwise Initialization Example

Here's a working version of the previous chunk of code. Use `cd` to move back up to the `projects` directory and then into the directory named `chap9_6`. The source code for this example is in the file named `mmbrwise.cpp`. Compile and link the source code by typing this line at the DOS prompt:

```
sc mmbrwise.cpp
```

The compiler will compile your source code, and the linker will link it into an executable file named `mmbrwise.exe`. Run your newly created executable by typing

```
mmbrwise
```

at the DOS prompt. Here's what you'll see:

```
Original constructor...
Copy constructor...
Original constructor...
```

```
Name: Dave Mark
Name: Dave Mark
Name: Andrew Schulman
```

Let's take a look at the source code.

The mmbrwise Source Code

`mmbrwise.cpp` starts by including `<iostream.h>` and `<string.h>`:

```
#include <iostream.h>
#include <string.h>
```

The `Name` class includes two data members, `last` and `first`:

```
//------------------------------------ Name

class Name
{
  private:
    char  *last;
    char  *first;
```

The first `Name()` constructor is for regular `Name` objects; the second constructor is our copy constructor:

```
public:
      Name( char *firstParam, char *lastParam );
      Name( const Name &original );
```

The destructor frees up the memory allocated for `first` and `last`:

```
~Name();
```

The `Display()` function is used to display the data members of the current `Name` object:

```
void  Name::Display();
```

The Name class's operator=( ) function provides a service similar to the Name( ) copy constructor. When the compiler encounters an expression of the form

```
myObject = yourObject
```

where both operands belong to the same class, it performs a memberwise copy of the right operand to the left operand. If the class in question provides an operator=( ) function in the proper form, the operator=( ) function is called in lieu of performing the memberwise copy:

```
    Name  &Name::operator=( const Name &original );
};
```

The regular Name( ) constructor uses new to allocate memory for first and last:

```
Name::Name( char *firstParam, char *lastParam )
{
  first = new char[ strlen(firstParam) + 1 ];
  last = new char[ strlen(lastParam) + 1 ];
```

Next, strcpy( ) is called to copy the two parameters into their associated data members:

```
  strcpy( first, firstParam );
  strcpy( last, lastParam );
```

Then, a message is printed to let us know which constructor we're in:

```
  cout << "Original constructor...\n";
}
```

When the copy constructor is called, the current object is the new Name object. The parameter passed in is the original Name object from which the data is being copied:

```
Name::Name( const Name &original )
{
```

```
first = new char[ strlen(original.first) + 1 ];
last = new char[ strlen(original.last) + 1 ];

strcpy( first, original.first );
strcpy( last, original.last );
```

Once again, a message is printed telling us which constructor we're in:

```
cout << "Copy constructor...\n";
}
```

The destructor deletes the char arrays pointed to by first and last:

```
Name::~Name()
{
  delete [] first;
  delete [] last;
}
```

Again, the Display() function prints the current Name:

```
void  Name::Display()
{
  cout << "Name: " << first << " " << last << "\n";
}
```

The operator=() function starts by checking to see whether the left and right operands are the same object, as in this expression:

```
myObject = myObject;
```

Why is this case special? As you'll see, before we copy the right operand to the left operand, we delete any memory allocated to the left operand. If the left and right objects are the same object, we'll lose data if we delete:

```
Name  &Name::operator=( const Name &original )
{
  if ( this == &original )
    return( *this );
```

Once we know we're dealing with two different objects, we start by deleting any previously allocated memory. Remember, the left-hand operand is the current object; the right-hand operand is passed in as the parameter `original`:

```
delete [] first;
delete [] last;
```

The next four lines are lifted right from the copy constructor:

```
first = new char[ strlen(original.first) + 1 ];
last = new char[ strlen(original.last) + 1 ];

strcpy( first, original.first );
strcpy( last, original.last );
```

Finally, we return the current object as the result of the = operation:

```
return( *this );
}
```

`main()` starts by creating an original `Name`, reflecting the identity of your hard-working author:

```
//------------------------------------- main()

int main()
{
  Name  yourAuthor( "Dave", "Mark" );
```

This results in a call of the original constructor, and the following message appears in the console window:

```
Original constructor...
```

Next, another `Name` is created using the copy constructor:

```
Name  aCopy = yourAuthor;
```

This results in the following line of output:

```
Copy constructor...
```

The third Name object is used to test our `operator=( )` function:

```
Name  anotherAuthor( "Andrew", "Schulman" );
```

This results in the following line of output:

```
Original constructor...
```

When `yourAuthor.Display( )` is called, the contents of the original Name are printed:

```
yourAuthor.Display( );
```

Here's the result:

```
Name: Dave Mark
```

When `aCopy.Display( )` is called, the contents of the copy are printed:

```
aCopy.Display( );
```

Here's the result:

```
Name: Dave Mark
```

Next, the = operator is used to copy `anotherAuthor` to `aCopy`. Before the copy is done, `aCopy` has the name *Dave Mark* and `anotherAuthor` has the name *Andrew Schulman*:

```
aCopy = anotherAuthor;

aCopy.Display( );

return 0;
}
```

This call of `aCopy.Display( )` results in the following line of output:

```
Name: Andrew Schulman
```

If you have any doubts about memberwise initialization, add some additional output statements to the program to verify that a copied object has its own unique memory allocated for it. To do this, print the addresses of `first` and `last` in both the original and the copy.

Summary OK, time to break out the good champagne (grab a Perrier if you're driving). You have now officially made it through the basics of C++. Although there are still many interesting things to learn, you've mastered the essentials and you're ready to code. Chapter 10 offers a look at some C++ class libraries and development environments. Let's rip!

Chapter 10

Moving On

Now that you've mastered the basics of C++ programming, you're ready to develop some applications. This chapter takes a look at a variety of Windows development environments and class libraries.

This Chapter at a Glance

WHAT DOES IT TAKE TO DEVELOP A C++ APPLICATION? The answer depends on the computer and operating system under which your application will ultimately run. Are you building a program destined for a text-based environment like DOS or Unix? Are you writing an application that will run only in Windows? Are you trying to write an application that will run on a variety of platforms?

The User Interface

If you can live within the confines of a text-oriented user interface, almost any C++ development environment will work for you. By taking advantage of the `iostream` library, you can build a C++ application with a completely portable user interface. The upside here is that you can develop an application on a PC, copy the source code to a Sun workstation, recompile, and (with some minor retooling, perhaps) you'll have a perfectly acceptable Unix application.

The down side is that a text-oriented user interface is limited. The console works, but it isn't pretty. (If you tried to fob off an `iostream`-based user interface on a seasoned Windows user, you might get run out of town.) Most graphical user interfaces (GUIs, pronounced "gooeys") require strict adherence to a set of **interface guidelines**. In general, these guidelines are specified in the manuals that come with your development environment. The Windows environment has its own interface guidelines, as do GUIs such as the Macintosh, Motif, and OpenLook.

If you can live within the confines of `iostream`, you'll have the ultimate in application portability. If you want to create an application with the look and feel of the environment it's running under, you'll have some extra work to do. First, you must become an expert user of the destination environment. You'll need to recognize each of the elements that make up that environment's user interface, as well as the proper behavior of each element. When a window is in front, does it look different than when it is behind another window? What's the proper way to disable a menu item? Where do scroll bars usually appear? How do you resize a window? When you've mastered this **interface vocabulary**, you're ready to design your application's interface.

If you plan to develop an application that will run on more than one platform, you have even more work to do. First, you must absorb the interface vocabulary for each platform you plan to support.

Next, you'll have to make some decisions about your user interface. Your programming task will be simpler if you build your interface by using elements common to all of the platforms your application will run on. For example, unless all of the candidate platforms support pop-up menus, you might consider leaving them out of your interface. Each special case that you support will make your software more difficult to maintain.

Another option is to take advantage of a cross-platform development system, a development environment that can generate versions of your application for several different platforms, all from the same specifications/code. The upside to a cross-platform development system is the ease with which you can maintain your product. Instead of updating your product on each platform you support, you'll only have to make your changes once.

There are several down sides. Most cross-platform development systems are very expensive (thousands of dollars). Some restrict their feature set to the smallest common denominator of the features offered by all supported platforms. In other words, if a specific feature is not found on each and every platform, you won't be able to use it at all.

The Windows API

For the moment, let's assume that you wish to use your newfound C++ talents to build a Windows application with all of the user-interface elements that Windows users have come to know and love. Fortunately, each of the Windows development environments comes with a set of class and/or function libraries containing all of the user-interface routines you'll need to implement the look and feel of Windows.

For example, the user-interface libraries that come with Symantec C++ for Windows contain some functions that create windows on the screen and others that draw text in these windows. There are functions for drawing shapes, lines, and dots in color and in black and white. These libraries provide more than a thousand functions that put the entire Windows interface at your disposal.

With the advent of Windows 3.1, Microsoft has worked hard to ensure that each new Windows program adheres strictly to the Windows interface standards. They even have a program set up to review your application for any discrepancies. When you send your program to Microsoft, they go over it with a fine-tooth comb and then work with you to standardize your interface. Once it passes Microsoft's tough inspection, your application will be "Microsoft Windows Compatible" and you can put a symbol that says so on your packaging and in your program's displays.

The "Windows Logo" program is absolutely free. It usually takes about a month for Microsoft to evaluate your application, so plan ahead. To find out more, call (206) 936-2880 and ask for your Windows Logo Kit.

The Windows Class Libraries

Since most development environments come with all the necessary graphics routines, you could design your own set of classes to implement the Windows interface. You might build one group of classes to create and manage windows and another group of classes to implement your program's menus.

This approach is just fine, though it will probably take you an incredible amount of time to build all the necessary classes. A better alternative is to take advantage of one of the existing Windows class libraries.

There are several class libraries designed specifically to simplify the process of creating a Windows application. Probably the most famous of these class libraries is the Microsoft Foundation Class (MFC) Library, which contains classes that implement every nook and cranny of the Windows interface. The MFC classes are organized in a treelike hierarchy, known as an **application framework**. This application framework is much more than just an object-oriented translation of the Windows interface. Think of it as a generic application, complete with menu and window-handling code in place and ready to go. Rather than starting from scratch, your job is to customize this generic application, shaping its look and behavior to suit your design. For the most part, you do this by deriving new classes from the existing MFC classes and then adding your own classes as the need arises. Symantec C++ for Windows ships with the complete Microsoft Foundation Class Library.

Another popular class library is the Object Windows Library (OWL), which is brought to you by Borland. The OWL classes are also organized hierarchically as an application framework. Just as with MFC, you start with a generic OWL application and then customize it to suit your needs.

Class Library Economics

MFC and OWL are the main players in the application framework wars, but there are a few other choices. Which class library should you choose—MFC, OWL, or one of the others? All of these libraries are Windows specific, so you won't be able to use them to create a Unix or Macintosh application. Some people feel that OWL is more robust, while others swear by MFC. Some of the less known class libraries promise a better framework design with faster execution times.

Unfortunately, there is no simple method for selecting the class library that's best for you. Do your friends use one particular class library over another? If so, stick with your friends—at least you'll have someone close at hand who can help you come up to speed.

Check out trade magazines like *Dr. Dobbs' Journal* and *Byte*. They periodically run comparisons of the major development environments, describing the pros and cons associated with each.

Three primary C++ development environments take advantage of the MFC and OWL class libraries: Microsoft Visual C++, Symantec C++ for Windows, and Borland C++. Microsoft Visual C++ and Symantec C++ for Windows both work exclusively with the Microsoft Foundation Class Library, while Borland C++ works exclusively with the Object Windows Library.

Each of these environments lists for just under $500, so price isn't really a consideration. Each provides all the tools you'll need to get the job done. Though there are differences between them, the trade-offs are pretty reasonable. If you're getting ready to make your development-environment buying decision, here's some information you can use to get in touch with these companies. Each company will be more than happy to provide you with information on its particular development environment.

To find out more about Microsoft Visual C++ and the Microsoft Foundation Class Library, get in touch with the Microsoft Developer Network (described later in this chapter). To get in touch with Symantec, call (408) 253-9600. To reach Borland International, call (408) 438-8400.

Waiting for Bedrock

Just when you thought you had this class library thing figured out, along comes a new wrinkle—Bedrock. Bedrock is a class library that is being developed by Symantec and is scheduled for release in early 1994. Bedrock is intended as *the* standard cross-platform class library, capable of generating applications that will run under Windows as well as on the Macintosh and under Unix. While you will be able to use Bedrock exclusively for the creation of Windows applications, the beauty of Bedrock is that by changing a few settings, you can use the same source code to generate applications that will run on multiple platforms. Since Bedrock isn't shipping yet, we'll have to wait and see. In the short term, any time you invest in learning an existing Windows class library will pay off in the long run.

Books and Other References

Once you've decided on a class library, you'll be ready to turn your sights to the specifics of Windows development. If you're new to Windows, you'll be glad to know that there's a lot of reading material available to help ease you through the learning curve associated with Windows programming.

The Microsoft Developer Network

The Microsoft Developer Network is the official source for Microsoft's developer technical material. Anyone can join the Network (the cost is $195 per year). What do you get? For starters, you get the *Microsoft Developer Network News*, a bimonthly newspaper filled with up-to-the-minute information about Microsoft's systems strategy, development products, and services. You also get a quarterly CD-ROM containing thousands of pages of articles, product information, and sample code. To find out more about the Microsoft Developer Network, give them a call at (800) 227-4679, x11771.

The *Microsoft Systems Journal*

Published monthly by M&T Publishing, the *Microsoft Systems Journal* (or *MSJ*) is jam-packed with all kinds of tips and tidbits for aspiring Windows programmers. You definitely want to subscribe to this excellent magazine! For information on subscriptions, call M&T at (800) 666-1084. Outside the U.S. and Canada, call them at (303) 447-9330.

The *Windows Tech Journal*

Another excellent publication, the *Windows Tech Journal* (or *WTJ*), is not quite as popular as the *Microsoft Systems Journal*, but it is definitely worth a look. It is published monthly by Oakley Publishing in Springfield, Oregon. To subscribe, call (800) 234-0386 or (503) 747-0800. A one-year subscription costs $29.95.

The Bibliography

Be sure to check out the bibliography in Appendix H, where you'll find a list of books that will help ease your transition into Windows C++ programming. Now that you've mastered the basics of C++, you should pick up a good reference guide to help complete your education. *The C++ Programming Language* by Bjarne Stroustrup (the principal architect of C++) is a must. *C++ Primer* by Stanley Lippman is also very helpful. Make sure you get the second edition of both books. Finally, get hold of a copy of *The Annotated C++ Reference Manual* (also known as the *ARM*) by Margaret Ellis and Bjarne Stroustrup. Although it was written with the expert C++ programmer in mind, the *ARM* provides a complete and authoritative C++ reference.

Go Get 'Em... Well, that's it. I hope you enjoyed reading *Learn C++ on the PC* as much as I enjoyed writing it. Above all, I hope you are excited about C++. Now go out there and write some source code!

Glossary

abstract class: A base class whose sole purpose is to provide a basis for derived classes. You'll never create an object based on an abstract class.

access specifier: One of `public`, `private`, or `protected`, the access code defines which of your program's functions has access to the specified data member or function.

access function: A function designed specifically to provide access to a data member. See *setter* or *getter function*.

application framework: A collection of classes that implement a generic application. Typically, the classes in an application framework act as placeholders. The programmer overloads various parts of the framework to give the application the desired look and feel.

base class: A class used as the basis for the declaration of a second class, known as a derived class. The derived class inherits all the members of the base class.

class: A C++ structure that encapsulates data and functions, known as data members and member functions.

class derivation: The technique of deriving classes based on other classes.

class library: A collection of classes, sometimes used to implement a platform's user interface. Many class libraries come in the form of an application framework.

constructor function: A member function having the same name as its class. The constructor function is typically used to initialize an object's data members.

copy constructor: A constructor designed to provide an alternative to memberwise initialization for copying one object to another.

current object: The object that launched the current member function. The members of the current object may be referred to from within a member function without using the normal object notation. `this` is always a pointer to the current object.

data member: One of the data elements of a class.

declaration: A statement that creates a reference to an object or a function, without actually allocating memory for the object or function.

default argument initializer: A function argument with an associated default value. If the function is called and no value is passed in corresponding to the argument, the argument is initialized to its default value.

definition: A statement that causes memory to be allocated for a variable or function. A function prototype is a declaration. The entire function, including curly braces and all the statements between, is known as the function definition.

derivation chain: The chain of classes running from a root class, through a sequence of derived classes, to the ultimate derived class, which is the last class in the derivation chain.

derived class: A class declared using a base class. The derived class inherits all the members of its base class.

destructor function: A member function having the same name as its class preceded by the ~ character. The destructor function is typically used to delete any member allocated for an object.

extraction operator: The >> operator, part of `iostream`, that allows you to extract data from a stream.

formatting flags: A series of flags maintained by the `ios` class used to control various `iostream` formatting features.

function name overloading: A feature that allows you to create several functions with the same name, but having different signatures. Each call of an overloaded function is compared against the available signatures and the matching function is called. If no match is found, the compiler reports an error.

inheritance: The technique wherein a derived class inherits the characteristics of its base class.

inline function: A function declared using the `inline` keyword. The body of an inline function is actually copied into the calling function, allowing you to bypass the overhead normally associated with calling a function.

insertion operator: The `<<` operator, part of `iostream`, that allows you to insert data into a stream.

interface guidelines: A document that guides you through the process of designing a user interface for a specific platform.

interface vocabulary: A language that describes the elements in a platform's user interface. The terms *scroll bar*, *window*, and *pull-down menu* are all part of the Windows interface vocabulary.

manipulator: A special function, provided as part of the `iostream` library, that allows you to perform a specific I/O operation while you are in the middle of an insertion or extraction.

member function: One of the functions declared as part of a class.

member initialization list: The list that optionally follows a constructor's parameter list, used to initialize an object's members. The member initialization list is always preceded by a `:`.

memberwise assignment: The process of copying the value of the data members of one object to the data members of another object belonging to the same class, one at a time.

memberwise initialization: A special form of initialization used to copy one object to another. The first object's data members are copied to those of the second, one at a time.

multiple inheritance: The technique of defining a class derived from more than one class.

object: Any C++ entity that occupies memory.

operator overloading: Similar to function overloading, the technique of assigning more than one meaning to one of the built-in C++ operators. Overloaded operators rely on functions having the name `operator`, followed by the name of the operator being overloaded. For example, the function `operator+( )` overloads the + operator.

project: A collection consisting of a project file and all the other files that contribute to a particular program.

project file: A file used by Symantec's development environments to manage all of a program's source and object code. By convention, project files usually end in ".prj".

project window: A window that appears when you open a project using Symantec C++ for Windows. The window that describes all the source code file and library files that make up the project.

read-only memory (ROM): Computer memory that can only be read from, not written to.

reference variable: A variable designed to act as an alias to another variable of the exact same type. To denote a variable as a reference variable, precede its name with an & in its definition. Reference variables must be initialized (set to alias another variable) at the same time they are defined.

root base class: The ultimate base class in a derivation chain.

scope: A variable's scope defines the availability of the variable throughout the rest of the program.

scope resolution operator: The scope resolution operator, ::, precedes a variable, telling the compiler to look outside the current block for a variable of the same name. The scope resolution operator is also used to refer to a class's static members.

signature: A function's parameter list. A function's name and signature combine to distinguish it from all other functions. A function's return type is not part of its signature.

smart pointer: An overloaded version of the -> operator, used to walk down a chain of pointers.

state bits: A series of bits that reflect the current status of a stream. The bits are `goodbit`, `eofbit`, `failbit`, and `badbit`.

static member: A data member or member function declared using the `static` keyword. A static data member is shared by the entire class, rather than allocated for each object of the class. A static member function is typically created to control access to a static member. The `this` pointer is unavailable in a static member function.

template: A function or class definition containing a series of placeholders, each of which represents a type that isn't provided until the function is called or until an object of the class is defined.

template argument list: The list of type placeholders following the `template` keyword in a function or class template.

template instantiation: A function or class defined based on a template.

virtual base class: A root base class having all derived classes marked using the `virtual` keyword. This ensures that a derived class having more than one path back to the virtual base class will not instantiate more than one copy of the root base class.

Source Code Listings

addtime (Chapter 7)

```cpp
#include <iostream.h>


//--------------------------------------- Time

class Time
{
//      Data members...
   private:
      short hours;
      short minutes;
      short seconds;

//      Member functions...
      void  NormalizeTime();
   public:
            Time();
            Time( short h, short m, short s );
```

```cpp
         void   Display();
         Time   operator+( Time &aTime );
         void   operator*=( short num );
};

Time::Time()
{
   seconds = 0;
   minutes = 0;
   hours = 0;
}

Time::Time( short h, short m, short s )
{
   seconds = s;
   minutes = m;
   hours = h;

   NormalizeTime();
}

void   Time::NormalizeTime()
{
   hours += ((minutes + (seconds/60)) / 60);

   minutes = (minutes + (seconds/60)) % 60;

   seconds %= 60;
}

void   Time::Display()
{
   cout << "(" << hours << ":" << minutes
        << ":" << seconds << ")\n";
}

Time   Time::operator+( Time &aTime )
{
   short h;
   short m;
   short s;
```

```
   h = hours + aTime.hours;
   m = minutes + aTime.minutes;
   s = seconds + aTime.seconds;

   Time  tempTime( h, m, s );

   return tempTime;
}

void  Time::operator*=( short num )
{
   hours *= num;
   minutes *= num;
   seconds *= num;

   NormalizeTime();
}


//------------------------------------- main

int  main()
{
   Time  firstTime( 1, 10, 50 );
   Time  secondTime( 2, 24, 20 );
   Time  sumTime;

   firstTime.Display();
   secondTime.Display();

   cout << "---------\n";

   sumTime = firstTime + secondTime;
   sumTime.Display();

   cout << "*       2\n";
   cout << "---------\n";

   sumTime *= 2;
   sumTime.Display();

   return 0;
}
```

caller (Chapter 7)

```
#include <iostream.h>


//--------------------------------------- Item

class Item
{
   private:
      float     price;

   public:
                  Item( float itemPrice );
         float operator()( float taxRate = 0 );
};

Item::Item( float itemPrice )
{
   price = itemPrice;
}

float Item::operator()( float taxRate )
{
   return( ((taxRate * .01) + 1) * price );
}


//--------------------------------------- main()

int    main()
{
   Item   stimpyDoll( 36.99 );

   cout << "Price of Stimpy doll: $" << stimpyDoll();
   cout << "\nPrice with 4.5% tax:  $" << stimpyDoll( 4.5 );

   return 0;
}
```

cin (Chapter 4)

```
#include <iostream.h>

const short kMaxNameLength = 40;

int    main()
{
    char   name[ kMaxNameLength ];
    short myShort;
    long   myLong;
    float myFloat;

    cout << "Type in your first name: ";
    cin >> name;

    cout << "Short, long, float: ";
    cin >> myShort >> myLong >> myFloat;

    cout << "\nYour name is: " << name;
    cout << "\nmyShort: " << myShort;
    cout << "\nmyLong: " << myLong;
    cout << "\nmyFloat: " << myFloat;

    return 0;
}
```

cout (Chapter 4)

```
#include <iostream.h>

int    main()
{
    char   *name = "Dr. Crusher";

    cout << "char:     " << name[ 0 ] << '\n'
    << "short:    " << (short)(name[ 0 ]) << '\n'
    << "string:   " << name << '\n'
    << "address: " << (unsigned long)name;

    return 0;
}
```

derived (Chapter 6)

```
#include <iostream.h>


//------------------------------------ Base

class Base
{
//        Data members...
    private:
       short baseMember;

//        Member functions...
    protected:
       void  SetBaseMember( short baseValue );
       short GetBaseMember();
};

void  Base::SetBaseMember( short baseValue )
{
    baseMember = baseValue;
}

short Base::GetBaseMember()
{
    return baseMember;
}


//------------------------------------ Base:Derived

class Derived : public Base
{
//        Data members...
    private:
       short derivedMember;

//        Member functions...
    public:
       void  SetMembers( short baseValue,
                         short derivedValue );
       void  PrintDataMembers();
};
```

```
void  Derived::SetMembers( short baseValue,
                     short derivedValue )
{
   derivedMember = derivedValue;
   SetBaseMember( baseValue );
}

void  Derived::PrintDataMembers()
{
   cout << "baseMember was set to "
      << GetBaseMember() << '\n';

   cout << "derivedMember was set to "
      << derivedMember << '\n';
}


//------------------------------------ main()

int   main()
{
   Derived      *derivedPtr;

   derivedPtr = new Derived;

   derivedPtr->SetMembers( 10, 20 );

   derivedPtr->PrintDataMembers();

   return 0;
}
```

employee (Chapter 5)

```cpp
#include <iostream.h>
#include <string.h>

const short kMaxNameSize = 20;

class Employee
{
//        Data members...
   private:
       char   employeeName[ kMaxNameSize ];
       long   employeeID;
       float  employeeSalary;

//        Member functions...
   public:
           Employee( char *name, long id, float salary );
           ~Employee();
       void   PrintEmployee();
};

Employee::Employee( char *name, long id, float salary )
{
   strncpy( employeeName, name, kMaxNameSize );

   employeeName[ kMaxNameSize - 1 ] = '\0';

   employeeID = id;
   employeeSalary = salary;

   cout << "Creating employee #" << employeeID << "\n";
}

Employee::~Employee()
{
   cout << "Destroying employee #" << employeeID << "\n";
}

void  Employee::PrintEmployee()
{
   cout << "-----\n";
   cout << "Name:    " << employeeName << "\n";
```

```
   cout << "ID:      " << employeeID << "\n";
   cout << "Salary: " << employeeSalary << "\n";
   cout << "-----\n";
}

int    main()
{
   Employee employee1( "Dave Mark", 1, 200.0 );
   Employee *employee2;

   employee2 = new Employee( "Steve Baker", 2, 300.0 );

   employee1.PrintEmployee();
   employee2->PrintEmployee();

   delete employee2;

   return 0;
}
```

equals (Chapter 7)

```cpp
#include <iostream.h>
#include <string.h>


//------------------------------------ String

class String
{
   private:
      char      *s;
      short     stringLength;

   public:
                String( char *theString );
                ~String();
      void      DisplayAddress();
      String    &operator=( const String &fromString );
};

String::String( char *theString )
{
   stringLength = strlen( theString );
   s = new char[ stringLength + 1 ];

   strcpy( s, theString );
}

String::~String()
{
   delete [] s;
}

void  String::DisplayAddress()
{
   cout << "String address: " << (unsigned long)s << "\n";
}

String    &String::operator=( const String &fromString )
{
   delete [] s;
```

```
    stringLength = fromString.stringLength;

    s = new char[ stringLength + 1 ];

    strcpy( s, fromString.s );

    return( *this );
}


//------------------------------------- main()

int   main()
{
    String      captain( "Picard" );
    String      doctor( "Crusher" );

    captain.DisplayAddress();
    doctor.DisplayAddress();

    cout << "-----\n";

    doctor = captain;

    captain.DisplayAddress();
    doctor.DisplayAddress();

    return 0;
}
```

formattr (Chapter 8)

```
#include <iostream.h>


//----------------------------------- main()

int    main()
{
    cout << 202 << '\n';

    cout.width( 5 );
    cout.fill( 'x' );
    cout.setf( ios::left, ios::adjustfield );

    cout << 202 << '\n';

    cout.width( 10 );
    cout.fill( '=' );
    cout.setf( ios::internal, ios::adjustfield );

    cout << -101 << '\n';

    cout.width( 10 );
    cout.fill( '*' );
    cout.setf( ios::right, ios::adjustfield );

    cout << "Hello";

    return 0;
}
```

friends (Chapter 5)

```
#include <iostream.h>
#include <string.h>


const short kMaxNameSize = 20;

class Employee;


//-------------------------------------- Payroll

class Payroll
{
//      Data members...
   private:

//      Member functions...
   public:
            Payroll();
            ~Payroll();
      void  PrintCheck( Employee *payee );
};

//-------------------------------------- Employee

class Employee
{
   friend void Payroll::PrintCheck( Employee *payee );

//      Data members...
   private:
      char  employeeName[ kMaxNameSize ];
      long  employeeID;
      float employeeSalary;

//      Member functions...
   public:
            Employee( char *name, long id, float salary );
            ~Employee();
      void  PrintEmployee();
};
```

```
//------------------- Payroll Member Functions

Payroll::Payroll()
{
    cout << "Creating payroll object\n";
}

Payroll::~Payroll()
{
    cout << "Destroying payroll object\n";
}

void  Payroll::PrintCheck( Employee *payee )
{
    cout << "Pay $" << payee->employeeSalary
        << " to the order of "
        << payee->employeeName << "...\n\n";
}


//------------------- Employee Member Functions

Employee::Employee( char *name, long id, float salary )
{
    strncpy( employeeName, name, kMaxNameSize );

    employeeName[ kMaxNameSize - 1 ] = '\0';

    employeeID = id;
    employeeSalary = salary;

    cout << "Creating employee #" << employeeID << "\n";
}

Employee::~Employee()
{
    cout << "Destroying employee #" << employeeID << "\n";
}

void  Employee::PrintEmployee()
{
```

```
        cout << "-----\n";
        cout << "Name:    " << employeeName << "\n";
        cout << "ID:      " << employeeID << "\n";
        cout << "Salary: " << employeeSalary << "\n";
        cout << "-----\n";
}


//------------------------------------- main

int   main()
{
    Employee *employee1Ptr;
    Payroll      *payroll1Ptr;

    payroll1Ptr = new Payroll;

    employee1Ptr = new Employee( "Carlos Derr", 1000, 500.0 );

    employee1Ptr->PrintEmployee();

    payroll1Ptr->PrintCheck( employee1Ptr );

    delete employee1Ptr;
    delete payroll1Ptr;

    return 0;
}
```

gramps (Chapter 6)

```cpp
#include <iostream.h>


//------------------------------------- Gramps

class Gramps
{
//      Data members...

//      Member functions...
   public:
           Gramps();
           ~Gramps();
};

Gramps::Gramps()
{
    cout << "Gramps' constructor was called!\n";
}

Gramps::~Gramps()
{
    cout << "Gramps' destructor was called!\n";
}


//------------------------------- Pops:Gramps

class Pops : public Gramps
{
//      Data members...

//      Member functions...
   public:
           Pops();
           ~Pops();
};

Pops::Pops()
{
    cout << "Pops' constructor was called!\n";
}
```

```
Pops::~Pops()
{
   cout << "Pops' destructor was called!\n";
}


//-------------------------------  Junior:Pops

class Junior : public Pops
{
//       Data members...

//       Member functions...
   public:
            Junior();
            ~Junior();
};

Junior::Junior()
{
   cout << "Junior's constructor was called!\n";
}

Junior::~Junior()
{
   cout << "Junior's destructor was called!\n";
}


//--------------------------------------- main

int   main()
{
   Junior        *juniorPtr;

   juniorPtr = new Junior;

   cout << "----\n";

   delete juniorPtr;

   return 0;
}
```

hello (Chapter 2)

```
#include <iostream.h>

int   main()
{
    cout << "Hello, world!";

    return 0;
}
```

init (Chapter 9)

```cpp
#include <iostream.h>


//------------------------------------- MyClass

class MyClass
{
   public:
      const short     kMaxNameLength;
      short           &numberAlias;
      short           number;

      MyClass( short constValue );
};

MyClass::MyClass( short constValue )
   : kMaxNameLength( constValue ), numberAlias( number )
{
   number = kMaxNameLength;

   cout << "Before: number = "
      << number << "\n";

   numberAlias += 10;

   cout << "After:  number = "
      << number << "\n";
}


//------------------------------------- main()

int    main()
{
   MyClass      myObject( 10 );

   return 0;
}
```

inline (Chapter 4)

```cpp
#include <iostream.h>

inline   long power( short base, short exponent );

int   main()
{
   cout << "power( 2, 3 ): " <<
         power( 2, 3 ) << "\n";

   cout << "power( 3, 6 ): " <<
         power( 3, 6 ) << "\n";

   cout << "power( 5, 0 ): " <<
         power( 2, 0 ) << "\n";

   cout << "power( -3, 4 ): " <<
         power( -3, 4 ) << "\n";

   return 0;
}

inline   long power( short base, short exponent )
{
   long  product = 1;
   short i;

   if ( exponent < 0 )
      return( 0 );

   for ( i=1; i<=exponent; i++ )
      product *= base;

   return product;
}
```

mmbrwise (Chapter 9)

```cpp
#include <iostream.h>
#include <string.h>


//------------------------------------- Name

class Name
{
    private:
        char  *last;
        char  *first;

    public:
            Name( char *firstParam, char *lastParam );
            Name( const Name &original );
            ~Name();
        void  Display();
        Name  &operator=( const Name &original );
};

Name::Name( char *firstParam, char *lastParam )
{
    first = new char[ strlen(firstParam) + 1 ];
    last = new char[ strlen(lastParam) + 1 ];

    strcpy( first, firstParam );
    strcpy( last, lastParam );

    cout << "Original constructor...\n";
}

Name::Name( const Name &original )
{
    first = new char[ strlen(original.first) + 1 ];
    last = new char[ strlen(original.last) + 1 ];

    strcpy( first, original.first );
    strcpy( last, original.last );

    cout << "Copy constructor...\n";
}
```

```
Name::~Name()
{
   delete [] first;
   delete [] last;
}

void  Name::Display()
{
   cout << "Name: " << first << " " << last << "\n";
}

Name  &Name::operator=( const Name &original )
{
   if ( this == &original )
      return( *this );

   delete [] first;
   delete [] last;

   first = new char[ strlen(original.first) + 1 ];
   last = new char[ strlen(original.last) + 1 ];

   strcpy( first, original.first );
   strcpy( last, original.last );

   return( *this );
}


//------------------------------------- main()

int   main()
{
   Name   yourAuthor( "Dave", "Mark" );
   Name   aCopy = yourAuthor;
   Name   anotherAuthor( "Andrew", "Schulman" );

   yourAuthor.Display();
   aCopy.Display();

   aCopy = anotherAuthor;

   aCopy.Display();

   return 0;
}
```

menu (Chapter 7)

```
#include <iostream.h>
#include <string.h>

const short kMaxNameLength = 40;

//------------------------------------- MenuItem

class MenuItem
{
   private:
      float     price;
      char      name[ kMaxNameLength ];

   public:
                MenuItem( float itemPrice, char *itemName );
      float     GetPrice();
      float     operator+( MenuItem item );
      float     operator+( float subtotal );
};

MenuItem::MenuItem( float itemPrice, char *itemName )
{
   price = itemPrice;
   strcpy( name, itemName );
}

float MenuItem::GetPrice()
{
   return( price );
}

float MenuItem::operator+( MenuItem item )
{
   cout << "MenuItem::operator+( MenuItem item )\n";

   return( GetPrice() + item.GetPrice() );
}

float MenuItem::operator+( float subtotal )
{
   cout << "MenuItem::operator+( float subtotal )\n";
```

```
    return( GetPrice() + subtotal );
}


//------------------------------------  operator+()

float operator+( float subtotal, MenuItem item )
{
    cout << "operator+( float subtotal, MenuItem item )\n";

    return( subtotal + item.GetPrice() );
}


//------------------------------------  main()

int   main()
{
    MenuItem chicken( 8.99, "Chicken Kiev with salad" );
    MenuItem houseWine( 2.99, "Riesling by the glass" );
    MenuItem applePie( 3.99, "Apple Pie a la Mode" );
    float    total;

    total = chicken + houseWine + applePie;

    cout << "\nTotal: " << total
        << "\n\n";

    total = chicken + (houseWine + applePie);

    cout << "\nTotal: " << total;

    return 0;
}
```

multiinh (Chapter 9)

```
#include <iostream.h>
#include <string.h>

const short kMaxStringLength = 40;


//--------------------------------------- Predator

class Predator
{
   private:
      char   favoritePrey[ kMaxStringLength ];

   public:
            Predator( char *prey );
            ~Predator();
};

Predator::Predator( char *prey )
{
   strcpy( favoritePrey, prey );

   cout << "Favorite prey: "
      << prey << "\n";
}

Predator::~Predator()
{
   cout << "Predator destructor was called!\n\n";
}


//--------------------------------------- Pet

class Pet
{
   private:
      char   favoriteToy[ kMaxStringLength ];

   public:
```

```
          Pet( char *toy );
          ~Pet();
};

Pet::Pet( char *toy )
{
   strcpy( favoriteToy, toy );

   cout << "Favorite toy: "
      << toy << "\n";
}

Pet::~Pet()
{
   cout << "Pet destructor was called!\n";
}


//------------------------- Cat:Predator,Pet

class Cat : public Predator, public Pet
{
   private:
      short        catID;
      static short    lastCatID;

   public:
            Cat( char *prey, char *toy );
            ~Cat();
};

Cat::Cat( char *prey, char *toy ) :
   Predator( prey ), Pet( toy )
{
   catID = ++lastCatID;

   cout << "catID: " << catID
      << "\n---------\n";
}

Cat::~Cat()
{
```

```
    cout << "Cat destructor called: catID = "
        << catID << "...\n";
}

short Cat::lastCatID = 0;


//------------------------------------- main()

int    main()
{
    Cat    TC( "Mice", "Ball of yarn" );
    Cat    Benny( "Crickets", "Bottle cap" );
    Cat    Meow( "Moths", "Spool of thread" );

    return 0;
}
```

new (Chapter 7)

```cpp
#include <iostream.h>


//------------------------------------- Blob

class Blob
{
   public:
      void   *operator new( size_t blobSize );
      void   operator delete( void *blobPtr, size_t blobSize );
};

void   *Blob::operator new( size_t blobSize )
{
   cout << "new: " << blobSize << " byte(s).\n";

   return new char[ blobSize ];
}

void   Blob::operator delete( void *blobPtr, size_t blobSize )
{
   cout << "delete: " << blobSize << " byte(s).\n";

   delete [] blobPtr;
}


//------------------------------------- main()

int   main()
{
   Blob   *blobPtr;

   blobPtr = new Blob;

   delete blobPtr;

   return 0;
}
```

newtestr (Chapter 4)

```
#include <iostream.h>
#include <new.h>

const short false = 0;
const short true = 1;

void    NewFailed( void );

char    gDone = false;
char    *gSpareBlockPtr = 0;

int    main()
{
   char    *myPtr;
   long    numBlocks = 0;

   cout << "Installing NewHandler...\n";

    set_new_handler( NewFailed );
   gSpareBlockPtr = new char[20480];

    while ( gDone == false )
   {
      myPtr = new char[1024];
      numBlocks++;
   }

   cout << "Number of blocks allocated: " << numBlocks;

   return 0;
}

void    NewFailed()
{
   if ( gSpareBlockPtr != 0 )
   {
      delete gSpareBlockPtr;
      gSpareBlockPtr = 0;
   }

    gDone = true;
}
```

nonvirt (Chapter 9)

```
#include <iostream.h>


//-------------------------------------- Root

class Root
{
   public:
      Root();
};

Root::Root()
{
   cout << "Root constructor called\n";
}


//-------------------------------------- Base1

class Base1 : public Root
{
   public:
      Base1();
};

Base1::Base1()
{
   cout << "Base1 constructor called\n";
}


//-------------------------------------- Base2

class Base2 : public Root
{
   public:
      Base2();
};

Base2::Base2()
```

```
{
   cout << "Base2 constructor called\n";
}


//-------------------------------------- Derived

class Derived : public Base1, public Base2
{
   public:
      Derived();
};

Derived::Derived()
{
   cout << "Derived constructor called\n";
}


//-------------------------------------- main()

int   main()
{
   Derived      myDerived;

   return 0;
}
```

overload (Chapter 4)

```
#include <iostream.h>

void  Display( short shortParam );
void  Display( long longParam );
void  Display( char *text );

int   main()
{
   short myShort = 3;
   long  myLong = 12345678L;
   char  *text = "Make it so...";

   Display( myShort );
   Display( myLong );
   Display( text );

   return 0;
}

void  Display( short shortParam )
{
   cout << "The short is: " << shortParam << "\n";
}

void  Display( long longParam )
{
   cout << "The long is:  " << longParam << "\n";
}

void  Display( char *text )
{
   cout << "The text is:  " << text << "\n";
}
```

overlod2 (Chapter 8)

```
#include <iostream.h>
#include <fstream.h>
#include <string.h>

const short kMaxNameLength = 40;

//-------------------------------------- MenuItem

class MenuItem
{
   private:
      float    price;
      char     name[ kMaxNameLength ];

   public:
      void     SetName( char *itemName );
      char     *GetName();
      void     SetPrice( float itemPrice );
      float    GetPrice();
};

void  MenuItem::SetName( char *itemName )
{
   strcpy( name, itemName );
}

char  *MenuItem::GetName()
{
   return( name );
}

void  MenuItem::SetPrice( float itemPrice )
{
   price = itemPrice;
}

float MenuItem::GetPrice()
{
   return( price );
}
```

```
//------------------------  iostream operators


istream &operator>>( istream &is, MenuItem &item )
{
    float itemPrice;
    char  itemName[ kMaxNameLength ];

    is.getline( itemName, kMaxNameLength );
    item.SetName( itemName );

    is >> itemPrice;
    item.SetPrice( itemPrice );

    is.ignore( 1, '\n' );

    return( is );
}

ostream &operator<<( ostream &os, MenuItem &item )
{
    os << item.GetName() << " ($"
       << item.GetPrice() << ") ";

    return( os );
}


//------------------------------------- main()

int   main()
{
    ifstream    readMe( "menuitms.txt" );
    MenuItem item;

    while (  readMe >> item )
       cout << item << "\n";

    return 0;
}
```

prototst (Chapter 4)

```
#include <iostream.h>

void  MyFunc( short param1,
          short param2 = 0,
          short param3 = 0 );

int   main()
{
   MyFunc( 1 );
   MyFunc( 1, 2 );
   MyFunc( 1, 2, 3 );

   return 0;
}

void  MyFunc( short param1,
          short param2,
          short param3 )
{
   cout << "MyFunc( " << param1
      << ", " << param2
      << ", " << param3
      << " )\n";
}
```

readme (Chapter 8)

```
#include <iostream.h>
#include <fstream.h>

int    main()
{
    ifstream    readMe( "myfile.txt" );
    char        c;

    while ( readMe.get( c ) )
        cout << c;

    return 0;
}
```

refrence (Chapter 4)

```
#include <iostream.h>

void  CallByValue( short valueParam );
void  CallByReference( short &refParam );

int   main()
{
   short number = 12;
   long  longNumber = 12L;

   cout << "&number:      " <<
      (unsigned long)&number << "\n";

   cout << "&longNumber: " <<
      (unsigned long)&longNumber << "\n\n";

   CallByValue( number );
   cout << "After ByValue: " << number << "\n\n";

   CallByReference( number );
   cout << "After ByRef( short ): " << number << "\n\n";

// This next line will generate a warning. Do you see why?
   CallByReference( longNumber );
   cout << "After ByRef( long ): " << longNumber << "\n";

   return 0;
}

void  CallByValue( short valueParam )
{
   cout << "&valueParam: " <<
       (unsigned long)&valueParam << "\n";
   valueParam *= 2;
}

void  CallByReference( short &refParam )
{
   cout << "&refParam:    " <<
       (unsigned long)&refParam << "\n";
   refParam *= 2;
}
```

scopetst (Chapter 4)

```cpp
#include <iostream.h>

short myValue = 5;

int    main()
{
    short yourValue = myValue;

    cout << "yourValue: " << yourValue << "\n";

    short myValue = 10;
    yourValue = myValue;

    cout << "yourValue: " << yourValue << "\n";

    yourValue = ::myValue;
    cout << "yourValue: " << yourValue << "\n";

    return 0;
}
```

smartptr (Chapter 7)

```
#include <iostream.h>
#include <string.h>

const short kMaxNameLength = 40;


//-------------------------------------- Name

class Name
{
   private:
      char      first[ kMaxNameLength ];
      char      last[ kMaxNameLength ];

   public:
                Name( char *lastName, char *firstName );
         void   DisplayName();
};

Name::Name( char *lastName, char *firstName )
{
   strcpy( last, lastName );
   strcpy( first, firstName );
}

void  Name::DisplayName()
{
   cout << "Name: " << first << " " << last;
}


//-------------------------------------- Politician

class Politician
{
   private:
      Name      *namePtr;
      short     age;

   public:
```

```
                 Politician( Name *namePtr, short age );
        Name   *operator->();
};

Politician::Politician( Name *namePtr, short age )
{
   this->namePtr = namePtr;
   this->age = age;
}

Name   *Politician::operator->()
{
   return( namePtr );
}


//----------------------------------- main()

int   main()
{
   Name           myName( "Clinton", "Bill" );
   Politician  billClinton( &myName, 46 );

   billClinton->DisplayName();

   return 0;
}
```

square (Chapter 6)

```cpp
#include <iostream.h>


//------------------------------------- Rectangle

class Rectangle
{
//       Data members...
   protected:
      short height;
      short width;

//       Member functions...
   public:
            Rectangle( short heightParam, short widthParam );
      void  DisplayArea();
};

Rectangle::Rectangle( short heightParam, short widthParam )
{
   height = heightParam;
   width = widthParam;
}

void  Rectangle::DisplayArea()
{
   cout << "Area is: " <<
      height * width << '\n';
}


//------------------------------------- Rectangle:Square

class Square : public Rectangle
{
//       Data members...

//       Member functions...
   public:
            Square( short side );
};
```

```
Square::Square( short side ) : Rectangle( side, side )
{
}


//------------------------------------- main()

int    main()
{
    Square      *mySquare;
    Rectangle   *myRectangle;

    mySquare = new Square( 10 );
    mySquare->DisplayArea();

    myRectangle = new Rectangle( 10, 15 );
    myRectangle->DisplayArea();

    return 0;
}
```

statebts (Chapter 8)

```cpp
#include <iostream.h>

const short true = 1;
const short false = 0;

int    main()
{
    char    done = false;
    char  c;
    short number;

    while ( ! done )
    {
        cout << "Type a number: ";
        cin >> number;

        if ( cin.good() )
        {
            if ( number == 0 )
            {
                cout << "Goodbye...";
                done = true;
            }
            else
                cout << "Your number is: " << number << "\n\n";
        }
        else if ( cin.fail() )
        {
            cin.clear();

            cin.get( c );
            cout << c << " is not a number...";
            cout << "Type 0 to exit\n\n";
        }
        else if ( cin.bad() )
        {
            cout << "\nYikes!!! Gotta go...";
            done = true;
        }
    }

    return 0;
}
```

strstrea (Chapter 8)

```
#include <iostream.h>
#include <strstrea.h>

const short kBufferSize = 10;

//------------------------------------- main()

int   main()
{
    char        buffer[ kBufferSize ];
    ostrstream  ostr( buffer, kBufferSize );
    short       i = 0;

    while ( ostr << (char)('a' + i) )
        i++;

    cout << "Number of characters written: "
        << i << '\n';

    buffer[ kBufferSize - 1 ] = '\0';

    cout << "Buffer contents: " << buffer;

    return 0;
}
```

subscrpt (Chapter 7)

```
#include <iostream.h>
#include <string.h>

const short kMaxNameLength = 40;

//-------------------------------------- Name

class Name
{
   private:
      char       nameString[ kMaxNameLength ];
      short      nameLength;

   public:
              Name( char *name );
      void  operator()();
      char  &operator[]( short index );
};

Name::Name( char *name )
{
   strcpy( nameString, name );
   nameLength = strlen( name );
}

void  Name::operator()()
{
   cout << nameString << "\n";
}

char& Name::operator[]( short index )
{
   if ( ( index < 0 ) || ( index >= nameLength ) )
   {
      cout << "index out of bounds!!!\n";
      return( nameString[ 0 ] );
   }
   else
      return( nameString[ index ] );
}
```

```
//-------------------------------------- main()

int    main()
{
   Name       pres( "B. J. Clinton" );

   pres[ 3 ] = 'X';
   pres();

   pres[ 25 ] = 'Z';
   pres();

   return 0;
}
```

template (Chapter 9)

```
#include <iostream.h>

const short kNumElements = 10;

//------------------------------------ Array

template <class T>
class Array
{
   private:
      short    arraySize;
      T            *arrayPtr;
      T            errorRetValue;

   public:
               Array( short size );
               ~Array();
      T        &operator[]( short index );
};

template <class T>
Array<T>::Array( short size )
{
   arraySize = size;
   arrayPtr = new T[ size ];
   errorRetValue = 0;
}

template <class T>
Array<T>::~Array()
{
   delete [] arrayPtr;
}

template <class T>
T  &Array<T>::operator[]( short index )
{
   if ( ( index < 0 ) || ( index >= arraySize ) )
   {
      cout << "index out of bounds(" << index << ")\n";
```

```
         return( errorRetValue );
      }
   else
         return( arrayPtr[ index ] );
}


//--------------------------------------- Power

template <class T>
T  Power( T base, T exponent )
{
   T  i, product = 1;

   for ( i=1; i<=exponent; i++ )
      product *= base;

   return( product );
}


//--------------------------------------- main()

int   main()
{
   Array<short>    myRay( kNumElements );
   Array<long>     myLongRay( kNumElements );
   short        i, shortBase = 4;
   long         longBase = 4L;

   for ( i=0; i<=kNumElements; i++ )
      myRay[ i ] = Power( shortBase, i );

   cout << "----\n";

   for ( i=0; i<kNumElements; i++ )
      cout << "myRay[" << i << "]: " << myRay[ i ] << "\n";

   for ( i=0; i<kNumElements; i++ )
      myLongRay[ i ] = Power( longBase, (long)i );

   cout << "----\n";
```

```
for ( i=0; i<kNumElements; i++ )
    cout << "myLongRay[" << i
        << "]: " << myLongRay[ i ] << "\n";

return 0;
}
```

virtual (Chapter 9)

```
#include <iostream.h>


//------------------------------------- Root

class Root
{
   protected:
      short num;

   public:
           Root( short numParam );
};

Root::Root( short numParam )
{
   num = numParam;

   cout << "Root constructor called\n";
}


//------------------------------------- Base1

class Base1 : public virtual Root
{
   public:
      Base1();
};

Base1::Base1() : Root( 1 )
{
   cout << "Base1 constructor called\n";
}


//------------------------------------- Base2

class Base2 : public virtual Root
{
```

```
  public:
      Base2();
};

Base2::Base2() : Root( 2 )
{
   cout << "Base2 constructor called\n";
}


//--------------------------------------- Derived
class Derived : public Base1, public Base2
{
   public:
              Derived();
        short GetNum();
};

Derived::Derived() : Root( 3 )
{
   cout << "Derived constructor called\n";
}

short Derived::GetNum()
{
   return( num );
}


//--------------------------------------- main()
int   main()
{
   Derived      myDerived;

   cout << "-------\n"
      << "num = " << myDerived.GetNum();

   return 0;
}
```

whatami (Chapter 6)

```cpp
#include <iostream.h>


//------------------------------------- Shape

class Shape
{
//       Data members...

//       Member functions...
   public:
      virtual void   WhatAmI();
};

void  Shape::WhatAmI()
{
   cout << "I don't know what kind of shape I am!\n";
}


//------------------------------------- Shape:Rectangle

class Rectangle : public Shape
{
//       Data members...

//       Member functions...
   public:
      void  WhatAmI();
};

void  Rectangle::WhatAmI()
{
   cout << "I'm a rectangle!\n";
}


//------------------------------------- Shape:Triangle

class Triangle : public Shape
{
```

```
//        Data members...

//        Member functions...
   public:
      void  WhatAmI();
};

void  Triangle::WhatAmI()
{
   cout << "I'm a triangle!\n";
}



//------------------------------------ main()

int    main()
{
   Shape *s1, *s2, *s3;

   s1 = new Rectangle;
   s2 = new Triangle;
   s3 = new Shape;

   s1->WhatAmI();
   s2->WhatAmI();
   s3->WhatAmI();

   return 0;
}
```

fstream.h

```
// IOStreams Package
// Steve Teale April 1992
// Copyright Symantec Corp 1990-1992. All Rights Reserved.

#ifndef __FSTREAM_H
#define __FSTREAM_H

#include <iostream.h>

#pragma pack(__DEFALIGN)
class filebuf : public streambuf {

// This is a streambuf class specialized for handling files.
// The get and put pointers are locked together so that reads and writes
// happen at the same offset into the file.

public:
    enum { openprot = 0644 };

    filebuf();
// The default constructor. Creats a filebuf that is not associated
// with any file. open() or attach() can then be used to connect
// to a file.
```

```
    filebuf(int file_descriptor, int io_mode = ios::in|ios::out
#if M_UNIX || M_XENIX
        );
#else
        |ios::translated);
#endif
// Constructs a filebuf for the open file attached to the argument
// file descriptor. More comprehensive io_mode information can
// be specified e.g. ios::app, if required

    filebuf(int descriptor, char *memory, int length,
                    int io_mode = ios::in|ios::out
#if M_UNIX || M_XENIX
        );
#else
        |ios::translated);
#endif
// Constructs a filebuf for the open file attached to the
// file_descriptor, and sets the buffer to "memory", which is of
// "length" bytes in size. If memory is 0 or length is <= 0,
// it is taken as a request that the file be unbuffered.

    ~filebuf();

    filebuf *attach(int file_descriptor,
                    int io_mode = ios::in|ios::out
#if M_UNIX_ || M_XENIX
        );
#else
        |ios::translated);
#endif
// Attaches an open file to a filebuf. Returns "this" if successful,
// 0 if the filebuf is already attached to a file.

    filebuf *close();
// Flushes output, closes the file, and detaches the file from this
// filebuf. Clears the error state unless there is an error flushing
// the output. Will always close the file and detach it from the
// filebuf, even if there are errors.

    int fd() const { return file; };
// Returns the file descriptor for the connected file. If the
// filebuf is closed or not attached to a file, returns EOF.
```

```
    int is_open() const { return file != EOF; };
// Returns non-zero when this filebuf is attached to a file,
// otherwise returns zero.

    filebuf *open(const char *name, int io_mode,
                  int protection = openprot);
// Opens the file "name", and connects it to this filebuf.
// io_mode is a bit-mask containing one or more of the values of
// enum open_mode:
// ios::in     Open for reading.
// ios::out    Open for writing.
// ios::ate    Position to the end-of-file.
// ios::app    Open the file in append mode.
// ios::trunc  Truncate the file on open.
// ios::nocreate   Do not attempt to create the file if it
//          does not exist.
// ios::noreplace  Cause the open to fail if the file exists.
// ios::translate  Convert CR/LF to newline on input and
//          vice versa on output

    streampos seekoff(streamoff offset, ios::relative_to,
                      int which);
// Relative seek the get and put pointers within the file.
// The get and put pointers of a filebuf always point to the
// same byte of the file.

    streambuf *setbuf(char *memory, int length);
// Set the buffer to use "memory", of "length" bytes.
// If memory == 0 or length <= 0, it is taken as a request that
// I/O to the file be unbuffered.

    int sync();
// Flush any bytes in the get buffer, and re-position the file so
// that is appears they were never read. Write any bytes in the
// put buffer to the file.

#if __SC__ > 0x214
    int overflow(int c);
#else
    int overflow(int c = EOF);
#endif
// Flush bytes in the put area to the file.
```

```
    int underflow();
// Get more bytes for reading.

protected:
    int doallocate();

    int pbackfail(int c);
// Called to atempt recovery if putback attempted at
// start of get buffer

private:

    void buffer_setup();
            // Internal. Set up I/O buffer.
    int newlines();
            // count newline chars in the get buffer
    int syncin();
    int syncout();
            // two halves of sync() function
    int fillbuf();
    int flushbuf();
            // Functions which actually transfer to/from
            // the file

    int file;    // File descriptor for the associated file.
    short mode;  // I/O mode from the argument to open().
    char unbuf[2];
            // pseudo buffer for unbuffered operation
    char *gptr_;
    char *egptr_;
            // Save old gptr() & egptr() while using the
            // pushback buffer.
    char pushback_buf[4];
            // Reserve buffer for pushback.
            // Only used if there is no room for pushback in
            // the regular buffer.
    char do_not_seek;
            // Set if the file (device) does not support seeks.
            // This is set for a TTY, or a Unix pipe.
    char own_file_descriptor;
            // Set if the file descriptor is from open, and
            // the file should be closed by the destructor.
```

```
      static const int lseek_consts[3];
                // A look up table for the lseek constants from
                // the appropriate C header file
};

class fstream_common : virtual public ios {

// Features common to ifstream, ofstream, and fstream.

public:

    void attach(int file_descriptor, int io_mode);
// Attach the filebuf to the argument file descriptor, error state
// set to ios::failbit|ios::badbit on failure.

    void close();
// Flush the filebuf, and close the file attached to it. Error state
// set ios::failbit|ios::badbit if rdbuf()->sync() fails. File closed
// regardless.

    void open(const char *name, int io_mode,
                int protection = filebuf::openprot);
// Open a file, and attach it to the filebuf. Error state set to
// ios::failbit|ios::badbit on failure

    void setbuf(char *memory, int length)
    {
        buffer.setbuf(memory, length);
    }
// Use the argument memory, of the given length, as the I/O buffer.
    filebuf *rdbuf() { return &buffer; }
// Note that fstream_common::rdbuf returns a filebuf*
// instead of a streambuf*.

protected:
    fstream_common();
    filebuf buffer;
};

class ifstream : public fstream_common, public istream {
public:
    ifstream();
// Create an ifstream not attached to any file.
```

```
    ifstream(const char *name, int io_mode = ios::in | ios::nocreate
#if M_UNIX || M_XENIX
      ,int protection = filebuf::openprot);
#else
      | ios::translated, int protection = filebuf::openprot);
#endif
// Open the argument file and create an ifstream attached to it.

    ifstream(int file_descriptor, int io_mode = ios::in
#if M_UNIX || M_XENIX
      );
#else
      | ios::translated);
#endif
// Create an ifstream attached to the argument file descriptor.

    ifstream(int file_descriptor, char *memory, int length,
                                  int io_mode = ios::in
#if M_UNIX || M_XENIX
      );
#else
      | ios::translated);
#endif
// Create an ifstream attached to the argument file descriptor, and
// using the argument memory as the I/O buffer.

    ~ifstream();

    void attach(int file_descriptor, int io_mode = ios::in
#if M_UNIX || M_XENIX
      )
#else
      | ios::translated)
#endif
    {
      fstream_common::attach(file_descriptor, io_mode);
    }

    void open(const char *name, int io_mode = ios::in
#if M_UNIX || M_XENIX
      ,int protection = filebuf::openprot)
#else
      | ios::translated, int protection = filebuf::openprot)
```

```
#endif
    {
        fstream_common::open(name, io_mode, protection);
    }

};

class ofstream : public fstream_common, public ostream {
public:
    ofstream();
// Create an ofstream not attached to any file.

    ofstream(const char *name, int io_mode = ios::out
#if M_UNIX || M_XENIX
        ,int protection = filebuf::openprot);
#else
        | ios::translated, int protection = filebuf::openprot);
#endif
// Open the argument file and create an ofstream attached to it.

    ofstream(int file_descriptor, int io_mode = ios::out
#if M_UNIX || M_XENIX
        );
#else
        | ios::translated);
#endif
// Create an ofstream attached to the argument file descriptor.

    ofstream(int file_descriptor, char *memory, int length,
                            int io_mode = ios::out
#if M_UNIX || M_XENIX
        );
#else
        | ios::translated);
#endif
// Create an ofstream attached to the argument file descriptor, and
// using the argument memory as the I/O buffer.

    ~ofstream();

    void attach(int file_descriptor, int io_mode = ios::out
#if M_UNIX || M_XENIX
        )
```

```
#else
      | ios::translated)
#endif
    {
        fstream_common::attach(file_descriptor, io_mode);
    }

    void open(const char *name, int io_mode = ios::out
#if M_UNIX_ || M_XENIX
      ,int protection = filebuf::openprot)
#else
      | ios::translated, int protection = filebuf::openprot)
#endif
    {
        fstream_common::open(name, io_mode, protection);
    }

};


class fstream : public fstream_common, public iostream {
public:
    fstream();
// Create an fstream not attached to any file.

    fstream(const char *name, int io_mode = ios::in|ios::out
#if M_UNIX || M_XENIX
      ,int protection = filebuf::openprot);
#else
      | ios::translated, int protection = filebuf::openprot);
#endif
// Open the argument file and create an fstream attached to it.

    fstream(int file_descriptor, int io_mode = ios::in | ios::out
#if M_UNIX || M_XENIX
      );
#else
      | ios::translated);
#endif
// Create an fstream attached to the argument file descriptor.

    fstream(int file_descriptor, char *memory, int length,
                        int io_mode = ios::in | ios::out
```

```
#if M_UNIX || M_XENIX
        );
#else
        | ios::translated);
#endif
// Create an fstream attached to the argument file descriptor, and
// using the argument memory as the I/O buffer.

    ~fstream();

    void attach(int file_descriptor, int io_mode = ios::in | ios::out
#if M_UNIX || M_XENIX
        )
#else
        | ios::translated)
#endif
    {
        fstream_common::attach(file_descriptor, io_mode);
    }

    void open(const char *name, int io_mode = ios::in | ios::out
#if M_UNIX || M_XENIX
        ,int protection = filebuf::openprot)
#else
        | ios::translated, int protection = filebuf::openprot)
#endif
    {
        fstream_common::open(name, io_mode, protection);
    }

};
#pragma pack()
#endif    // __FSTREAM_H
```

iomanip.h

```
// IOStreams Package
// Steve Teale April 1992
// Copyright Symantec Corp 1990-1992. All Rights Reserved.

#ifndef __IOMANIP_H
#define __IOMANIP_H

#include <iomdefs.h>

#pragma pack(__DEFALIGN)
ios &_iomanip_resetiosflags(ios&, long);
inline SMANIP<long> resetiosflags(long f)
   { return SMANIP<long>(_iomanip_resetiosflags,f); }

ios &_iomanip_setfill(ios&, int);
inline SMANIP<int> setfill(int filler)
   { return SMANIP<int>(_iomanip_setfill,filler); }

ios &_iomanip_setiosflags(ios&, long);
inline SMANIP<long> setiosflags(long f)
   { return SMANIP<long>(_iomanip_setiosflags,f); }
```

```
ios &_iomanip_setprecision(ios&, int);
inline SMANIP<int> setprecision(int n)
   { return SMANIP<int>(_iomanip_setprecision,n); }

ios &_iomanip_setw(ios&, int);
inline SMANIP<int> setw(int w)
   { return SMANIP<int>(_iomanip_setw,w); }

ios &_iomanip_setbase(ios&, int);
inline SMANIP<int> setbase(int n)
   { return SMANIP<int>(_iomanip_setbase,n); }

#pragma pack()
#endif  // __IOMANIP_H
```

iostream.h

```
// IOStreams Package
// Steve Teale April 1992
// Copyright Symantec Corp 1990-1992. All Rights Reserved.

#ifndef __IOSTREAM_H
#define __IOSTREAM_H
#include <stddef.h>
#include <2comp.h>

#define seek_dir relative_to

#ifndef EOF
const int EOF = -1;
#endif

const int _ios_default_decimal_precision = 6;
const int _ios_n_extended_format_words = 10;
// This is the number of extended format state words reserved for use
// by derived classes and user inserters. This value should be reasonably
// small, as it inflates the size of each instance of ios.

#pragma pack(__DEFALIGN)
class streampos {
```

```
friend class streamoff;
public:
    streampos(long elems, size_t elemsize = 1) : ne(elems),
es(elemsize) {}
    operator long() const { return (ne == -1)? EOF: ne*es; }
private:
    long ne;
    size_t es;
};

class streamoff {
public:
    streamoff(long elems, size_t elemsize = 1) : ne(elems),
es(elemsize) {}
    streamoff(streampos &a) : ne(a.ne), es(a.es) {}
    size_t stepsize() const { return es; }
    long steps() const { return ne == -1? 0: ne; }
    streamoff& operator += (long o) { ne += o; return *this; }
    streamoff& operator -= (long o) { ne -= o; return *this; }
    operator long() const { return steps()*es; }

private:
    long ne;
    size_t es;
};

class streambuf;
class ostream;
class istream;


class ios {

// This is the base class for istream and ostream, and all of their
// derivations.

friend ostream &endl(ostream &);

public:
    enum io_state {
        goodbit=0,
// No errors - everything hunky dory!
        eofbit=1,
```

```
// Normally set when underflow failed because there was no more file.
        failbit=2,
// An error has ocurred, but it is probably recoverable, and the
// stream is still in a useable state
        badbit=4
// A fatal error has ocurred
    };


// This is called seek_dir in the AT & T version, which is misleading.
// A define is included above for compatibility. These enumerators are
// used to specify relative seeks in streams.
    enum relative_to {
        beg,
// For seek operations relative to the beginning of the stream (file),

        cur,
// relative to the current position in the stream (file),

        end
// and relative to the end of the stream (file)
    };

// The following enumeration applies to file related derivatives.
    enum open_mode {
        in=0x1,
// Input allowed

        out=0x2,
// Output allowed

        ate=0x4,
// A seek to the end of the file to be performed during open.

        app=0x8,
// All writes are to the end of the file - implies out

        trunc=0x10,
// Existing contents of the file to be discarded. Implies out
// unless ate or app specified as well.

        nocreate=0x20,
// Open will fail if the file does not already exist
```

```
      noreplace=0x40,
// Open will fail if the file does already exist

      translated = 0x80
// CR/LF pairs to be translated to newline characters on input
// and newline characters to be translated to CR/LF pairs on
// output (the normal behaviour for DOS)
    };
```

```
// The formatting state is a bit-mask used to control some of the
// inserters and extractors. All of the bits of the format state
// can be manipulated by flags(), setf(), and unsetf(). Some
// specialized parts of the formatting state can be manipulated
// by fill(), width(), and precision() . Here are the meanings
// of the various bits:
```

```
   enum format_mode {
        skipws = 0x1,
// Skip past leading white space when extracting.
// Since zero-width fields are considered an
// error by the numeric extractors, attempting
// to extract white-space into a number without
// this bit set will set an error flag.

        left = 0x2,
// Left-adjust values when inserting (fill on the right).

        right = 0x4,
// Right-adjust values when inserting (fill on the left).

        internal = 0x8,
// When inserting, fill _between_ the numeric sign or
// base indicator and the value.

        dec = 0x10, oct = 0x20, hex = 0x40,
// Default radix for integers. If neither dec, octal,
// or hex is set, integer inserters use base 10, and
// integer extractors interpret numbers according to the
// C++ lexical convention: "0x" precedes a base-16 number,
// and a number with a leading zero is base-8.

        showbase = 0x80,
// If this is set, base-16 numbers will be inserted with a
// leading "0x", and base-8 numbers will have a leading zero.
```

```
        showpoint = 0x100,
// If this is set, the floating-point inserters will print a
// decimal point and trailing zeroes, even when the trailing
// places are not significant.

        uppercase = 0x200,
// If this is set, "E" instead of "e" will be used to indicate
// the exponent of a floating point number, and "A" through "F"
// will be used to represent base-16 numerals instead of "a"
// through "f".
//
// If uppercase and showbase are both set, the string "0X"
// instead of "0x" will be used to indicate a base-16 number.

        showpos = 0x400,
// If this is set, positive numbers will be inserted with a
// leading "+".

        scientific = 0x800,
// If this is set, the floating-point inserters will print a
// number with one digit before the decimal point, and the
// number of digits after the decimal point equal to the
// value of precision(). The character "e" will introduce the
// exponent.

        fixed = 0x1000,
// If this is set, the floating-point inserters will use
// precision() to determine the number of digits after the
// decimal point.
//
// If neither scientific or fixed is set, numbers with
// exponents smaller than -4 or greater than precision() will
// be printed as if scientific were set. Other numbers will
// be printed using zeroes to explicitly show the decimal place.

        unitbuf = 0x2000,
// When this is set, a flush is performed after each insertion
// (by ostream::osfx()). This is more efficient than using
// unbuffered output, but provides most of the same advantages.

        stdio = 0x4000
// When this is set, streams using stdiobufs will flush stdout and
// stderr after each insertion.
```

```
// Note that it is not possible to use bit 0x8000 in this way,
// as this evaluates to an enumerator with a negative value and
// lots of bits set.
    };    // end enum format_mode

    static const long stickywidth;
    static const long spacing;

    enum format_mode_mask {
        defaults = right|skipws,
        basefield = dec|oct|hex,
        adjustfield = left|right|internal,
        floatfield = scientific|fixed
    };

public: // just a reminder!

    ios(streambuf *buffer);
// Construct an ios associated with the argument streambuf.
// "buffer" should not be null.

    virtual ~ios();

//////////////////////////////////////////////////////////////
//
// Functions to interrogate/set the error state

    int good() const { return error_state == 0; };
// If there are no error bits set, this returns non-zero, otherwise
// it returns zero.

    int eof() const { return error_state & eofbit; };
// If eofbit is set in the error state, this return non-zero, otherwise
// it returns zero. This indicates that end-of-file has been reached
// while reading the character stream.

    int fail() { return error_state & (badbit | failbit); }
// If badbit or failbit is set in the error state, return non-zero.
// Otherwise, return zero. Failbit generally indicates that some
// extraction has failed, but the stream may still be used once
// failbit has been cleared.
```

```
    int bad() const { return error_state & badbit; }
// Returns non-zero if badbit is set in the error state. This
// indicates some unrecoverable error, generally an I/O error.

    int operator!() const
    {
        return error_state & (badbit|failbit);
    }
// Return non-zero if badbit or failbit is set in the error state,
// which allows expressions of the form:
//   if ( !cout )

    operator void*()
    {
        return (error_state & (badbit|failbit))?
            0: this;
    }
// Convert an ios to a value that can be compared to zero, but can
// not be easily used accidentally. The return value is a void pointer
// that will be zero if failbit or badbit is set in the error state,
// and non-zero otherwise. This allows an iostream to be used
// in conditional expressions that test its state, as in:
// if ( cin ) and if ( cin >> variable )

    int rdstate() const { return error_state; };
// Returns the current error state.

    void clear(int new_state = 0) { error_state = new_state; }
// Stores "new_state" as the error state.
//
// To set a bit without clearing others requires something like
// clear(bits_to_set | rdstate()) .

//////////////////////////////////////////////////////////////////
//
// Functions to set/interrogate various options

    char fill(char new_value)
    {
        char old_value = padding_character;
        padding_character = new_value;
        return old_value;
    }
```

```
// Sets the fill character, and returns the old value. This is the
// character used to pad output when the left, right, or internal
// adjustments are in effect.

    char fill() const { return padding_character; }
// Returns the fill character.

    int precision(int new_value)
    {
        int old_value = decimal_precision;
        decimal_precision = new_value >= 0?
            new_value: _ios_default_decimal_precision;
        return old_value;
    }
// Sets the decimal precision, and returns the old value.
// This controls the number of digits inserted after the decimal
// point by the floating-point inserter.

    int precision() const { return decimal_precision; }
// Returns the current decimal precision.

    ostream *tie(ostream * new_value)
    {
        ostream *old_value = tied_ostream;
        tied_ostream = new_value;
        return old_value;
    };
// Facilitate automatic flushing of iostreams.
// Associate this ios to an ostream such that the ostream will be
// flushed before this ios makes a request for characters, or flushes
// output characters. These ties exist by default:
//   cin.tie(cout);
//   cout.tie(cerr);
//   cout.tie(clog);
//
// For other instances of ios, the tie is set to zero by default.
//
// This returns the old value.

    long flags() const { return format_state; }
// Return the format state flags.
```

```
    long flags(long new_value)
    {
        long old_value = format_state;
        format_state = new_value;
        return old_value;
    }
// Sets the format state flags, returning the old values.

    long setf(long bits_to_set, long mask = 0)
    {
        long old_value = format_state;
        format_state = (format_state & ~mask)
                | bits_to_set;
        return old_value;
    }
// Clears the bits corresponding to mask in the format state, and
// then sets only those bits from the value of bits_to_set.

    long unsetf(long bits_to_clear)
    {
        long old_value = format_state;
        format_state &= ~bits_to_clear;
        return old_value;
    };
// Clears flags in the format state.

    ostream *tie() const { return tied_ostream; };
// Return the current "tied" ostream.

    int width(int new_value);
// Sets the field width used by inserters.
// When the width is zero, inserters will use only as many characters
// as necessary to represent a value. When the width is non-zero,
// inserters will insert at least that many characters, using the
// fill character to pad out the field. Inserters will never truncate,
// so they may output more characters than the current width.

    int width() const { return field_width; };
// Returns the current width.
```

```
////////////////////////////////////////////////////////////////
//
// Other utilities

    streambuf *rdbuf() { return buf; }
// Returns a pointer to the streambuf associated with this ios.

    static void sync_with_stdio();
// Use this when mixing C and C++ in the same program.
// It resets cin, cout, cerr, and clog to use stdiobufs, and
// thus makes I/O to these streams compatible with the C stdio.
// Invoking this degrades performance.

////////////////////////////////////////////////////////////////
//
// Functions to manipulate user defined format flags and control
// words.

    static int bitalloc();
// Returns an int with one previously-unallocated bit set.
// This allows users who need an additional format flag to
// get one. Note that this allocation is global for class ios,
// not local to any instance of class ios.

    static int xalloc();
// Returns a previously-unused index into an array of words usable
// as format-state variables by derived classes.

    long &iword(int index)
    {
        return extended_format_words[index].l;
    }
// Returns a reference to one of the auxillary format state words
// reserved for use by derived classes and user inserters, where
// index is a value returned by xalloc().

    void* &pword(int index)
    {
        return extended_format_words[index].vp;
    };
```

```
// Returns a reference to a pointer to one of the auxillary format
// state words reserved for use by derived classes and user
// inserters, where index is a value returned by xalloc().

protected:
    void set_buffer(streambuf *b) { buf = b; }

private:
    streambuf   *buf;
    ostream     *tied_ostream;
    long        format_state;
    char        error_state;
    char        padding_character;
    short       decimal_precision;
    short       field_width;
    union {
        void *vp;
        long l;
    } extended_format_words[_ios_n_extended_format_words];

    ios(const ios&);
    ios &operator=(const ios&);
// These copying functions are private so that the compiler
// will complain about an attempt to assign an ios. It is not
// actually defined. Instead of copying an ios, assign a pointer
// to it.

};

///////////////////////////////////////////////////////////////
//
// Manipulator functions

ios &dec(ios&);
// Set the default integer radix to 10.
// Invoke this (and the other manipulators) this way:
// stream >> dec;
// stream << dec;

ios &hex(ios&);
ios &oct(ios&);
ios &defaults(ios&);
```

```
class streambuf {
// Streambuf abstracts the operations used to perform I/O on a character
// stream such as a computer terminal, a file or a string.
//
// The two basic operations are "get", which fetches characters from the
// stream, and "put", which places characters on the stream. Some streambufs
// are unidirectional, in which case they support the "get" operation but
// not "put", or vice-versa.
//
// Some streambufs are bi-directional, with the "get" and "put" offsets
// at different locations in the stream. Some streambufs may implement
// a circular buffer between the "get" and "put" offsets, as in a FIFO.
// Some streambufs lock the "get" and "put" offset together, as in a
// UNIX file.
// Some streambufs provide buffered I/O on the underlying character streams
// for efficiency.
//
// Streambufs contain a buffer, a get area, and a put area. Usually, the
// get area and put area overlap the buffer, but do not overlap each other.

public:

    streambuf();
// The default constructor.

    streambuf(char *memory, int length);
// Constructs a streambuf, possibly using the argument buffer.
    virtual ~streambuf();

    void dbp();
// Write debugging information about the streambuf on file
// descriptor 1. Nothing about the form of that information
// is specified.

    int in_avail() const { return _egptr - _gptr; }
// Return the number of characters that can be read immediately
// with a guarantee that no errors will be reported.

    int out_waiting() const { return _pptr - _pbase; }
// Return the number of characters that have not
// been flushed away, or EOF if there are no characters.
```

```
    virtual streambuf *setbuf(char *memory, int length);
```
// Requests that this streambuf use the argument memory buffer.
// Special case: a null memory argument, or a length argument that is
// zero or negative, is taken as a request that this streambuf be
// unbuffered.
//
// If the request to set the buffer is honored, return "this",
// otherwise return 0.
//
// * Use of this interface, except by a derived class of streambuf,
// is discouraged. It is not protected for compatibility with the
// original stream package in Stroustrup.
//
// The default version of this member will honor the request if no
// buffer has been allocated.

```
    virtual streampos  seekpos(streampos position,
                                int which=ios::in|ios::out);
```
// Performs an absolute seek of the get or put pointers, or both, to
// "position". Position is an implementation-dependent value which
// should not have arithmetic performed on it. "which" signifies what
// pointer is to be affected: ios::in signifies the get pointer, and
// ios::out signifies the put pointer. The two "which" values may be
// or-ed together, in which case the operation affects both pointers.
//
// * The default version of this member returns
//   seekoff(position, ios::beg, which)
// thus is is only necessary for a derived class to define
// seekoff(), and use the inherited seekpos().

```
    virtual streampos seekoff(streamoff offset, ios::relative_to pos,
                                int which=ios::in|ios::out);
```
// Performs a relative seek of the get or put pointers, or both, by
// "offset". Position is a byte offset, and may be negative.
// "pos" may be ios::beg, which signifies a seek relative to
// the beginning of the stream; ios::cur, which signifies a seek
// relative to the current position in the stream; and ios::end, which
// signifies a seek relative to the end of the stream.
// "which" signifies what pointer is to be affected: ios::in
// signifies the get pointer, and ios::out signifies the put pointer.
// The two "which" values may be or-ed together, in which case the
// operation affects both pointers.
//   * The default version of this member always returns EOF.

```
    int sgetc()
    {
        return _gptr < _egptr?
                    (unsigned char) *_gptr: underflow();
    }
// Returns the character at the get pointer, without moving the get
// pointer.

    int sbumpc()
    {
        return _gptr < _egptr?
                    (unsigned char) *_gptr++: sbumpc_special();
    }
// Moves the get pointer forward one character, and return the
// character it moved past.

    int sgetn(char *buffer, int count);
// Fetch the "count" characters following the get pointer, and
// stores them in "buffer". If there are less than "count" characters,
// the number remaining are fetched. The get pointer is repositioned
// after the fetched characters, and the number of characters fetched
// is returned.

    int snextc()
    {
        return _gptr+1 < _egptr?
                    ((unsigned char) *(++_gptr)): underflow();
    }

// Skip past the character at the get pointer, and return the
// character after that, or EOF.

    int sputbackc(char c)
    {
        return _gptr > _gbase?
                    (*(-_gptr) = c, 0): pbackfail(c & 0x00ff);
    }
// Move the get pointer back one character. If c is not the last
// character retrieved, the effect is undefined. In this implementation
// it should work
```

```
    int sputc(int c)
    {
        return _pptr < _epptr?
                        (*_pptr++ = c, 0): overflow(c & 0x00ff);
    }
```
// Store c on the character stream, advancing the "put" pointer.
// Return EOF when an error occurs.

```
    int sputn(const char *string, int length);
```
// Store "n" characters on the character stream, advancing the "put"
// pointer past the stored characters. Return the number of characters
// stored, which may be less than "n" if there is an error.

```
    void stossc()
    {
        if (_gptr < _egptr) ++_gptr;
    }
```
// Skip the "get" pointer forward, wasting one character of input.
// If the get pointer is already at the end of the sequence
// this has no effect.

```
    virtual int sync();
```
// Make the external character stream and the streambuf consistent
// with each other. This usually means:
// 1. If there are characters in the get area, return them to the
//   stream, or throw them away. Re-position the stream so that
//   it appears that the characters that had been in the get area
//   had never been taken from the stream.
// 2. If there are characters in the put area, store them to the
//   stream. Re-position the stream immediately after the characters
//   just stored.
// 3. Return EOF if there's an error, otherwise return some other
//   value.
//   * The default version of this member will return 0 if the get area
// is empty, otherwise it returns EOF.

```
    virtual int overflow(int c = EOF);
```
// This is called to store characters in the character stream, usually
// when the put area is full. It generally stores all of the characters
// that are in the put area, stores c if it is not EOF, and calls
// setp() to establish a new put area. It should return EOF if it
// has an error, otherwise return some other value.

```
    virtual int underflow();
// This is called to read characters from the character stream,
// usually when the get area is empty. It should read one or more
// characters, and place them in the get area. It should return the
// first character in the get area, without incrementing the get
// pointer. It should return EOF if there's a problem.

protected:

// Buffer base and one past the end
    char *base() const { return _base; }
    char *ebuf() const { return _ebuf; }
// Get pointer, pushback limit, and one past end of put area
    char *gptr() const { return _gptr; }
    char *eback() const { return _gbase; }
    char *egptr() const { return _egptr; }
// Put pointer, and one past end of put area
    char *pbase() const { return _pbase; }
    char *pptr() const { return _pptr; }
    char *epptr() const { return _epptr; }

    int blen() const { return _ebuf-_base; }
// Return the size in characters of the buffer.

    int allocate();
// Try to set up the buffer. If one already exists or unbuffered() is
// non-zero, return 0 without doing anything. If something goes wrong,
// return EOF. Otherwise, return 1. This function is only called by
// virtual members of the base class streambuf, thus you can override
// everything that uses it.

    virtual int doallocate();
// This is called when allocate() determines that space is needed.
// This function must call setb() to set up the buffer, and return
// a non-eof value, or return EOF if it can not get space.
// This function is only called if unbuffered() is zero, and base()
// is zero.
//
// * The default version allocates a buffer using operator new.

    virtual int pbackfail(int c);
// This is called by sputbackc() when the get pointer is equal to
// the base of the get area, and there is thus no space to put back
```

```
// characters. It may try to re-arrange the buffer so that it is
// possible to put back characters, and then put back c. If it
// succeeds it should return c, otherwise it should return EOF.
//        * The default version of this member always returns EOF.

    void setg(char *base, char *get, char *end)
    {
        _gbase = base;
        _gptr = get;
        _egptr = end;
    }
// Sets the base of the get area, the get pointer, and the end of
// the get area.

    void setp(char *base, char *end)
    {
        _pbase = _pptr = base;
        _epptr = end;
    }
// Sets the base of the put area, the put pointer, and the end of
// the put area.

    void setb(char *base, char *end, int own = 0);
// Sets the base and end of the buffer. If own is true, then this
// streambuf will delete base in its destructor or if setb() is called
// again.

    void gbump(int n) { _gptr += n; }
    void pbump(int n) { _pptr += n; }

    int unbuffered() const { return _unbuffered; }
    void unbuffered(int u) { _unbuffered = u; }


private:
    char * _base;
    char * _ebuf;
    char * _gbase;
    char * _gptr;
    char * _egptr;
    char * _pbase;
    char * _pptr;
    char * _epptr;
```

```
        char _unbuffered;
        char _owned;

        char unbuf[2];
// This is big enough to deal with the translated case when unbuffered

        int     sbumpc_special();
// Called by sbumpc() when get_pointer == get_area_end.
// Simply calls overflow(), increments the get pointer, and
// returns the value returned by overflow(). It's here so that
// the special-case code does not have to be inlined.
};

class ostream : virtual public ios {

// This is the class used for formatted character output.
// The various "operator << (...)" members are called "inserters",
// because they insert information into the character stream.
//
// Unless otherwise noted, all of the functions here that do output set
// the error state on failure.
//
// Where the inserters perform conversions of numbers to a readable string,
// the conversion is affected by the format state flags in ios::flags().

public:
        ostream(streambuf * buffer);
// Construct an ostream associated with the argument streambuf.

        virtual ~ostream();

        ostream &flush();
// Flush any characters queued for output.

        int opfx();
// Perform output-prefix operations.
// If the error state is non-zero, return zero immediately.
// If there is a tied ostream (see ios::tie()), flush it.
// Return non-zero. If you define your own inserter that directly
// manipulates the streambuf instead of calling other inserters,
// it should call this when it starts.
```

```
     void osfx();
// Perform output-suffix operations.
// If ios::unitbuf is set in the format state, flush output.
// If ios::stdio is set, flush stdio and stderr.
// If you define your own inserter that directly manipulates the
// streambuf, it should call this just before returning.
// All of the inserters in ostream call this.
// The binary put() and write() functions do not call this.

     ostream &put(char c);
// Inserts a character

     ostream &seekp(streampos position);
// Absolute seeks the output stream to "position".

     ostream &seekp(streamoff offset, seek_dir direction);
// Relative seeks the output stream. See streambuf::seekoff()

     streampos tellp();
// Returns the current position in the output stream.

     ostream &write(const void *data, size_t size);
     size_t pcount() { return write_count; }
// Inserts the block of "size" bytes starting at "data". Does not
// perform any formatting. The number of characters successfully
// output can be determined by a following call to ostream::pcount().

     ostream &operator<<(const char *string);
     ostream &operator<<(const signed char *string)
          { return operator<<((const char *) string); }
     ostream &operator<<(const unsigned char *string)
          { return operator<<((const char *) string); }
// Insert a null-terminated string.

     ostream &operator<<(char c);
     ostream &operator<<(signed char c)
   { return operator<<((char) c); }
     ostream &operator<<(unsigned char c)
   { return operator<<((char) c); }
// Insert a single character.

     ostream &operator<<(short v)
          { return _2Comp::insert(*this,&v,sizeof(short),1); }
```

```
    ostream &operator<<(int v)
        { return _2Comp::insert(*this,&v,sizeof(int),1); }
    ostream &operator<<(long v)
        { return _2Comp::insert(*this,&v,sizeof(long),1); }
    ostream &operator<<(unsigned short v)
        { return _2Comp::insert(*this,&v,sizeof(unsigned short),0); }
    ostream &operator<<(unsigned v)
        { return _2Comp::insert(*this,&v,sizeof(unsigned),0); }
    ostream &operator<<(unsigned long v)
        { return _2Comp::insert(*this,&v,sizeof(unsigned long),0); }

#if macintosh
    ostream &operator<<(float v) { return operator<<((long double) v); }
    ostream &operator<<(double v) { return operator<<((long double) v); }
    ostream &operator<<(long double);
#else
    ostream &operator<<(float v) { return operator<<((double) v); }
    ostream &operator<<(double);
#endif


    ostream &operator<<(void *);
// Convert a pointer to a hex integer, and insert.

    ostream &operator<<(streambuf *source);
// Insert all of the characters that can be fetched from the streambuf.

    ostream &operator<<(ostream &(*manipulator)(ostream &))
        { return (*manipulator)(*this); }
// Parameterless manipulators are implemented by providing an
// inserter for the type pointer to function taking an ostream reference
// argument and returning an ostream reference. The specified function
// is simple executed for the current ostream.

    ostream &operator<<(ios &(*manipulator)(ios &))
    {
        (*manipulator)(*this);
        return *this;
    }
// Similar facility to insert a pointer to function taking an ios
// reference argument.
```

```
// This isn't in the draft standard, but it is so useful in the
// implementation of inserters that it is made public here.
    int pad(int where, int wide);

protected:
    ostream();  // ios will be initialized by derived class
private:
    size_t write_count;
// Records number of bytes actually put out by a write()

    void eof_fail() { clear(ios::badbit | ios::failbit | ios:: eofbit); }
// Internal. Set error flags after an output EOF error.

#if macintosh
    int fixed_point(long double, char *);
#else
    int fixed_point(double, char *);
#endif
// Internal. Convert double to fixed-point string.

#if macintosh
    int sci_notation(long double, char *, int &);
#else
    int sci_notation(double, char *, int &);
#endif
// Internal. Convert double to scientific-notation string.

    int adjust(int bit_to_test, int field_width);
// Manages padding
    void flush_stdio();
// Called by osfx() if ios::stdio is set.  This function is in a
// separate module to prevent the stdio stuff from being pulled
// in when it is not required.
};

// The following functions provide parameterless inserters of the
// type noted above. They have to be real functions because we
// need to take their address.

ostream &ends(ostream&);
// Ends a string by inserting a null character. Use this on strstreams
// before you call ostrstream::freeze().
```

```
//
// stream << "whatever" << ends;

ostream &flush(ostream&);
// Flushes output on an ostream.
//
// stream << "whatever" << flush

ostream &endl(ostream &);
// Inserts the appropriate new-line character(s) for the system, and flushes
// output. On Unix the new-line character is inserted. On DOS, the
// carriage-return and new-line characters are inserted. Thus, using endl
// instead of '\n' or "\r\n" is more portable.
//
// stream << "whatever" << endl;

ostream &stickywidth(ostream &);
// Sets the state so that width is not reset after each insertion
// unlatch this by a call to width() or use setw manipulator.

ostream &spacing(ostream &);
ostream &nospacing(ostream &);
// Sets the state so that a space is output after any item which
// makes a call to osfx() except the endl manipulator.

ostream &fixed(ostream &);
ostream &scientific(ostream &);
ostream &showpoint(ostream &);
ostream &floating(ostream &);
ostream &uppercase(ostream &);
// Manipulate the floating point format, floating sets the default
// state.

ostream &leftjust(ostream &);
ostream &rightjust(ostream &);
ostream &internal(ostream &);
ostream &showbase(ostream &);
// Set a justify mode

// types used by istream dfa extractor function
typedef void (*translate_function_t)(void *, const char *, void *);
typedef int (*helper_function_t)(int, char, void *);
```

```
class istream : virtual public ios {

// This is the class used for character input.
// The various "operator>>(...)" members are called "extractors", because
// they extract information from the character stream.
//  * Where the extractors perform conversions of a string to a number,
// the conversion is affected by the format state flags in ios::flags().
// Each of the extractors calls ipfx() first, and returns immediately if
// ipfx returns zero. Extractors indicate errors by setting bits of the
// error state. ios::failbit means the input characters weren't a
// representation of the required type. ios::badbit means that the I/O
// system failed to get the required characters.
//  * The unformatted extractors (get(), getline()) will set ios::failbit
// only if they are not able to extract at least one character.
//  * Caveat: The ATT version ignores overflow. This version attempts to
// set the error flags on overflow.

public:
    static int is_white_space(char c);
// Internal. Return 1 if the argument character is white-space,
// otherwise return 0.

    istream(streambuf *buffer);
// Construct a new istream associated with the argument streambuf.

    virtual ~istream();

    size_t gcount() { return read_count; }
// Return the number of characters extracted by the last unformatted
// input function. Other input functions may call the unformatted
// input functions, so this counter is only accurate immediately
// after a call to an unformatted input function.

    istream &get(char *data, int length, char delimiter = '\n');
    istream &get(signed char *data, int length, char delimiter = '\n');
    istream &get(unsigned char *data, int length, char delimiter = '\n');
// Both of these extract up to "length" characters, storing them in
// "data". If a character equal to "delimiter" is seen, it is pushed
// back on the input stream and extraction stops.

    istream &get(char &destination);
    istream &get(signed char &destination);
```

```
    istream &get(unsigned char &destination);
// Extract a single character.

    istream &get(streambuf &destination, char delimiter = '\n');
// Call ipfx(0), and if the result is non-zero, get characters until
// the delimiter is seen or EOF, and stuff the characters into the
// streambuf. Doesn't extract the delimiter character. Only sets
// ios::badbit if it can't extract at least one character.

    int get();
// Get one character, and return it in an int. Return EOF if there's
// an error.

    istream &getline(char *data, int length, char delimiter = '\n');
    istream &getline(signed char *data, int length,
                    char delimiter = '\n');
    istream &getline(unsigned char *data, int length,
                    char delimiter = '\n');
// These two are like get(char *data, int length, char delimiter),
// except that they extract the terminating delimiter instead of
// pushing it back.

    istream &ignore(int length = 1, int delimiter = EOF);
// Extract and throw away up to "length" characters. Extraction
// stops if "delimiter" is extracted, or at EOF. If "delimiter"
// is EOF, it won't match any character, and thus will not stop
// extraction.

    int ipfx(int need = 0);
// Perform input-prefix operations.
// The argument "need" is the number of characters that will be
// required, or 0 if you don't know how many you'll need. The
// formatted input functions call this with 0, and the unformatted
// input functions call it with 1.
//     * If the error state is non-zero, this returns zero immediately.
// Otherwise, it returns non-zero when finished.
// If there is a tied stream (see ios::tie()) and need is 0 or greater
// than the number of immediately available characters, the tied
// iostream is flushed.
//     * If ios::skipws is set in the format state, and "need" is zero,
// leading white-space characters are thrown away and the stream
// is advanced to the first available character.
```

```
// This returns zero if there is an error while skipping a
// white-space character, otherwise it returns non-zero.

    int peek();
// Calls ipfx(1). If that returns zero, or if the input character
// stream is at EOF, return EOF. Otherwise return the next character
// without extracting it from the input stream.

    istream &putback(char c);
// Attempt to push the last character read back onto the input stream.
// "c" must be the last character read. This does not call ipfx(), but
// it will return without doing anything if the error state is
// non-zero.

    istream &read(void *data, int size);
// Extracts a block of "size" bytes and stores them at "data".
// If EOF is reached before "size" bytes are extracted,
// ios::failbit is set. The number of characters actually
// extracted is available as the return value of istream::gcount().

    istream &seekg(streampos position);
// Absolute-seek the input character stream to "position".

    istream &seekg(streamoff offset, seek_dir direction);
// Relative-seek the input character stream by "offset" relative to
// the current position.

    int sync();
// Establishes consistency between the internal data structure
// and the external character source. This usually means that
// characters that were buffered for input are thrown away, and
// the file pointer is decremented so that it appears that the
// buffered characters were never read.

    streampos tellg();
// Return the current file position. The value returned is a magic
// cookie that is usable only as an argument to seekg(streampos).
// Don't perform arithmetic on the return value.

    istream &operator>>(char *);
    istream &operator>>(signed char *s)
        { return operator>>((char *) s); }
```

```
    istream &operator>>(unsigned char *s)
        { return operator>>((char *) s); }
// For the string extractors, characters are extracted until a
// white-space is seen. The white-space is pushed back on the
// incoming character stream. If width() is non-zero, it is taken
// as the size of the argument character array, and no more than
// width()-1 characters are extracted. A terminating null character
// is ALWAYS stored, even when nothing else is done because of
// the error state.

    istream &operator>>(char &);
// Extracts a single character, similar to get()
    istream &operator>>(signed char &c)
    { return operator>>((char) c); }
    istream &operator>>(unsigned char &c)
    { return operator>>((char) c); }

// Extract byte wide integers -128 - +127 and 0 - 255 respectively

    istream &operator>>(short &v)
        { return _2Comp::extract(*this,&v,sizeof(short)); }
    istream &operator>>(int &v)
        { return _2Comp::extract(*this,&v,sizeof(int)); }
    istream &operator>>(long &v)
        { return _2Comp::extract(*this,&v,sizeof(long)); }
    istream &operator>>(unsigned short &v)
        { return _2Comp::extract(*this,&v,sizeof(unsigned short)); }
    istream &operator>>(unsigned int &v)
        { return _2Comp::extract(*this,&v,sizeof(unsigned int)); }
    istream &operator>>(unsigned long &v)
        { return _2Comp::extract(*this,&v,sizeof(unsigned long)); }

    istream &operator>>(float &);
    istream &operator>>(double &);
#if macintosh
    istream &operator>>(long double &);
#endif

    istream &operator>>(streambuf*);
// Calls ipfx(0), and if the result is non-zero, extracts characters
// and stuffs them into the argument streambuf until EOF is reached.
// Only sets ios::badbit if it can't get at least one character.
```

```
    istream &operator>>(istream &(*manip)(istream&))
    {
        (*manip)(*this);
        return *this;
    }
// Provides an pseudo extractor which allows for parameterless
// manipulators. The target type is pointer to function returning
// istream reference and taking istream reference argument.

    istream &operator>>(ios &(*manip)(ios&))
    {
        (*manip)(*this);
        return *this;
    }
// Similar facility to manipulate an ios object directly

protected:
    istream();   // derived class will initialize ios directly

private:
friend istream &_2Comp::extract(istream&, void *, int);

// The extract function provides for general type translation using
// a character set string and a DFA transition table
    istream &extract(void *type, const char *okchars, int *tt,
            translate_function_t tf, helper_function_t hf, void *tds);
    size_t read_count;
};

istream &ws(istream&);
// Manipulator to skip white-space, positioning the input
// character stream to the first available non-white-space
// character.

class iostream : public istream, public ostream {

// A stream that supports both insertion and extraction.

public:
    iostream(streambuf *buf);
// Construct an iostream associated with the argument streambuf.
```

```
    virtual ~iostream();
protected:
    iostream(); // derived class will initialize ios directly

};

// Iostream classes that support assignment.
//
// They're used for cin, cout, cerr, and clog, but you should not use
// them for anything else. Instead, use a regular stream and assign a
// pointer to it.

class istream_withassign : public istream {
public:
    istream_withassign();
    istream_withassign(streambuf *);
    ~istream_withassign();
    istream_withassign &operator=(istream &);
    istream_withassign &operator=(istream_withassign &s) {return
operator=((istream &)s);}
    istream_withassign &operator=(streambuf *);
private:
    short assigned_to;
};

class ostream_withassign : public ostream {
public:
    ostream_withassign();
    ostream_withassign(streambuf *);
    ~ostream_withassign();
    ostream_withassign &operator=(ostream &);
    ostream_withassign &operator=(ostream_withassign &s) {return
operator=((ostream &)s);}
    ostream_withassign &operator=(streambuf *);
private:
    short assigned_to;
};

class iostream_withassign : public iostream {
public:
    iostream_withassign();
    iostream_withassign(streambuf *);
    ~iostream_withassign();
```

```
    iostream_withassign &operator=(ios &);
    iostream_withassign &operator=(iostream_withassign &s)
        {return operator=((ios &)s);}
    iostream_withassign &operator=(streambuf *);
private:
    short assigned_to;
};

extern istream_withassign cin;
extern ostream_withassign cout;
extern ostream_withassign cerr;
#if M_UNIX || M_XENIX
extern ostream_withassign  clog;
#endif

class IosTie {
public:
    IosTie(ios *a, ostream *b) {a->tie(b);
#if THINK_CPLUS
                        ios::sync_with_stdio();
#endif
                        }
};

class IosUnitbuf {
public:
   IosUnitbuf(ios *a) { a->setf(ios::unitbuf); }
};

#pragma pack()

#endif  // __IOSTREAM_H
```

strstrea.h

```
#ifndef __SSTREAM_H
#define __SSTREAM_H

// Iostreams Package
// Bruce Perens, July-August 1990
//
// Modified Steve Teale April 1991
// Copyright Zortech 1990-1991. All Rights Reserved.

#include <iostream.h>

const int default_allocation = 32;

#pragma pack(__DEFALIGN)
class strstreambuf : public streambuf {

// This is a streambuf that holds a character array, and I/O is to that
// character array instead of a file or some external character stream.
// There is a dynamic-allocation mode that allocates space for characters
// as needed. Get, put, and seeks are supported within the character array.
// The call freeze() returns a pointer to the array, so that the data may
// be read by conventional string-handling routines.
```

```
public:

// state flags
   enum sstream_flags {
       statmem = 1,
// Set if the buffer was set with an argument to the constructor or
// setbuf, and I should not do dynamic allocation if it runs out of
// space.

       frozen = 2,
// Set when the buffer is frozen.
       merged = 4,
// Set if the get and put areas are considered to be overlapped. This
// will be the case if the strstreambuf is dynamic, or if a simultaneous
// seek of both the get and put pointers has been done.
       rdonly = 0x10
// Puts are not allowed.
   };

   strstreambuf(int chunksize = default_allocation);
// Create a strstreambuf in dynamic-allocation mode, with the initial
// allocation at least "chunksize" bytes long, defaulted to default
// allocation

   strstreambuf(char *memory, int length = 0,
                   char *start_of_put_area = 0);
// Create a strstreambuf using the static buffer at "memory".
// If "length" is positive, that is taken as the length of the
// buffer. If it is zero, the length is taken from strlen(memory).
// If "length" is negative, the buffer is assumed to be of infinite
// length.
//
// The get pointer is initialized to "memory". If "start_of_put_area"
// is zero, the get area covers the entire buffer and a put will be
// considered an error. If "start_of_put_area" is non-zero, the
// get area consists of the bytes between "memory" and
// "start_of_put_area" - 1, and the put area consists of the bytes
// between "start_of_put_area" and the end of the buffer.

   strstreambuf(unsigned char *memory, int length = 0,
                   unsigned char *start_of_put_area = 0);
// Same as above, but for an unsigned character buffer.
```

```
     strstreambuf(void * (*allocate_function)(size_t),
                    void (*free_function)(void *),
                    int chunksize = default_allocation);
// Create a streambuf in dynamic allocation mode. Use
// void * allocate_function(size_t length) to allocate memory,
// and void free_function(void * memory) to free it. Allocation
// chunk size can be specified.

     ~strstreambuf();

     void freeze(int on = 1);
     void unfreeze() { freeze(0); }
// If the argument is non-zero, "freeze" the strstreambuf. This
// inhibits automatic deletion of the current character buffer.
// This is only important in dynamic-allocation mode. Stores into
// the buffer are invalid when it is "frozen". Calling this with
// a zero argument "un-freezes" the buffer. Deleting a strstreambuf
// will not de-allocate a frozen buffer - you must delete it yourself.

     int pcount() const { return pptr()-pbase(); }
// Return the number of characters inserted. Not accurate after
// a seek.

     char *str();
// Freeze the buffer and return a pointer to its first byte.
// The pointer may be null if no bytes have been stored and the
// buffer is in dynamic-allocation mode. The buffer may be "un-frozen"
// by calling freeze(0). Deleting a strstreambuf will not de-allocate
// a frozen buffer - you must delete it yourself.

     streambuf *setbuf(char *memory, int length);
// The memory argument is not used. The next time the streambuf
// does dynamic allocation, it will allocate at least "length" bytes.
// This function in fact sets the allocation granularity.

#if __SC__ > 0x214
     int overflow(int c = EOF);
#else
     int overflow(int c);
#endif
```

```
    int underflow();
    streampos seekoff(streamoff offset, ios::seek_dir direction,
                      int which =ios::in|ios::out);
    int sync();
// All of these are virtual functions derived from streambuf.
// There's more documentation on them in iostream.h .

protected:
    int doallocate();

private:
    short sflags;
    int chunk;
// The minimum amount to allocate when doing dynamic allocation.

    void *(*allocate_function)(size_t size);
// Points to the function used to allocate memory.

    void (*free_function)(void *memory);
// Points to the function used to free memory.

    void buffer_setup(char *memory, int length,
                      char *start_of_put_area);
};

class istrstream : public istream {

// A class of istream that takes as input a character array, and extracts
// information from it.

public:
    istrstream(char *memory, int length = 0);
// Create an istrstream attached to the character array at "memory",
// of length "length". If length is zero, strlen() is used, if length
// is negative, the stream is considered to be of a length equivalent
// to the maximum value of type size_t.

    ~istrstream();
    strstreambuf *rdbuf() { return &buffer; }

private:
    strstreambuf buffer;
};
```

```
class ostrstream : public ostream {

// A class of ostream that inserts information into a character array.

public:
    ostrstream();
// Create an ostrstream in dynamic-allocation mode.

    ostrstream(char *memory, int length, int mode=ios::out);
// Create an ostrstream attached to the character array at "memory",
// of length "length". If ios::ate or ios::app is set in "mode",
// the buffer is assumed to contain a null-terminated string, and
// the put area begins at the null character. Otherwise the put
// area will begin at "memory".

    ~ostrstream();

    int pcount() const { return buffer.pcount(); }
// Returns the number of bytes that have been put into the buffer.

    char *str();
// Freezes the buffer, and returns a pointer to the first byte of the
// buffer. Once the buffer is frozen it will not be deleted by
// the destructor of the stream: it becomes the user's responsibility
// to delete it.
    void unfreeze();
// Unfreeze the buffer and unconditionally clear the state flags.

    strstreambuf *rdbuf() { return &buffer; }
private:
    strstreambuf buffer;
};


class strstream : public iostream {

// A class of iostream that inserts and extracts information in a character
// array.

public:
    strstream();
// Create a strstream in dynamic-allocation mode.
```

```
    strstream(char *memory, int length = 0, int mode =
ios::in|ios::out);
// Create a strstream attached to the character array at "memory",
// of length "length". If length is zero, then "memory" is assumed to
// contain a null terminated string, and the langth is taken from
// strlen. If ios::ate or ios::app is set in "mode", the buffer is
// assumed to contain a null-terminated string, and the put area begins
// at the null character. Otherwise the put area will begin at "memory".

    ~strstream();

    char *str();
// Freezes the buffer, and returns a pointer to the first byte of the
// buffer. Once the buffer is frozen it will not be deleted by
// the destructor of the stream: it becomes the user's responsibility
// to delete it.
    void unfreeze();
// Unfreeze the buffer and unconditionally clear the state flags.

    strstreambuf *rdbuf() { return &buffer; }

private:
    strstreambuf buffer;
};

#pragma pack()
#endif // __SSTREAM_H
```

The Complete Symantec C++ Development Environment

NOW THAT YOU'VE WORKED WITH A SCALED-DOWN version of Symantec C++, you'll want to upgrade to the full version. Symantec C++ Professional v6.0 contains many new features, including:

- Inline assembler
- Integrated debugger
- Visual Programmer
- Microsoft Foundation Classes v2.0
- Win32s

This appendix will describe some of those features.

You've had your first taste of the Symantec C++ environment working with the special version of the product included with this book. In the full version of the product, however, you can take advantage of many additional features, such as the IDDE (Integrated Development and Debugging Environment), full source-level debugging capabilities, and an inline assembler. The MFC (Microsoft Foundation Class) libraries give you object-oriented building blocks. In addition, with the complete version of Symantec C++, you can build your own 32-bit Windows applications.

Special Upgrade Offer

Symantec will upgrade owners of *Learn C++ on the PC* to the complete Symantec C++ development environment for a special price. See the back page for further details and an upgrade coupon.

Overview of the Symantec C++ Environment

Symantec C++ is a unique development environment for the PC. It features very fast C and C++ compilers, a resource editor, the fastest linker (OPTLINK), an integrated source editor, an auto-make facility, and a project manager that holds all the pieces together. Because the editor, the compilers, and the linker are all components of the same application, Symantec C++ knows when edited source files need to be recompiled.

Symantec C++ is a complete, integrated environment, not just a C++ compiler for the PC. Traditional development environments consist of three separate applications: the editor, the compiler, and the linker. It is up to you to create your source files with a text editor, run each file through the compiler, and finally, link all your object files. In Symantec C++, the project manager oversees the operation of the compilers, the linker, and the editor. They all work in concert as part of the same application. This way, the project manager knows when you've edited a file. You can run your program from Symantec C++ as you work on it. The standard C libraries include all the functions specified in the

ANSI C standard, as well as some additional Unix operating system functions. The C++ libraries include IOStreams, a flexible expandable class library for doing input and output.

With the Visual Programmer, you can create your application graphically just by clicking and dragging dialogs, buttons, and other objects. The Visual Programmer can be used for fast prototyping or even to generate the full C or C++ source code for your application.

The Project

The project is at the heart of the Symantec C++ IDDE. The project maintains the dependencies and connections among your source code modules. It keeps track of files that need to be recompiled or that depend on an edited `#include` file. You can have C, C++, resource files, and libraries in the same project. The project window contains a list of all the files that comprise your program. When you edit a source file, the project manager marks it for recompilation. When you edit a `#include` file, the project manager marks all the files that use it.

The Editor

Once you've created a project document, the next step is to add your source files. Symantec C++ source files are standard text files, so you'll be able to use existing source files. The Symantec C++ editor uses color syntaxing so that keywords, comments, and constants are in different colors. Its search facilities include a pattern-matching option based on Grep, and a multi-file search that looks for strings in any file in your project. You can open and edit as many files as the memory in your PC will allow, and each file appears in its own edit window. Although you usually create and open source or header files, you can also use the Symantec C++ editor to open any text file.

Fast Turnaround

Symantec C++ lets you run your program directly from the environment. With the single command Run, the project manager automatically recompiles any source files that are new or have changed. The Symantec C++ linker links all your code together instantly and then executes your application.

Source-level Debugging

To help get your program working correctly, you can use Symantec C++'s source level debugger. The Symantec C++ debugger lets you debug your code the way you wrote it: in C or C++. You can set breakpoints, step through your code, debug objects, examine variables, and change their values while your program is running. You can set conditional breakpoints that stop execution only when certain conditions are true. You can debug inline functions and templates. The data/object window shows you the values of your local and global variables. The Source window contains the source text of your program and the current line of execution. The title of the Source window is the name of the source file. The breakpoint window shows the list of breakpoints that are set in the current project. The Source window shows the source text of your program. When you start the debugger, this window shows the file that contains the `main()` (or `WinMain()`) routine of your application. A diamond to the left of a source line indicates a breakpoint. An arrow to the left of a source line indicates the current line of execution. You can set breakpoints by dragging a line from the Source window to the breakpoint window.

Inline Assembler

Symantec C++ lets you use assembly language in your C and C++ programs. You can use the built-in inline assembler for assembly language in your source files, or you can use object files generated by other assemblers. The Symantec C++ inline assembler supports every Intel assembly instruction including those for the Pentium.

Visual Programmer

The Visual Programmer, supplied by Blue Sky Software, is a complete prototyping and code generation facility for creating Windows applications. The Visual Programmer is very intuitive. Adding or changing the functionality of buttons, menu items, and dialogs is as easy as pointing and clicking. You can prototype an entire application without writing a single line of code.

Why Upgrade? As you can see, the full version of Symantec C++ offers a host of features not included in this special book-version of the product: the Visual Programmer, integrated source-level debugging, inline assembler, the MFC Libraries, and more. As you develop your skills as a DOS or Windows programmer, you'll want the power and flexibility the Symantec C++ development environment offers. Don't forget to check out the upgrade coupon at the back of the book.

Appendix H

Bibliography

1. *The C++ Programming Language*, 2nd ed., Bjarne Stroustrup, 1991, Addison-Wesley Publishing Company, Reading, MA.

2. *C++ Primer*, 2nd ed., Stanley B. Lippman, 1991, Addison-Wesley Publishing Company, Reading, MA.

3. *Advanced C++: Programming Styles and Idioms*, James Coplien, 1992, Addison-Wesley Publishing Company, Reading, MA.

4. *Undocumented Windows*, Schulman, Maxey, and Pietrek, 1992, Addison-Wesley Publishing Company, Reading, MA.

5. *Programming Windows 3.1*, Charles Petzold, 1992, Microsoft Press, Redmond, WA.

6. *Windows API Bible*, James L. Conger, 1992, The Waite Group, Corte Madera, CA.

7. *Programming in C++*, Stephen C. Dewhurst and Kathy T. Stark, 1989, Prentice-Hall, Englewood Cliffs, NJ.

8. *The Annotated C++ Reference Manual*, Margaret Ellis and Bjarne Stroustrup, 1990, Addison-Wesley Publishing Company, Reading, MA.

Index